Sport Policy in Small States

For small nations like Grenada, New Zealand and Norway, medal counts relative to population are increasingly touted as the most meaningful comparisons with sporting superpowers China, the United States and Germany. In acknowledging that 60% of the world's states have populations of less than 10 million and 48% of these have less than 5 million inhabitants, this book explores how the 'minnows' can build or sustain their sport programmes.

Despite the immense variation among and between small states, this book suggests that scale 'matters'. The contributors, from Antigua and Barbuda, Finland, Lebanon, Norway, New Zealand and Sweden demonstrate the challenges and opportunities of governing sport in their respective countries. These works highlight the distinctive policy 'ecologies' of sport in small states, marked by the unique responses to global pressures, the domestic realities of having limited resources and by the close-knit networks of accountability. This volume will help scholars and policy makers to better understand the significance of having fewer 'degrees of separation' and the implications this has for sport.

This book was published as a special issue of the *International Journal of Sport Policy and Politics*.

Michael P. Sam is a Senior Lecturer at the University of Otago where he teaches organisational aspects of sport and sport/leisure policy. His research interests broadly encompass areas of policy, politics and governance as they relate to the public administration/management of sport.

Steven J. Jackson is a Professor at the University of Otago who specialises in the area of sociology of sport and sport media. His research focuses on globalisation, national identity, media and advertising cultures.

BARNSLEY COLLEGE

00140375

30013736

Sport Policy in Small States

Edited by
Michael P. Sam and Steven J. Jackson

Routledge
Taylor & Francis Group

LONDON AND NEW YORK

First published 2017
by Routledge

2 Park Square, Milton Park, Abingdon, Oxfordshire OX14 4RN
711 Third Avenue, New York, NY 10017

Routledge is an imprint of the Taylor & Francis Group, an informa business

First issued in paperback 2018

Copyright © 2017 Taylor & Francis

All rights reserved. No part of this book may be reprinted or reproduced or
utilised in any form or by any electronic, mechanical, or other means, now known
or hereafter invented, including photocopying and recording, or in any information
storage or retrieval system, without permission in writing from the publishers.

Notice:
Product or corporate names may be trademarks or registered
trademarks, and are used only for identification and explanation without intent to
infringe.

British Library Cataloguing in Publication Data
A catalogue record for this book is available from the British Library

ISBN: 978-1-138-93888-5 (hbk)
ISBN: 978-0-367-02886-2 (pbk)

Typeset in TimesNewRomanPS
by diacriTech, Chennai

Publisher's Note
The publisher accepts responsibility for any inconsistencies that may have arisen
during the conversion of this book from journal articles to book chapters, namely
the possible inclusion of journal terminology.

Disclaimer
Every effort has been made to contact copyright holders for their permission to
reprint material in this book. The publishers would be grateful to hear from any
copyright holder who is not here acknowledged and will undertake to rectify any
errors or omissions in future editions of this book.

MIX
Paper from
responsible sources
FSC
www.fsc.org   FSC™ C013985

Printed in the United Kingdom
by Henry Ling Limited

Contents

Citation Information

The chapters in this book were originally published in the *International Journal of Sport Policy and Politics*, volume 7, issue 3 (September 2015). When citing this material, please use the original page numbering for each article, as follows:

Chapter 6

Sport policy and transformation in small states: New Zealand's struggle between vulnerability and resilience
Michael P. Sam
International Journal of Sport Policy and Politics, volume 7, issue 3 (September 2015) pp. 407–420

Chapter 7

Finland as a small sports nation: socio-historical perspectives on the development of national sport policy
Pasi Koski and Jari Lämsä
International Journal of Sport Policy and Politics, volume 7, issue 3 (September 2015) pp. 421–441

Chapter 8

Sport, policy and politics in Lebanon
Nadim Nassif and Mahfoud Amara
International Journal of Sport Policy and Politics, volume 7, issue 3 (September 2015) pp. 443–455

For any permission-related enquiries please visit:
http://www.tandfonline.com/page/help/permissions

Notes on Contributors

Mahfoud Amara is an Assistant Professor in Sport Management and Policy at the College of Arts and Sciences, Qatar University, Qatar. His research focuses on sport business, culture and politics in Arab and Muslim contexts. He is a co-editor of *Sport in Islam and Muslim Communities* (Routledge, 2015).

Natalie Darko is a Lecturer in the College of Arts and Science, School of Science & Technology, Nottingham Trent University, UK. She specialises in Caribbean sport policy and development. Her publications have appeared in journals such as the *International Journal of Sport and Society* and the *Journal of Men's Health*.

Inger Eliasson is an Associate Professor in the Department of Education, University of Umea, Sweden. Her research focuses on the areas of sports science, gender studies, qualitative ethnography and cultural sociology. Her work has appeared in journals such as the *International Review for the Sociology of Sport* and the *International Journal of Sport Policy and Politics*.

Josef Fahlén is an Associate Professor in the Department of Education at the University of Umea, Sweden. He specialises in the area of sport management in Sweden. His articles have appeared in the *International Review for the Sociology of Sport* and the *International Journal of Sport Policy*.

Barrie Houlihan is a Professor of Sport Policy at Loughborough University, UK. His research interests include elite sport development systems, anti-doping and diplomacy and sport. He has published several books in the field of sport policy, including *Youth Olympic Games* (Routledge, 2014) and *Anti-doping Governance, Research and Policy* (Routledge, 2013). He is the Editor in Chief of the *International Journal of Sport Policy and Politics*.

Steven J. Jackson is a Professor at the University of Otago who specialises in the area of sociology of sport and sport media. His research focuses on globalisation, national identity, media and advertising cultures.

Pasi Koski is a Professor of Physical Education at the University of Turku, Finland. He specialises in youth sport and physical activity, as well as sport policy and governance.

Jari Lämsä is the Chief Specialist in the Department of Social Sciences of Sport at KIHU (Research Institute for Olympic Sports), Jyväskylä, Finland. He is also a former Finnish triple jumper.

NOTES ON CONTRIBUTORS

Christopher Mackintosh is a researcher in the School of Sport Studies, Leisure and Nutrition at Liverpool John Moores University, UK. He is interested in sport development evaluation, implementation and qualitative methodologies. His most recent publications have appeared in such journals as *Qualitative Research in Sport, Exercise and Health* and *Leisure Studies*.

Nadim Nassif is an Assistant Professor in the Department of Psychology, Education and Physical Education at Notre Dame University, Zouk Mosbeh, Lebanon. His research focuses on elite sport and sport policy and culture in Lebanon. He is the author of *Sport Policy in Lebanon* (2010).

Lars Tore Ronglan is a researcher in the Department of Coaching and Psychology at the Norwegian School of Sport Sciences, Norway. His research focuses on youth in sport.

Michael P. Sam is a Senior Lecturer at the University of Otago where he teaches organisational aspects of sport and sport/leisure policy. His research interests broadly encompass areas of policy, politics and governance as they relate to the public administration/ management of sport.

Kim Wickman is an Associate Professor in the Department of Education, University of Umea, Sweden. Her teaching and research interests include sport, gender and disability.

Jinming Zheng is a PhD candidate at Loughborough University, UK. His thesis compares the policy processes of elite sport development in China and the UK.

Sport and small states: the myths, limits and contradictions of the legend of David and Goliath

The legendary tale of David and Goliath is an enduring story about the underdog. It is the ultimate metaphor for 'improbable victory', of slight over might, whereby a small opponent defeats a larger giant. As the story is often told a colossal, heavily armoured Philistine warrior, named Goliath challenges the Israelites to send a warrior to engage in face to face combat in the Elah valley. To everyone's surprise a relatively small young shepherd, named David, steps forth armed with only a slingshot that he uses to wound and eventually kill Goliath. This is the romanticised, mythical version of the giant killer story that has become the defining metaphorical narrative for small versus big. However, as Gladwell (2013) reveals, people have misunderstood and misrepresented this story throughout history. In reality, it was Goliath's massive size, his specialist position as a heavy infantryman, which demanded the use of heavy armour, and his apparent medical condition, which blurred his vision that not only hindered his movement but put him at a significant disadvantage. Or, stated another way, David's mobility (aided by his small stature), choice of weapon and strategic assessment of the strengths and weaknesses of his opposition actually gave him an enormous advantage. The lesson in recasting this well-known (though perhaps misinterpreted) story is that physical size is not everything. More specifically, according to Gladwell, there are two key points to consider in the David and Goliath narrative. First, giants are not always what we think and often not as strong as we imagine, and, second, being a small underdog may enable or force people to think, adapt and act in innovative ways, allowing them to succeed despite what appear to be over-whelming odds.

The demystified version of the David and Goliath story is relevant to how we perceive and understand the advantages and disadvantages of large and small states. Within the context of sport, serious questions are being asked about how small states are supposed to compete against giants like the USA, China, Russia, Brazil and Germany. How much money should be spent on elite sport development and/or the hosting of sport mega-events in what is quickly becoming the equivalent of a 'sporting arms race'? At first glance, the fate and future of small states seems obvious. For example, according to recent estimates, China has 400 million basketball participants (Anon 2014). Even if this is an over-estimation, it provides a significant contrast to observations that 60% of the world's states have populations of less than 10 million and 48% of states have less than 5 million inhabitants. When it comes to sport, size 'matters', and hence differences in scale have been a frequent independent variable in studies examining elite sport success (De Bosscher *et al.* 2008). Generating explanations regarding how and why size matters for sport raises numerous questions regarding the possible differences, challenges and oppor-tunities of being a small 'state'.

We are grateful to be given this opportunity to pursue our interests in this area. The seeds for this volume were planted at the 'Sport in Small Nations' International Symposium held at the University of Otago, Dunedin New Zealand. Three of the papers in the volume were presented in earlier versions at the symposium (Houlihan, Koski,

Ronglan) while others came from our general call for papers. In this introduction, we want to demonstrate the importance of scale in the development of policies and programmes around sport. We first outline the case for studying small states and consider the key characteristics that might distinguish small states from large ones, focusing in particular on the conceptual dimensions of vulnerability and resilience. Alongside the existing literature, we then synthesise the works from this volume to highlight the main issues and themes that underpin sport studies in small states. Our introduction concludes by suggesting that the importance of these works lies with the distinctive 'ecologies' of small states.

What is a small state?

The identification of small states is problematic given the myriad ways size can be expressed (Thorhallsson and Wivel 2006). Size is contested in theory and practice but for comparative purposes, three dimensions are relevant. The first is population and as one might expect there are a number of proposed cut-off points, ranging from 1 million to 20 million (Tõnurist 2010). In studies of Commonwealth countries, the threshold for small is set at under 1.5 million, a figure also generally accepted as the approximate cut-off for what are referred to as 'microstates'. The threshold for smallness thus generally depends on the interest of the academic field itself (Tõnurist 2010). In some European studies, for example, smallness as a function of population has been arbitrarily set in relation to the Netherlands (i.e., approximately 16 million) because of the wide gap between it and the next largest state, Poland (pop. 38 million) (Thorhallsson 2006). This collection uses an arbitrary population of under 10 million, a relatively high threshold in part because of the dearth of research scholarship on sport in states under 5 million. A second related dimension is geographical size, where small states are generally understood to have small land areas. Island states like Fiji and Samoa in the South Pacific, or Mauritius and Malta would fit this description. Here again, however, the size of a state is relative; some such as Mongolia (pop. 2.8 million) or Namibia (pop. 2.3 million) can have large land areas and therefore very low population densities. Ultimately, in light of the imprecise nature of definitions and thresholds, it has become accepted that smallness is best viewed as lying upon a continuum (Tõnurist 2010, Sutton 2011).

A third, more commonly used dimension in relation to small state studies is the size of its economy. This dimension is usually operationalised with reference to a state's Gross Domestic Product (GDP), narrow base for trade (e.g., agriculture or tourism), small domestic market, comparative expenditures on defence, health, etc. With respect to the sport sector, economic scale could be said to affect many facets of its development and sustainability. A smaller tax base means less revenue that can be used for the provision of sport and recreation facilities. A narrower economic base also translates into a smaller number of large companies that can limit the pool of potential corporate sponsors. This limited economic power has great relevance in the contemporary world of international professional sport. Larger markets typically command larger athlete salaries, pressuring small states to either meet expectations in their own domestic competitions and/or institute a range of policies discouraging player migration. The New Zealand Rugby Union, for example, has tried to discourage outward migration by negating a player's eligibility to play for the national team should they take up contracts in other leagues. For its part, however, NZ welcomes the migration of Samoan, Tongan and Fijian rugby players into its national ranks, contributing to the depletion of human capital in those comparatively smaller Pacific nations (Grainger 2009, Kanemasu and Molnar 2013).

Insofar as broadcasting revenue depends on the size of audiences, small states arguably have less control over the makeup of leagues or the timing of major events (see for example, Kanemasu and Molnar 2013). More significantly perhaps is that with the exception of Singapore, Qatar and the United Arab Emirates, small states are susceptible to the inflationary financial pressures around the hosting of events, rendering these beyond reach or causing the governments of small states to engage in a 'race to the bottom' (i.e., making commitments that can be ill-afforded in order to win the bid).

Taken together, a country's 'vulnerability' is what sets small states apart (Briguglio *et al.* 2009). For reasons of geography and economy, they are prone to economic shocks, and heavily constrained in their development by global forces beyond their control (Neumann and Gstöhl 2004). Houlihan and Zheng (this volume), for example, note the potential Olympic medals shock for Azerbajan and Georgia, had the IOC followed through on its proposal to remove wrestling from the Olympic programme. Globalisation is therefore an important theoretical dimension in relation to small states, as one of its key themes surrounds the vulnerability of the 'local' in relation to the 'global'. The fall of oil prices in the 1980s for instance resulted in a sharp economic downturn for states like Trinidad and Tobago, resulting in delayed social programmes (including sport) that would not be revisited until the late 1990s when commodity prices began to rise again (McCree 2009).

Small states and resilience

Where vulnerability emerged as the bridging concept in identifying small states, scholars sought to move away from pessimistic views of 'small as weak' that typified international relations literature. *Resilience* has since become an important part of the lexicon in small-state studies. Katzenstein's (1985) proposition in this regard is that through their experience of vulnerability at particular historical junctures (e.g., Great Depression, World War I) small states have developed political capacities to respond successfully. The adaptive effects of smallness thus include: (1) the establishment of corporatist institutions (i.e., government partnership with selected interest groups); (2) the development of policies aimed at social integration (e.g., language policy); and (3) the coordination of responses to public problems. Echoing these ideas, others point out that the resiliences of small nations lie with their capacities for social partnership, cooperation and sacrifice (Lowenthal 1987, Campbell and Hall 2009).

In reflecting on his own seminal book *Small States in World Markets* (1985), Katzenstein (2003, p. 11) remarked that the most 'important explanatory variable' 20 years later was that

> Small size was a code for something more important …What really mattered politically was the perception of vulnerability, economic and otherwise. Perceived vulnerability generated an ideology of social partnership that had acted like glue for the corporatist politics of the small European states.

The possibility of closer personal ties is thus what sets small states apart. More trusting relationships and repeated interactions act as a means to supplant stricter principal–agent relations. Put another way, the development of social capital serves to remove the distrust in impersonal contacts. Indeed, it would be difficult to challenge the notion that small states are also small societies (Benedict 1967) with highly personalised role relationships (Farrugia 1993) that can provide a capacity for resilience. And in light of the above, it is not surprising that small states should pursue sport as a means of inducing social integration and national unity.

In one of the few comparative studies focusing on small states, Girginov *et al.* (2006) explored the cultural orientations of sport managers in Malta, Cyprus, Iceland, Luxembourg, San Marino, Monaco and Liechtenstein. While the sample of individuals was small (n = 15 managers), the research acknowledged the cultural differences in how administrators deal with dilemmas. Germane to this volume is the observation that managers considered it normal to reconcile tensions and conflicts, as against the general tendency of western sport management to want to seek more definitive resolutions.

One explanation is that people in small states are accustomed to compromise, reflecting Lowenthal's (1987, p. 39) thesis of a 'managed intimacy', where:

> Small-state inhabitants learn to get along, like it or not, with folk they will know in myriad contexts over their whole lives. To enable the social mechanism to function without undue stress, they minimise or mitigate overt conflict. They become expert at muting hostility, deferring their own views, containing disagreement, avoiding dispute, in the interest of stability and compromise.

This is not to suggest that the sport sectors of small states would lack detractors but rather that small size perhaps necessitates 'sophisticated modes of accommodation' (Lowenthal, 1987, p. 39). Fahlén, Eliasson and Wickman's analysis of the Swedish government's 'sport-for-all' ambitions provides a case in point. Despite governmental efforts to induce broader gender-and-class equality aims, the study demonstrates that clubs are difficult to harness and that 'policy fails to survive the journey from top to bottom'. As the authors point out, this resistance is to some extent tacitly accepted, since it maintains the legitimacy of historically, trust-based relations.

Cases, contradictions and tensions

If fewer 'degrees of separation' and close ties provide a source of resilience, a significant counterbalance has been the transformation of small states to align with neoliberal institutions. Indeed, one important source of transformation for small states has been the role of international or supranational organisations such as the International Monetary Fund, World Bank and European Union. Given the legitimacy of these agencies and the interest they have in small states, it is not surprising that their prescriptions should influence domestic policies including those related to sport (cf. Girginov and Sandanski 2008, McCree 2009).

One prescription or strategy concerns the need for small states to specialise, to consolidate and target specific industries (Bray 1991, Sarapuu 2010). Smallness and the comparative resource scarcity that goes with it, thus invites consolidation, the narrowing of objectives, targeting and rationing. Hence in their wider economies, small states may choose to focus their investments in technology, agriculture or tourism (Browning 2006). Contemporary investment in sport falls under similar logic. The tendency to consolidate efforts around particular sports appears to be evident in both small and large nations – China, for example, has identified nine 'superior' sports (about the same number as New Zealand's targeted or 'priority' sports). However, it is doubtful that the narrowing of priorities in a large country distorts their sporting systems to the same degree.

In states like Singapore (pop. 5.4 million), New Zealand (4.3 million) and Finland (pop. 5.3 million), the doctrines of New Public Management (NPM) have been pursued with substantive effects on the organisation of sport. The governments of these countries have sought to achieve greater alignment between sport and business practices, while demonstrating a preference for using contracts and their associated targets, benchmarks and performance-based budgeting (cf. Collins 2011, Teo 2011, Sam 2012). Insofar as these strategies are largely premised on distrust, Sam's contribution to this volume suggests that small states may struggle to reconcile the ideals of social partnerships with the contemporary emphasis on accountability. Neoliberal doctrines, he argues, present small states with a paradox: scale invites consolidation, targeting and rationing, while also invoking strategies to break the very communal bonds that provide them with the 'fertile' conditions for growth and competitive advantage.

This paradox is certainly not a 'trajectory' that states are compelled to follow. While New Zealand's standing as the model neoliberal reformer has encouraged the development of a centralised system for elite sport, Nordic countries have by design maintained the autonomy of their sport organisations. Indeed, in Koski and Lamsa's contribution, the authors point out that Finland has eschewed the targeting of particular sports. Ronglan's essay details a similar outlook in Norway's system, one that owes much to the legitimacy of its traditional grassroots system and the representative structures of its umbrella organisation, the Norwegian Sports Federation. Clearly, then, the paradox between neoliberal reforms and small societies does not play out the same way, but it remains a recognisable tension and one in need of further analysis.

Common themes in small-state sports research

Perhaps the most common theme around small state sport is in regards to how sport is portrayed in the national psyche. Bairner's (1996) analysis of Sweden, Scotland and the Republic of Ireland is instructive in this regard, suggesting that the construction of 'sporting nationalisms' is shaped by dimensions of homogeneity and by the relative historical significance of national identity. In the Finnish context, Koski and Lamsa (this volume) maintain that sport strengthened national pride during that country's path to independence. It is Finland's unique history that resulted in the concept of *sisu* that relates to stamina – a type of endurance born out of a combination of a demanding natural environment, the protestant ethic, the struggle for political independence and the pursuit of a civil and equality-based society. Likewise, rugby's importance to the development of national identity is well documented in New Zealand (Phillips 1996, Scherer and Jackson 2010) as well as Fiji (Kanemasu and Molnar 2013). The contemporary use of sport as a means of projecting national identity is also an emerging theme, particularly in relation to the pursuit of events hosting by small (but economically successful) states such as Singapore (Fry and McNeill 2011) and Persian Gulf nations Bahrain, Qatar and United Arab Emirates (cf. Henry *et al.* 2003, Bromber and Krawietz 2013).

Another common theme in the narratives of small state sport relates to issues around migration. Two broad storylines appear in this regard. The first tells of the tendency for athletes (especially young athletes) to leave their home countries in search of more lucrative opportunities, producing a kind of 'brawn drain'. McGovern (2000), for example, documents the departure of Irish footballers to English Premier League clubs, suggesting that this contributes to football's underdevelopment in the Republic. The second storyline surrounds the initiatives of small states to develop their sporting capacities by effectively purchasing talent from abroad. Qatar has been the most forthright in this practice, having for instance purchased an entire weightlifting team from Bulgaria in the late 1990s (Girginov and Sandanski 2008) and naturalising a Kenyan steeplechase runner in 2003 to boost the country's standing in athletics (Hunter 2003). Houlihan and Zheng's essay also highlights this strategy's adoption in Singapore, where the country has experienced considerable success through its Foreign Sport Talent Scheme. To the extent that other states (e.g., New Zealand) also encourage this kind of resettlement through special immigration categories, we see that sporting talent is an increasingly valued 'skillset' and one that small states may be keen to attract. However, against the migratory patterns of elite athletes, coaches and technical directors, it is nevertheless evident that sport is an area of activity that is inherently 'nationalistic'. Home-grown talent may become more valued than imported talent or talent principally nurtured and developed in larger overseas 'hot houses' (e.g., USA colleges).

Yet another important theme is with respect to how small states attempt to coordinate the competing demands around sport. The tension between sport-for-all and elite sport is ubiquitous but it is notably more muted in Scandinavian countries characterised by strong member associations, links with workers' organisations and a longstanding public perception of sport as a social movement (Ronglan, this volume). Reflecting the imperative of maintaining legitimacy, Ronglan suggests that elite sport in Scandinavia requires a constant effort and a constructed connection between the specific medal performances and the characteristics/conditions of the wider sport movement.

However, the lack of a critical mass of athletes to provide high-level competition also features as problematic in small states. Reflecting this concern, a common issue raised in small state research relates to the coordination between the education and sport sectors. In the context of Barbuda and Antigua, Darko and Mackintosh's contribution points to the persistent compartmentalisation between physical education and sport, between levels of education and between layers of government. Paradoxically and speaking to the hegemony of sport, the authors observe that despite the unimportance accorded to physical education, Barbuda and Antigua maintains a national sport policy. In Sweden, the sport movement has begun to influence physical education in schools not simply by advancing sport's importance and status, but by becoming a primary 'supplier', offering coaches and programmes in the curriculum (Ferry *et al.* 2013). The growing tendency for outsourcing physical education to sport specialists is a trend in Singapore and New Zealand as well (Pope 2002, Fry and McNeill 2011) with the emergence of sport-specific boarding schools and academies in those countries further reflecting sport's importance in the market reforms of education sectors. Taken together, the tensions and coordination challenges between education and sport sectors (even in small states) point to the possibility that the schism is not easily reconciled.

If the combination of scale and neoliberalism potentially results in unwanted distortions, it is important to acknowledge that, at an individual level, there may be advantages for young athletes in small states. One advantage is that it is perhaps more likely that they will have the opportunity to compete internationally. In some cases, this may be through intentional government design; Namibia's Ministry of Youth, for example, has actively pursued international junior programmes in a number of sports (Chappell 2005). But even anecdotally, one could speculate that there is something significant in being the 'big fish in a small pond'. In a developed state like New Zealand, there are national representatives in many sports, from the major sports (such as cricket, rugby, netball and football) to comparatively minor sports (such as ice hockey and volleyball) and everything in between. Insofar as a country like this maintains a wide gamut of sports, the chances of rising to the top would seem to be proportionately greater than they would be otherwise. While it would be difficult to determine the statistical chances of being a national representative, the intuitive assumption is a dimension worth exploring. Indeed, is the wider range of possibilities to be a 'big fish' a help or hindrance with respect to participation patterns? What is the impact on 'sport-for-all' when role models are so accessible and characterized by only 'two degrees' of separation?

Conclusion

Though what defines a 'small state' is fairly fluid, it is generally agreed that scale 'matters'. How and why it matters, however, depends on the interplay between population size, geography, political economy and the subject area under analysis. It is these ecologies that render sport in small states an important vehicle through which to explore context-specific complexities and contradictions. For example, Nassif and Amara's profile of Lebanon points to the influence of entrenched divisions of power that ultimately present sport with a formidable set of intractable problems. Hence, while there is immense variation among and between small states, this volume suggests that sport yields distinctive responses compared to global 'superpowers', owing to the former's limited human and financial resources, close personal ties, and frameworks of legitimacy.

One proposition in this regard is that the small states would tend to mimic larger states because they are perceived to be successful. McCree's (2009) study of sport policy in the Caribbean, for example, notes that Trinidad and Tobago's policy was formulated using the Australian sport policy as a model, while Sam's research documents similar discourses in New Zealand's comparisons with Australia and the United Kingdom. Yet, the ways in which small states enact such modelling or mimicking must necessarily take place in an environment marked by each state's responses to global pressures, by the domestic realities of having limited resources, and by its close-knit networks of accountability. In this light, attention towards small states may help scholars and policy makers to better understand the significance of having fewer degrees of separation and the implications this has for sport.

Returning to the lessons of David and Goliath, while physical size in terms of geography and resources, including population, can certainly be an advantage, large states can also be myopic and have their own vulnerabilities. Moreover, for a wide range of reasons including cultural homogeneity, unique and highly efficient communicative and organisation networks, the need and ability to be innovative, flexible and resilient and, the high level of visibility and celebration of sporting victories may offer smaller states some distinct advantages. Indeed, according to Halpern's (2010) book *The hidden wealth of nations*, globalisation may be leading to a divergence of values between countries but a convergence within nations resulting in what he refers to as a 'soft' form of national identity that 'remains a powerful force' (p. 115).

References

Anon, 2014. *Sport in China* [online]. Wikipedia. Available from: http://en.wikipedia.org/wiki/Sport_in_China [Accessed 2014].

Bairner, A., 1996. Sportive nationalism and nationalist politics: a comparative analysis of Scotland, the Republic of Ireland, and Sweden. *Journal of sport & social issues*, 20 (3), 314–334. doi:10.1177/019372396020003006

Benedict, B., 1967. Sociological aspects of smallness. *In*: B. Benedict, ed. *Problems of smaller territories*. London: University of London/Athlone Press, 45–55.

Bray, M., 1991. *Making small practical: the organisation and management of ministries of education in small states*. London: Commonwealth Secretariat.

Briguglio, L., *et al.*, 2009. Economic vulnerability and resilience: concepts and measurements. *Oxford development studies*, 37 (3), 229–247. doi:10.1080/13600810903089893

Bromber, K. and Krawietz, B., 2013. The United Emirates, Qatar, and Bahrain as a modern sport hub. *In*: K. Bromber, B. Krawietz, and J. Maguire, eds. *Sport across Asia: politics, cultures and identities*. New York: Routledge, 189–212.

Browning, C.S., 2006. Small, smart and salient? Rethinking identity in the small states literature. *Cambridge review of international affairs*, 19 (4), 669–684. doi:10.1080/09557570601003536

Campbell, J.L. and Hall, J.A., 2009. National identity and the political economy of small states. *Review of international political economy*, 16 (4), 547–572. doi:10.1080/09692290802620378

Chappell, R., 2005. Sport in Namibia: conflicts, negotiations and struggles since independence. *International Review for the sociology of sport*, 40 (2), 241–254. doi:10.1177/1012690205057204

Collins, S., 2011. Finland. *In*: M. Nicholson, R. Hoye, and B. Houlihan, eds. *Participation in sport: international perspectives*. New York: Routledge, 109–125.

De Bosscher, V., *et al.*, 2008. *The global sporting arms race: an international comparative study on sports policy factors leading to international sporting success*. Oxford: Meyer & Meyer Verlag.

Farrugia, C., 1993. The special working environment of senior administrators in small states. *World development*, 21 (2), 221–226. doi:10.1016/0305-750X(93)90017-4

Ferry, M., Meckbach, J., and Larsson, H., 2013. School sport in Sweden: what is it, and how did it come to be? *Sport in society*, 16 (6), 805–818. doi:10.1080/17430437.2012.753530

Fry, J.M. and McNeill, M.C., 2011. 'In the Nation's good': physical education and school sport in Singapore. *European physical education review*, 17 (3), 287–300. doi:10.1177/1356336X11416730

Girginov, V., Papadimitriou, D., and López De D'amico, R., 2006. Cultural orientations of sport managers. *European sport management quarterly*, 6 (1), 35–66. doi:10.1080/16184740600798347

Girginov, V. and Sandanski, I., 2008. Understanding the changing nature of sports organisations in transforming societies. *Sport management review*, 11 (1), 21–50. doi:10.1016/S1441-3523(08)70102-5

Gladwell, M., 2013. *David and Goliath: underdogs, misfits and the art of battling giants*. New York: Allen Lane.

Grainger, A., 2009. Rugby, Pacific peoples, and the cultural politics of national identity in New Zealand. *The international journal of the history of sport*, 26 (16), 2335–2357. doi:10.1080/09523360903466776

Halpern, D., 2010. *The hidden wealth of nations*. Cambridge: Polity Press.

Henry, I.P., Amara, M., and Al-Tauqi, M., 2003. Sport, Arab nationalism and the Pan-Arab games. *International review for the sociology of sport*, 38 (3), 295–310. doi:10.1177/10126902030383003

Hunter, J., 2003. Flying the flag: identities, the nation, and sport. *Identities: global studies in culture and power*, 10 (4), 409–425. doi:10.1080/714947397

Kanemasu, Y. and Molnar, G., 2013. Collective identity and contested allegiance: a case of migrant professional Fijian rugby players. *Sport in society*, 16 (7), 863–882. doi:10.1080/17430437.2013.791158

Katzenstein, P.J., 1985. *Small states in world markets: industrial policy in Europe*. Ithaca, NY: Cornell University Press.

Katzenstein, P.J., 2003. Small states and small states revisited. *New political economy*, 8 (1), 9–30. doi:10.1080/1356346032000078705

Lowenthal, D., 1987. Social features. *In*: C. Clarke and T. Payne, eds. *Politics, security and development in small states*. London: Allen and Unwin, 26–49.

McCree, R., 2009. Sport policy and the new public management in the Caribbean: convergence or resurgence? *Public management review*, 11 (4), 461–476. doi:10.1080/14719030902989532

McGovern, P., 2000. The Irish brawn drain: English league clubs and Irish footballers, 1946–1995. *The British journal of sociology*, 51 (3), 401–418. doi:10.1080/00071310050131594

Neumann, I.B. and Gstöhl, S., 2004. *Lilliputians in Gulliver's world? Small states in international relations*. Reykjavik: University of Iceland.

Phillips, J., 1996. *A man's country? The image of Pakeha male, a history*. 2nd ed. Auckland: Penguin Books.

Pope, C.C., 2002. Plato makes the team: the arrival of secondary school sport academies. *Waikato Journal of education*, 8, 89–100.

Sam, M.P., 2012. Targeted investments in elite sport funding: wiser, more innovative and strategic? *Managing leisure*, 17 (2–3), 207–220. doi:10.1080/13606719.2012.674395

Sarapuu, K., 2010. Comparative analysis of state administrations: the size of state as an independent variable. *Administrative culture*, 11 (1), 30–43.

Scherer, J. and Jackson, S.J., 2010. *Globalization, sport and corporate nationalism: the new cultural economy of the New Zealand all blacks*. Oxford: Peter Lang.

Sutton, P., 2011. The concept of small states in the international political economy. *The round table*, 100 (413), 141–153. doi:10.1080/00358533.2011.565625

Teo, L., 2011. Singapore. *In*: M. Nicholson, R. Hoye, and B. Houlihan eds. *Participation in sport: international perspectives*. New York: Routledge, 183–208.

Thorhallsson, B., 2006. The size of states in the European Union: theoretical and conceptual perspectives. *Journal of European integration*, 28 (1), 7–31. doi:10.1080/07036330500480490

Thorhallsson, B. and Wivel, A., 2006. Small states in the European Union: what do we know and what would we like to know? *Cambridge review of international affairs*, 19 (4), 651–668. doi:10.1080/09557570601003502

Tõnurist, P., 2010. What is a 'small state' in a globalizing economy. *Halduskultuur – administrative culture*, 11 (1), 8–29.

Michael P. Sam and Steven J. Jackson
University of Otago

Small states: sport and politics at the margin

Barrie Houlihan[a,b] and Jinming Zheng[c]

[a]School of Sport, Exercise and Sport Sciences, Loughborough University, Loughborough, UK; [b]Department of Culture and Society, Norwegian School of Sport Sciences, Oslo, Norway; [c]School of Sport, Exercise and Health Sciences, Loughborough University, Loughborough, UK

The aims of this article are the identification of the objectives of small states for participation in international sport and investing in elite sport and the analysis of the strategies that small states adopt to maximize their ability to achieve their sport and non-sport objectives. The article discusses the problem of the definition of smallness and explores objective, relative and subjective definitions. There follows an analysis of the characteristics of vulnerability and capacity in relation to strategy development and a review of the utility of international relations theory for the analysis of small states. The article continues with the identification of five possible strategies that might be adopted by small states (independent/autonomous, isomorphist/imitative, isolationist, collective and camp follower) and the resources needed to operationalize the strategies. Following a brief review of the examples of Singapore and Ireland, the article concludes that the scope for the adoption of independent strategies is likely to narrow given the global ambitions of international federations and the International Olympic Committee. The conclusion also considers the prospects for stimulating research in the area of small state sport policy and argues that the prospects are not good.

Microstates, small states and major sports powers

In modern international sport events, small states are consistent in their presence and also in their marginality. The median population size of the 204 countries that participated in the London 2012 Olympic Games was just over 6.6 m and almost one-quarter (47) had a population of less than 1 m. Those countries with a population below 1 m accounted for just three Olympic medals in 2012, and the 102 countries with the smallest population accounted for just 11% (106) of the 962 medals won. The total number of athletes competing in London was approximately 10,800 with over half that number coming from just 17 countries. The median size of a national squad was 11 and of those countries below the median 70% were, not surprisingly, also below the population median of 6.6 m. The pattern of marginal presence and negligible success is also found in the analysis of the 2010 Commonwealth Games. Of the 71 countries and territories that took part, 52 had populations below 10 m of which 39 had populations below 1.5 m. Thirty-five countries did not win a single medal of which 23 had populations below 500,000. The aim of this article is to address this apparent paradox of presence yet marginality. The aim will be achieved by the identification of the objectives of small states for participation in international sport and investing in elite sport and the analysis of the strategies that small states adopt to maximize their ability to achieve their sport and non-sport objectives.

In discussions of the objectives of government involvement in sport, especially in elite sport, reference is often made, *inter alia*, to sport's perceived utility in developing and projecting national identity, providing economic benefits through regeneration or a strengthened balance of payments, delivering social benefits for individuals or communities and in adding to the repertoire of diplomatic resources (Arnaud and Riordan 1998, Preuss 2004, Houlihan 2006). However, the identification and analysis of governmental objectives is substantially based on the examination of the use of sport within a limited number of states whose main characteristics are wealth, large population and a long history of independence (notable exceptions include Beckles and Stoddart 1995, Cronin 1999, Sam 2003, and Andersen and Ronglan 2012). Yet, the vast majority of states that take part in major multi-sport events, such as the Olympic Games and the Commonwealth Games, and single sport world or regional championships, are 'small states'.

As a preliminary to the discussion of the two aims of the article, it is necessary to examine briefly the concept of a 'small state'. There is much debate, but little agreement on the definition of a small state (Duursma 1996, Maas 2009, Sutton 2011). Many attempts at developing a precise definition used a combination of population, usable land and GDP (for example, Taylor 1969, who found a high correlation between these characteristics) with the occasional addition of the dimensions of remoteness, because so many small states are islands, military assets and narrowness of the economic base (Thorhallsson 2000). While agreement on objective measures of smallness is not to be found, some indication of the objective characteristics of the type of states under discussion in this article is required. For the purposes of the following discussion, a small state will usually have a population below 10 m and a microstate a population below 1.5 m (Vital 1967, Bailes 2009). Even if a consensus did exist regarding the objective criteria by which a small state and a microstate could be defined, it would still be important to acknowledge that 'smallness' has significant relative and subjective aspects. For example, while North Korea has a population of 25 m, it is arguably 'small' in comparison with its regional neighbours, China (1352 m), Japan (128 m) and South Korea (50 m). Canada (population 35 m; per capita GDP US$42,000) is small in relation to its southern neighbour (population 314 m; per capita GDP US$52,000) with the latter having had a substantial impact on the development of elite sport in Canada, especially ice hockey and baseball. Furthermore, there is a subjective aspect to smallness insofar as a state may adopt the behaviour associated with small states because of a self-perception of weakness, for example, as is evident among some populous sub-Saharan states. While the ambiguity in the conceptualization of smallness need to be acknowledged, the problems of definition should not be allowed to justify the exclusion of small states from an analysis of the international politics of sport policy.

In addition to the ambiguity surrounding the concept of smallness, there is a similar degree of uncertainty regarding the concept of the state which requires brief comment. The 1933 Montevideo Convention on the Rights and Duties of States listed four criteria for statehood, namely defined territory, permanent population, effective government and a capacity to enter into relations with other states. Dissatisfaction with these criteria was soon apparent, but despite considerable debate in the intervening years, a consensus on a definition has proved elusive. The definition of statehood is relevant to this discussion insofar as there are some small and microstates that would not be able to operationalize their sport resources if it were not for external support (for example, of the Commonwealth Games Federation or Olympic Solidarity). Second, there are some territories whose claim to statehood is contested and who have been relatively effective in utilizing sport to support their claims to or aspirations for sovereignty/independence such as Palestine, Kosovo, Scotland and Catalonia. Finally, there is the example of Hong Kong which, while indisputably part of the People's Republic of China, aspires to distance itself symbolically from the central authority and position itself as a global rather than a Chinese region (Lau 2000, quoted in Ho and Bairner 2013, p. 353). Although this article will not explore these variations on statehood in detail, it is important to bear in mind that many of these territories will use sport in a broadly similar way to that under discussion for the generality of small states.

Domestic and international relations interests of small states

While other organizing principles such as culture (Francophone Games), religion (Maccabi Games) and sexuality (Gay Games) have been used independent of or in conjunction with statehood, in the study of international relations (IR), the state is the dominant organizing concept and unit of analysis and thus reinforces the state as the primary unit around which international sport is organized. It is argued in this article that not only do small states face similar political and sporting problems associated with recognition, voice and stakeholding and that elite level sport is often used as a resource in the pursuit of broader diplomatic goals, but also that the IR and sport policy interests of small states are generally under-researched by the academic community. Such interest as has been stimulated in the IR of small states was prompted in part by the rapid increase in the number of states between the 1960s and 1980s due to decolonialization. During those three decades, 36 states were admitted to the United Nations which had populations of around 1 m or less. The subsequent collapse of the Soviet Union and Yugoslavia provided a further incentive to address the IR of small states. However, much early research was often founded on a crude assumption that size equated to power and that small states were necessarily weak states (Neumann and Gstöhl 2004).

Much of the academic neglect of small states is due to the dominance of the realist paradigm in IR which, though centrally concerned with security (a primary concern of small states), emphasises (military and economic) capabilities, thus tending to privilege the study of the more powerful states. Small states are often seen, due to their perceived lack of capability, as mere irritants in great power politics (Lewis 2009) or as part of the supporting chorus of major sports-power politics. When the IR of small states has been considered, it has often been in terms of the threat they pose to the interests of major powers such as Cuba as a threat to the interests of the United States or Georgia and the Baltic states as threats to Russia. A parallel example in relation to sport would be the evidence of widespread doping and government neglect of anti-doping activity in Jamaica and Kenya which can be seen as a threat to the traditional prominence of the United States in track athletics.

A secondary aspect of the realist perspective on small states is a tendency to focus on what they lack and the ways in which they cope with economic vulnerability and political insecurity with some authors seeing vulnerability as the defining political characteristic of smallness (Commonwealth Secretariat 1997). As Bishop 2012 (p. 948) notes, 'the idea of vulnerability suggests that development is more fragile, ephemeral and potentially threatened than in larger societies'. Reflecting this concern, the United Nations published a 'vulnerability index' (Briguglio 1995) and the Commonwealth Secretariat commissioned a report on the impact of economic volatility (Atkins et al. 2000). In his review of the evidence on the association between population size and vulnerability, Payne (quoted in Sutton 2011, p. 151) concluded that 'it is vulnerabilities rather than opportunities ... that come through as the most striking manifestation of the consequences of smallness in global politics'. Much the same can be argued in relation to the consequences of smallness in global sport. For example, the narrow resource base of many small states, the limited domestic market and the concentration of elite sport resources in a narrow range of sports contribute to vulnerability and reflect the status of small states in international sport policy as predominantly policy-takers rather than policy-makers. It might also be argued that a further parallel could be drawn with the tendency of small states to specialize in one or two sports (Houlihan and Zheng 2013) and their consequent vulnerability to decisions by international sport organizations (such as the International Olympic Committee (IOC), Commonwealth Games Federation or major international federations (IFs)) to remove sports from multi-sport events or to change the format of single discipline competitions. For example, the decision (later reversed) by the IOC in 2013 to remove wrestling from the 2020 Olympic schedule would have been a major problem for Azerbaijan who won 7 of their 10 medals in the sport and Georgia who won all but 1 of their 7 medals in the sport.

Bishop (2012) cautions against a deterministic view of vulnerability as vulnerability should not be equated with poverty or economic weakness as the examples of Singapore, Monaco, Qatar and, though to a lesser extent, Cyprus and Malta illustrate. If the definition of state capabilities is broadened to include money, then realist theory can be used to analyse the capacity of small states such as Qatar (as hosts of the 2022 football World Cup), Singapore (host of the 2010 Youth Olympic Games) and Abu Dhabi (host of major tennis and golf championships) to challenge the traditional dominance of large states (sport powers) as hosts of major sports events.

To explore the sport politics of small states purely within the realist, paradigm would be unwise as there are plenty of examples from mainstream IR of small states confounding the assumptions made about them and demonstrating their capacity to pursue successfully their interests, often collectively, in the face of major power opposition. The 1997 international agreement to outlaw the use of anti-personnel mines and the 1998 agreement to establish an International Criminal Court to address the issue of war crimes were both achieved in the face of determined opposition from major powers, especially the United States, and not explicable in terms of conventional realist IR theorizing (Davenport 2002, see also Braveboy-Wagner 2010). A similar argument could be made regarding the role of African states in isolating South Africa from international sport during the apartheid period (Keech and Houlihan 1999).

The neoliberal paradigm gives less emphasis to capabilities and more to institutions and the institutionalization of interests. The paradigm also takes account of a broader range of political actors including non-governmental organizations (NGOs) such as the IOC, SportAccord and IFs, and encourages the exploration of the ways in which state interests are pursued beyond the concentration on state to state relations. While small states were seen as sharing many of the concerns of large states (such as recognition, self-determination and the maintenance of the integrity of borders), many had more intense concerns with environmental and trade issues as a direct consequence of their narrow economic base and their small geographical as well as population size. The neoliberal paradigm supports the examination of the use made by small states of international organizations and international policy regimes as arenas within which to pursue their national (sport) interests. Of particular relevance to sport policy is the extent to which small states can use (either individually or collectively) NGOs and sport policy regimes (such as those for anti-doping and development through sport) to pursue their sport and non-sport objectives. For example, some states (Norway, Denmark and New Zealand, for example) have, arguably at least, developed a stronger global profile on non-sport issues through their involvement in NGOs and sport policy regimes (in relation to anti-doping, integrity and child protection, for example). However, while neoliberal institutionalism gives greater scope for the exercise of influence by small states, it must be acknowledged that most policy regimes, such as those for anti-doping and elite sport competition, represent the institutionalization of major power interests.

Social constructivism draws attention to the processes by which perceptions of states, for example, as vulnerable, sovereign, honest, trustworthy, efficient or corrupt, are established and maintained. The awareness of the importance of image is easily illustrated. In the early part of the present century, Norway used consultants to inform its public diplomacy strategy. The outcome was the formulation of four 'image and value platforms ... around which coherence in presenting Norway to the world should be built: a humanitarian superpower/a peacemaker; a society living with nature; a society with a high level of equality; [and] an internationalist society/a society with a spirit of adventure' (Batora 2005, p. 16, see also Leonard and Small 2003). The prominence of Norway in sport for development and peace initiatives, the promotion of community sport, hosting environmentally sensitive sports events and in anti-doping action all indicate the scope for sport to play an important part in the construction of the four value platforms and the fulfilment of the country's public diplomacy objectives.

According to Lee and Smith (2010, p. 1092), 'rather than treating smallness as an analytical category ... it can be understood as a discursive construction'. For many small states, a key challenge is to achieve recognition of their right to self-determination and claims to sovereignty. International sports events and organizations provide important opportunities for small states to assert and receive acknowledgement of their sovereignty. In addition to using sport as an opportunity to acquire quasi-legal recognition by other states, international sport helps small states project a degree of cultural distinctiveness which reinforces their sovereign status. As Grant (1997, p. 638) comments, 'nationals of microstates are often indistinguishable from nationals of their larger neighbours at least in terms of race, language, religion and tradition'. A number of small states saw the 2012 London Olympics as an opportunity to raise their profile (for example, Lesotho, Smith 2012, a landlocked country in Southern Africa) and/or to promote their claims to statehood (Palestine, Sherwood 2012, and Kosovo, BBC 2012). International sport presents many highly visible opportunities for small states whose claims to statehood are vulnerable and contested to do things that are 'characteristically state-like' (Grant 1997, p. 656). The Olympic Games and the Commonwealth Games give many small and microstates the rare opportunity to share a formal symbolic equality of status with the major (sports) powers most evident in the opening and closing ceremonies. Additional opportunities for symbolic demonstrations of statehood are offered by the IFs that operate on a one nation – one vote principle. As Grant (1997, p. 675) noted, in the struggle that many small and especially microstates face to assert and protect their status the most convincing evidence of statehood 'is their admission into international organizations'. Sport provides an important arena in which often limited tangible resources can be utilized to generate disproportionately effective symbolic strategies to manage the perception of statehood so as to protect or further claims to de facto and de jure recognition (Chong 2010).

The role of some small states as 'norm entrepreneurs' (Ingebritsen 2006) is an important concept that can be operationalized within both the neoliberal and social constructivist paradigms where much greater account is taken of the diplomatic skills of states. Norway's skill as a norm entrepreneur is evidenced and facilitated by the state's prominence in the World Anti-Doping Agency (WADA) and in the number of bilateral anti-doping agreements in which it has been involved.

Sport as a resource for small states: soft power and sport

Discussions of the motives for governments to invest in sport – mainly based on analyses of major states – often distinguish between domestic and diplomatic motives (Houlihan 2007, Horne *et al.* 2013). Among the domestic motives are urban regeneration, nation building, social integration and social control while diplomatic motives include expressing support or displeasure for the actions of other states, image building and the building of tentative diplomatic links. Whether these preoccupations are shared with small states is rarely explored although it is likely that small states do indeed share many of the concerns of larger states especially those related to improving health and maintaining social stability. However, as many small states are ex-colonies, it is likely that differentiation from their former colonial power is a significant motive for government interest in and funding of elite sport. Furthermore, for many small states, differentiation from the former colonial power is paralleled by the need to differentiate themselves from the neighbours who are often culturally similar. Many of the small states in the Caribbean are ethnically/ culturally homogeneous, but less ethnically/culturally distinct from their close neighbours. Singapore is an example from Southeast Asia. For these countries, differentiation is more important than integration. As regards diplomatic or external relations, the motives may be the same as those of major states, but they are likely to be more intense. Diplomatic recognition, security of borders and access to trade are motives not peculiar to small states, but they are often much more urgent concerns for the reasons previously discussed. With this range of domestic and diplomatic motives in mind, it is pertinent to ask what strategies are available to small states to protect and advance their interests.

It is possible to identify five potential sport strategies that are available to small states in pursuit of their objectives: independent (autonomous), isomorphist/imitative, isolation-ist, collective and camp follower. While the choice of strategy can be affected (and mainly constrained) by many factors, the most significant will be the degree of internal stability/ unity, uncertainty/hostility of the external environment and domestic resources. Domestic resources refer not only to wealth, population and sport facilities, but also to the nature and depth of the existing sport culture. The nature and depth of the sport culture is both a resource for, and a constraint on, government and needs to be recognized as retaining a degree of autonomy from the state in many countries. For example, the popularity of the sport of shooting migratory birds in Malta is a diplomatic embarrassment rather than a diplomatic soft power resource.

Few small states have the option of adopting an *independent strategy* and those that do tend to be wealthy such as Abu Dhabi, Qatar, Singapore and Bahrain, all of whom have used state resources not only to attract major global sports events in football, golf, tennis, rugby, Youth Olympic Games and Formula 1, but also to establish a presence in the sporting infrastructure of other major (sports) states through the ownership of commercial football clubs (such as Paris St Germain which is owned by Qatar Sports Investment and Manchester City which is owned by a member of the Abu Dhabi royal family) and by sponsorship of global sports brands such as Barcelona FC (shirts sponsored by Qatar) and the Tour de France (Qatar Air as the official airline). These small states are able to accrue a degree of status, international visibility and influence which eludes many medium-range states. However, an independent strategy does not have to be based solely on wealth as a deeply rooted and distinctive sporting culture might be an alternative resource. A small state such as Ireland, which has a deeply rooted national sporting culture (focused on the games of hurling and Gaelic football), continues to pursue, even if only partially, an independent strategy (partial because of the state's increasing engagement with Olympic sport and football). Norway similarly has relied on its moral resources to pursue an independent strategy on issues such as youth elite sport and anti-doping.

A much more common strategy is one of policy *isomorphism/imitation* according to which states seek to protect their interests by adopting the sporting interests of a sports power or a cluster of sports powers. For a large number of ex-colonies, such as many Caribbean islands, isomorphism takes the form of retaining selected benign colonial links in the form of the sporting culture of the former imperial power – for example, cricket in the case of many British ex-colonies. Isomorphism can also take the form of adopting the sporting culture of a powerful neighbour, such as the United States, illustrated by the popularity of the sports of baseball and basketball in the Caribbean. Similar patterns of isomorphism can be found among the many small states that associate themselves with the Olympic movement and the Commonwealth Games. The extent to which isomorphism is a strategic choice rather than an unavoidable default position is debatable, but it does give small states access to an international stage and often to development funding from the resources of Olympic Solidarity, the Commonwealth and the major IFs. A variation on the strategy of isomorphism is the *camp follower* strategy in which small states seek to gain advantage by ingratiating themselves with major states or with major international sport organizations. The most effective way of pursuing this strategy is by making their votes available to states or, more commonly to leaders of IFs, in return for which they receive development funding.

The adoption of an *isolationist* strategy is increasingly rare as states, whether large or small, find it difficult to ignore the diplomatic opportunities that involvement in international sport offers. It would be hard to imagine a state emulating the isolationism of China in the 1960s and 1970s, a period during which it had very little international sporting contact and did not participate in the Olympic Games. One of the few countries occasionally to consider isolationism as a viable strategy is North Korea, but even that state's leadership seems to have doubts about its utility in furthering the state's interests. The isolationist strategy contrasts with the much more common *collective* strategy where small states cooperate to protect and promote their collective interests. The organization of the Games of Small States of Europe[1] is one example of small states protecting their interests in relation to participation in elite level sport. A second example of a collective strategy is the boycott by 32 states, many of which were small, of the 1986 Edinburgh Commonwealth Games over the issue of apartheid in South Africa. A third example would be the attempt by a group of mainly socialist states, including many small states, to organize a multi-sport event (Games of the New Emerging Forces – GANEFO) to rival the Olympic Games in the mid-1960s. However, political issues of the potency of apartheid capable of uniting a significant group of countries are less common today.

Accepting that the capacity of most small states to select their strategy is highly circumscribed, it is important to consider what resources they could utilize and how they might deploy them most effectively. Given the general lack of economic, military and population resources valued by the realist IR analysts, most small states need to rely on softer resources and on the careful husbanding of sporting talent, thereby acknowledging their willingness to test the assumptions of neoliberal and constructivist analysts. In recent years, there has been a growing interest among IR analysts in the nature and efficacy of soft power which is a valuable concept in understanding the motivations for small states to invest in elite sport not just in the hope of developing an Olympic medal contender, but more pragmatically to give them access to significant global arenas such as sport NGOs and mega-sports events. Small states potentially benefit from the greater awareness of the risks of deploying traditional military forms of power which, according to Nye (1990,

p. 167), has led to 'intangible power resources such as culture, ideology and institutions' becoming more important in interstate relations. Nye (2004, p. 2) defines power in terms of the ability to 'influence the behaviour of others to get the outcomes one wants' and sees soft power, the ability to 'attract and co-opt them to want what you want', as a complement to, and occasionally a substitute for, the exercise of hard power. According to Nye, three key sources of soft power are a state's culture, its political values and its foreign policy (Nye 2004, p. 11, 2008, p. 96).[2] Although an activist foreign policy, utilizing the conventional resources of wealth, trade and military power, is generally unavailable to small states, the other two elements of soft power – culture and political values – are more accessible and can be co-produced between the state and domestic sport organizations such as the NOC. As Bially Mattern (2007, p. 102) comments, in contrast to hard power, 'soft power is available to any actor that can render itself attractive to another'.

As Batoria (2005, p. 1) astutely observes, much of contemporary IR take place in 'a post-modern world of images and influences' in which there is a greater possibility for small states to shape the international agenda and further their domestic interests to a degree that exceeds their limited tangible resources. However, in order to take advantage of the opportunities for influence that soft power resources provide small states have to overcome the problem of their invisibility which requires the availability of some at least of the following resources:

- access to and voice within appropriate global arenas such as IFs, the IOC, WADA, United Nations Educational, Scientific and Cultural Organization (UNESCO) and Council of Europe (organizations which operate on the basis of one country-one vote offer greater scope for influence) or within the sporting cultural fabric of one or more major sports powers.
- access to and prominence within highly valued (culturally and politically) sports events such as the summer Olympic Games, which is usually achieved by the concentration of development resources on a small number of sports in which the state hopes to become prominent if not dominant. Examples would include New Zealand and rugby union and Jamaica and athletics.
- ideas, values and behaviour that are attractive to other states
- a concentrated focus on one or two issues
- prominent/charismatic advocates/ambassadors, which would normally be globally known athletes, for example, Alberto Juantorena of Cuba (member of IAAF Council), Frankie Fredericks of Namibia (IOC member; member of Champions for Peace[3]) and George Weah of Liberia (UNICEF Goodwill ambassador), but which might also be internationally known sporting institutions such as the Gaelic Athletic Association

The brief review of Singapore and Ireland illustrates not only the operationalization of these requirements, but also how they relate to the sport strategies adopted by two small states.

The examples of Singapore and Ireland

Singapore (population 5.3 m) is a small island city-state located within a complex geopolitical context. It is also a highly successful economy with the ninth highest per capita GDP in 2012. However, the current achievement of the 'Lion city' (Williams 2009) is hard-won. Colonial rule under the British Empire (Lim and Horton 2012), cruel occupation by Japanese Fascists (Lim and Horton 2011), traumatic separation from Malaysia (Chen 1988, Horton 2013), direct and indirect influence from, and connection with, China (Aplin & Quek 2002), and its geographical location of being sandwiched between two non-Chinese-dominated neighbours – Malaysia and Indonesia and its internal lack of resources and intricate racial composition – resulted in an 'ideology of survivalism' within the Singapore government (Ortmann 2009, p. 29, Long 2012). In terms of foreign affairs, Singapore has adopted a pragmatic diplomatic strategy since Lee Kuan Yew's tenure, and the security and development of Singapore are the overriding objectives. The independence from and balance between major powers (in spite of a certain degree of dependence on the US' military power for national defence) have been key features of the People's Action Party's diplomatic policies (Qie 2005, Wang and Jiang 2008). As a member of the Non-Aligned Movement (MFA 2013), Singapore has played an active role in international and regional affairs including economic development and cooperation, counterterrorism, disarmament and non-proliferation, and environment and peacekeeping operations and made a great contribution to the establishment of Association of South East Asian Nations (ASEAN). The political priorities for the Singapore government may be summarized as the maintenance of internal cohesion and the maintenance of its external security and sovereignty.

Although Singapore's hard power resource, economic strength, is a valuable diplomatic tool, the country has relied to a greater extent on a soft power strategy within which sport has become an increasingly important element (Horton 2013). During Lee Kuan Yew's prime ministership (1959–1990), sport mainly served the political objectives of social cohesion, racial harmony, national identity and the promotion of health and fitness with sporting excellence labelled as 'foolish and wasteful' (Horton 2002, p. 251). Indeed, Lee Kuan Yew, speaking in 1973 (quoted in Horton 2002, p. 251), said that 'There are no national benefits from gold medallists for smaller countries … it is foolish and wasteful for the smaller countries to do it'. However, his successor, Goh Chok Tong, took a different view and argued, in 1998, that 'The contribution of sports to nation building and national pride is far-reaching. When Singapore athletes win medals at international sports competitions, they bring immense pride and joy to our people. Sporting victories foster national joy and pride…' (quoted in Horton 2002, p. 258). The subsequent publication of ambitious sports strategies, for example, Sports Excellence 2000 (Ministry of Community Development 1993), the establishment of a sports ministry in 2000 and the government's considerable investment in the construction of the Sports Hub all took place against a background of a distinct lack of enthusiasm for participation in elite sport within the country.

The lack of domestic enthusiasm notwithstanding the Singapore state invested heavily in a range of elite and international sport initiatives reflecting the government's concern to pursue an independent strategy. The government's strategy to strengthen its profile at major international sports events was supported by a concentration on seven priority sports including table tennis, badminton and sailing and the offer of substantial financial rewards to medallists. Although its post-1990 strategy has had only limited success at the summer Olympics, the state has maintained its ranking in recent Asian Games and seen a substantial improvement in its medal total at the Commonwealth Games. A second element in the state sport strategy was to attract major sports and sports-related events which would give the country an international profile: these included hosting the 117th IOC session in 2005, hosting the Formula 1 Grand Prix since 2008, hosting the inaugural Youth Olympic Games in 2010 and the planned hosting of the Women's Tennis Association annual end of season competition from 2014 to 2018. The third element in the strategy is the investment in the 'High Performance Training Hub' (SSC 2009) which has attracted many international teams and star athletes such as Michael Phelps and Ronaldinho. The fourth element of the strategy focused on attracting international and continental sports federations and organizations to locate in the country. One of the first fruits of this strategy was the decision by the International Table Tennis Federation to move its Asia Pacific Office and Marketing Headquarters to Singapore in 2011 (SSC 2011, p. 50). The fifth element of the strategy was to seek the appointment of Singaporeans to influential posts in major international sport organizations. In addition to Ng Ser Miang, the current Vice President of the IOC, there are several Singaporean members on the executive boards or senior committees of the IFs of a number of Olympic sports including badminton, canoeing, equestrian, hockey, sailing and table tennis and within the WADA. The final element is the Foreign Sports Talent Scheme (FSTS) introduced in the early 1990s, in table tennis, with the aim of identifying and facilitating the migration and naturalization of foreign-born athletes. FSTS athletes are most common in the Singapore badminton and table tennis squads, but are also present in sports as diverse as football, water polo and hockey. Most FSTS athletes have come from China, but the Scheme has also attracted athletes from Nigeria, Brazil and England. The Scheme has brought considerable success. In the 2002 Commonwealth Games, Singapore won four gold medals in table tennis with a squad almost exclusively foreign-born; in 2007, FSTS athletes accounted for almost 35% of Singapore's gold medals in the SE Asian Games; the following year, a FSTS table tennis player won the country's first Olympic medal since 1960; and in the 2013, FSTS athletes won all the team table tennis gold medals for their newly adopted country.

Although Singapore is far from typical of small states, the evidence clearly indicates the extent to which the country has been able to incorporate sport into its wider diplomatic strategy. With its substantial economic resources, Singapore has been able to pursue an independent strategy for the maintenance of its sovereignty. With reference to the six resources which facilitate the utilization of sport as a soft power resource, Singapore was relatively successful in gaining access to positions of influence within some major global sport organizations, most obviously the IOC. Ng Ser Miang's senior position within the Olympic Movement also gave the state a prominent advocate on its behalf. The hosting of a number of globally significant sports events was also a notable resource. Singapore made less use of the opportunity to associate itself with a distinctive set of values or issues although it did have such an opportunity to raise its profile through the promotion of youth sport by virtue of being the inaugural host of the Youth Olympic Games.

However, the strategy has not been without controversy especially in relation to the FSTS which has divided domestic opinion with the national media clearly treating success by Singapore-born athletes much more positively. There have also been domestic expressions of concern that the domination of Chinese-born athletes in some sports, table tennis in particular, is contrary to the implicit policy of ethnic balance in Singapore public life. Furthermore, the Scheme has drawn criticism from Singapore's regional neighbours with Malaysia, Indonesia and Thailand accusing Singapore of employing foreign mercenaries.[4]

Ireland provides a significant contrast to Singapore. Ireland has a population of about 4.6 m and is culturally homogeneous with over 80% of the population describing themselves as Catholic. Until 1922, Ireland was a part of the United Kingdom. Upon independence, the island of Ireland was divided between the independent Republic in the south and six counties in the North East which remained part of the United Kingdom. For well over 100 years, sport has played a central role in Irish politics initially as a focus for cultural resistance to the United Kingdom and, since independence, as a focus for nation building and as a cultural representation of the irredentist claims to Northern Ireland. Unlike many other small states for much of its recent history, Irish sport, as with much of Irish politics in general, has been shaped by the country's relationship with the United Kingdom and the division of the island.

Central to the sport politics of Ireland has been, and continues to be, the Gaelic Athletic Association (GAA). The GAA was founded in 1884 and was central to the campaign of cultural resistance to British rule. The aim of the Association was to revive and promote traditional Irish sports such as hurling and Gaelic football and to resist the spread of alien English sports such as rugby, football and cricket, which were referred to as a 'demoralising and prostrating tide' (quoted in Mandle 1977, p. 420). The network of local clubs established by the GAA fostered a close relationship between Gaelic sport and nationalism. Following independence and a brief but bitter civil war, the government of Ireland was content to let the GAA take the lead in organizing the sporting life of the country partly because of the chronic shortage of public finance and partly because the GAA club network was reasonably comprehensive in its geographical coverage.

In more recent years, there has been a marked change in the attitude of the government towards sport in general and towards non-Gaelic sports in particular. Non-Gaelic sports such as football (soccer), rugby and a range of Olympic sports have steadily grown in popularity partly due to decline in the significance of the confrontation with the United Kingdom and partly due to membership of the European Union which has encouraged a regional outlook within the Irish government. Periodic international sporting success has also contributed to a lessening in the dominance of the GAA. The success of the Irish football team at the 1988 European Championships and at the 1990 and 1994 World Cup finals, Barry McGuigan's success in boxing, Michael Roche's victory in the 1987 Tour de France and medal success at the 1992 Olympic Games all contributed to changes in Irish sport politics.

The IR that have shaped Irish sport politics are, first, the relationship with the United Kingdom; second, the relationship with Northern Ireland; third, the relationship with the Irish diaspora and fourth, the relationship with other countries, especially in the European Union. Lacking the economic resources of a small state such as Singapore, Qatar or Monaco Ireland has had to rely more heavily on the distinctiveness of their sporting culture and wider range of strategies. The period from the establishment of the GAA in 1884 at least to the establishment of the Irish Free State in 1922 was characterized by a strategy of confrontational autonomy and sporting isolationism directed at Britain as the colonial power. The organization of sport in Ireland prior to independence was clearly divided along political lines, with the GAA enforcing rules which prevented its members playing 'British' sports and attempts to undermine the efforts of Unionist associations such as the Irish Amateur Athletics Association to promote track and field disciplines. The forceful nationalism of the GAA brought it regularly into violent confrontation with the British government. There were also many examples of harassment of the GAA by the British government such as the attempt to impose a tax on Gaelic sports, interference with the organization of transport for major sports events, occasional bans on Gaelic sports and police disruption of sports events (De Búrca 1980).

Since independence and the establishment of the Irish Republic in the 26 counties of the island of Ireland, the focus of Irish sport politics has been more specifically on the relationship with Northern Ireland. However, the strategy of the Irish state remained autonomous and defined by irredentism. From 1937 to 1998, the constitution of Ireland stated that 'The territory consists of the whole island of Ireland' (Article 2). Although the constitution was amended in 1998 as part of the process to end the civil war in Northern

Ireland to remove the claim of the Irish government to the six counties in the North, the new constitution still noted the right of 'every person born in the island of Ireland … to be part of the Irish nation'. Paralleling the claim of the Irish government to Northern Ireland, the GAA operates across all 32 counties of the two countries and is a significant cultural and political force within Northern Irish politics.

Complementing and reinforcing the pursuit of an autonomous and isolationist sport strategy in relation to Britain and more recently Northern Ireland, the Irish state through the GAA has also pursued a collective strategy aimed at other states with large Irish migrant populations, particularly the United States and Australia. Up until the 1980s, Irish sports diplomacy was limited to and defined by the Irish Diaspora and was concerned to maintain Irish cultural identity in overseas communities and also to support a lobby on behalf of Irish political interests (especially in terms of the country's relationship with Britain and Northern Ireland) in influential host countries.

It is only more recently, since membership of the European Union in 1973 and the Good Friday agreement in 1998 which changed the character and intensity of nationalist politics with regard to Northern Ireland, that the nature of the Irish sport strategy has altered significantly. While an autonomous strategy continues to define Irish sports diplomacy, it has become less exclusive and isolationist. Irish involvement in football and particularly in the Olympic Games has increased steadily in prominence both in terms of popular appeal and also in terms of government support.

As a small and, for many years, an impoverished state, Ireland demonstrated the capacity to define and pursue an independent sport strategy at the domestic and international levels. This capacity was the product of the politicization of culture in the anti-colonial struggle with the United Kingdom and the integration of cultural and political nationalism. The strategy was also shaped by the singularity of Irish political objectives namely independence from the United Kingdom and a united Ireland. Once those objectives had been partially achieved, an isolationist sport strategy became far less effective in supporting the diplomatic ambitions of the Irish state. However, while the Irish strategy has become more conventional, it still reflects a considerable capacity on the part of the Irish state to determine the nature of strategic change.

In contrast to Singapore, Ireland has utilized a different set of resources in its efforts to utilize sport as a soft power diplomatic instrument. Ireland does not have a strong current voice within major international sport organizations. Although Lord Killanin was the President of the IOC in the 1970s, it was a time when Olympic sport was a low priority for the GAA-dominated Irish government. Although Ireland has increased its involvement in global sports, it has not achieved a dominant or even prominent profile in any sport with the possible exception of rugby union. The independent and isolationist strategy of support for Gaelic sport has proved attractive to other states with a large Irish migrant population such as the United States and Australia, although the extent to which the prominence that support for Gaelic sport in migrant communities affects their host government policy in a way that is favourable to Irish interests in unclear.

The brief review of the cases of Singapore and Ireland illustrates the capacity of small states to utilize sport for both domestic and international political purposes, but they also highlight the constraints on strategy choice even for states that possess substantial resources – economic in the case of Singapore and cultural in the case of Ireland. However, these two cases, while far from being the only studies of sport as a policy resource in small states, draw attention to the lack of research into the sport policy objectives of small states, the strategies they develop to pursue their objectives and the extent to which they achieve their objectives.

The relative neglect of the study of small states is not just a feature of sport policy analysis, but is a characteristic of the study of both domestic politics and IR. In the field of IR, Christmas-Møller (1983 p. 39) referred to the 'benign neglect' of small states within the IR literature. Although Neumann and Gstöhl (2004, pp. 12–13) noted a revival in small state studies in the 1990s, they concluded that 'there has been no continuous flow of research on small states' and that 'the continued ... proliferation of small states ... must constitute a challenge to social scientists'. Part of the explanation for the relative neglect of small state studies in the field of sport policy is due, in part at least, to the sociology of knowledge within the field which is dominated and defined by the interests of academics in the 'sports powers' of western Europe and North America. Within this academic community, the study of small states, such as it is, is often confined to the sub-discipline of 'sport for development' which tends to treat small states as passive objects rather than active, or potentially active, subjects in the policy process.

A second explanation of the neglect of small states is the difficulty of studying them. Given that the location of much sport studies research is in higher-education institutions in large states, there are few small states that have the research capacity (for example, universities with sports studies departments) to undertake research or to partner researchers from abroad. Furthermore, it is arguable that selecting the study of small states as university career direction is probably not a wise move as expertise in the policy of major states is likely to be more attractive to university appointments committees and to academic publishers: the study of small states has a small audience and one that is likely to remain small. A third explanation for the inertia in this area of study is the problem that the IR field has experienced in defining (and theorizing) small states and the consequent attraction of moving on to other more amenable topics rather than address the definitional impasse and theoretical underdevelopment.

Small states and the future of international sport

Although it has been argued that there is a risk in overemphasizing the vulnerability of small states and underplaying their capacity, there are trends in international sport that add a degree of urgency to the study of small states. The first is the globalizing ambitions of the major IFs. The steady increase in the number of states participating in world championships puts at risk the success that some small states have managed to achieve in developing a niche sport such as Samoa, Tonga and even New Zealand in men's rugby union, Slovenia and Croatia in men's handball and Bulgaria and Cuba in men's volleyball. If these and other ambitious sports are successful in attracting the major sports powers to embrace their sport, then it may be more difficult for small states to preserve their niche position. A second trend which generally reinforces the ambitions of the IFs is the global objectives of the IOC. The steady growth in the number of states attending the summer Olympic Games has brought many small states into the Olympic Movement. The attraction of participation (even if only in the opening and closing ceremonies) and of access to Olympic Solidarity funding has a significant effect on domestic sport policy. Most states, even the wealthy, adopt an elite sport policy that is heavily influenced, if not determined, by the decisions of the IOC on the sports to be included in the summer and winter Games. The homogenizing effect of the dominance of the Olympic diet of sports is unlikely to benefit small states, but rather makes it even harder for them to identify a niche where they can develop and sustain a competitive advantage (and the associated international profile in sport). A final pressure on the strategies of small states is the increase in expenditure of the medium and major sport powers on elite athlete development (Houlihan and Zheng 2013) and particularly the increasing investment in sport science which may price many poorer countries out of an increasing range of sports.

Despite these potential additional pressures that small states face in developing and operationalizing an effective sport strategy in pursuit of domestic and especially international political objectives, there is sufficient evidence to suggest that small states can be adept at operating in the political and diplomatic interstices between the major powers. More systematic studies of the strategies and experiences of small states would not only enrich our understanding of sport policy processes in a distinctive and extensive group of states, but also enrich our understanding of the interface between international sport and IR beyond that of a narrow group of sports powers.

Notes

1. Games of the Small States of Europe website 2013: http://www.luxembourg2013.lu/index_en.htm
2. Justin Morris (2011) lists the English language, Greenwich Mean Time, the 'Westminster Model' of government, English Law and the BBC World Service among other 'soft power' assets belonging to Britain.
3. For more information on 'Peace and Sport', see http://www.peace-sport.org/en/ (accessed 24 January 2014).
4. 'The Flawed Foreign Sports Talent Scheme', http://www.askmelah.com/foreign-sports-talent-scheme/ (accessed 30 July 2014).

References

Andersen, S.S. and Ronglan, L.-T., 2012. *Nordic elite sport: same ambitions different tracks*. Oslo: Universitetsforlag.

Aplin, N.G. and Jong, Q.J., 2002. Celestials in touch: sport and the Chinese in colonial Singapore. *The international journal of the history of sport*, 19 (2–3), 67–98. doi:10.1080/714001763.

Arnaud, P. and Riordan, J., 1998. *Sport and international politics: the impact of fascism and communism on sport*. London: E & FN Spon.

Atkins, J., Mazzi, S., and Easter, C., 2000. *A commonwealth vulnerability index for developing countries: the position of small states*. London: Commonwealth Secretariat.

Bailes, A.J.K., 2009. *Does a small state need a strategy?* Occasional Paper, Centre for Small Sates Studies. Reykjavik: University of Iceland.

Batora, J., 2005. *Public diplomacy in small and medium-sized states: Norway and Canada*. Discussion Papers in Diplomacy. Clingendael: Netherlands Institute of International Relations.

Beckles, H. and Stoddart, B., 1995. *Liberation cricket: West Indies cricket culture*. Manchester: Manchester University Press.

BBC, 2012. London 2012: Judoka's Kosovo Olympic bid turned down. BBC. Available from: http://www.bbc.co.uk/sport/0/olympics/18205297 [Accessed 10 January 2014].

Bially Mattern, J., 2007. Why soft power isn't so soft: representational force and the sociolinguistic construction of attraction in world politics. *In*: F. Berenskoetter and M. Williams, eds. *Power in international relations*. London: Routledge, 98–119.

Bishop, M.L., 2012. The political economy of small states: enduring vulnerability? *Review of international political economy*, 19 (5), 942–960. doi:10.1080/09692290.2011.635118.

Braveboy-Wagner, J.A., 2010. Opportunities and limitations of the exercise of foreign policy power by a very small state: the case of Trinidad and Tobago. *Cambridge review of international affairs*, 23 (3), 407–427. doi:10.1080/09557571.2010.484049.

Briguglio, L., 1995. Small island developing states and their economic vulnerabilities. *World development*, 23 (9), 1615–1632. doi:10.1016/0305-750X(95)00065-K.

Chen, J., 1988. Singapore's diplomacy – the way in which it survives. *Southeast Asian studies*, 30 (1), 63–72.

Chong, A., 2010. Small state soft power strategies: virtual enlargement in the cases of the Vatican city state and Singapore. *Cambridge review of international affairs*, 23 (3), 383–405. doi:10.1080/09557571.2010.484048.

Christmas-Møller, W., 1983. Some thoughts on the scientific applicability of the small state concept: a research history and discussion. *In*: O. Höll, ed. *Small states in Europe and dependence*. Vienna: Braumüller, 35–53.

Commonwealth Secretariat, 1997. *A future for small states: overcoming vulnerabilities*. Report. London: Commonwealth Secretariat.

Cronin, M., 1999. *Sport and nationalism in Ireland: Gaelic games, soccer and Irish identity since 1884*. Dublin: Four Courts Press.

Davenport, D., 2002. The new diplomacy. *Policy review*, 116, 17–30.

De Búrca, M., 1980. *The GAA: A history of the Gaelic athletic association*. Dublin: Cuman Lúthchleas Gael.

Duursma, J.C., 1996. *Fragmentation and the international relations of micro-states: self-determination and statehood*. Cambridge: Cambridge University Press.

Grant, T.D., 1997. Between diversity and disorder. *American university international law review*, 12 (4), 629–686.

Ho, G. and Bairner, A., 2013. One country, two systems, three flags: imagining Olympic nationalism in Hong Kong and Macao. *International review for the sociology of sport*, 48 (3), 349–365. doi:10.1177/1012690212441160.

Horne, J., *et al.*, 2013. *Understanding sport: a socio-cultural analysis*. London: Routledge.

Horton, P.A., 2002. Shackling the lion: sport and modern Singapore. *The international journal of the history of sport*, 19 (2–3), 243–274. doi:10.1080/714001758.

Horton, P.A., 2013. Singapore: imperialism and post-imperialism, athleticism, sport, nationhood and nation-building. *The international journal of the history of sport*, 30 (11), 1221–1234. doi:10.1080/09523367.2013.794414.

Houlihan, B., 2006. Government objectives and sport. *In*: W. Andreff and S. Szymanski, eds. *Handbook on the economics of sport*. Cheltenham: Edward Elgar, 254–259.

Houlihan, B., 2007. Politics and sport. *In*: G. Ritzer, ed. *The Blackwell encyclopedia of sociology*. Oxford: Blackwell.

Houlihan, B. and Zheng, J., 2013. The Olympics and elite sport policy: where will it all end? *International journal of the history of sport*, 30 (4), 338–355. doi:10.1080/09523367.2013.765726.

Ingebritsen, C., 2006. Norm entrepreneurs: Scandinavia's role in world politics. *In*: C. Ingebritsen, *et al.*, eds. *Small states in international relations*. Seattle: University of Washington Press, 273–285.

Keech, M. and Houlihan, B., 1999. Sport and the end of apartheid. *The round table*, 88 (349), 109–121. doi:10.1080/003585399108306.

Lee, D. and Smith, N.J., 2010. Small state discourses in the international political economy. *Third world quarterly*, 31 (7), 1091–1105. doi:10.1080/01436597.2010.518750.

Leonard, M. and Small, A., 2003. *Norwegian public diplomacy*. London: The Foreign Policy Centre.

Lewis, V.A., 2009. Foreword: studying small states over the twentieth into the twenty-first centuries. *In*: A.F. Cooper and T.M. Shaw, eds. *The diplomacies of small states: between vulnerability and resilience*. Basingstoke: Palgrave Macmillan, vii–xv.

Lim, L.K. and Horton, P.A., 2011. Sport in Syonan (Singapore) 1942–1945: centralisation and nipponisation. *The international journal of the history of sport*, 28 (6), 895–924. doi:10.1080/09523367.2011.557910.

Lim, L.K. and Horton, P.A., 2012. Sport in the British colony of Singapore (1819–1900s): formation, diffusion and development. *The international journal of the history of sport*, 29 (9), 1325–1343. doi:10.1080/09523367.2012.694248.

Long, D., 2012. Predicament and transcendence: the deconstruction of Singapore's ASEAN strategy in the perspective on small state crisis consciousness. *Southeast Asian studies*, 54 (4), 27–38.

Maas, M., 2009. The elusive definition of the small state. *International politics*, 46 (1), 65–83. doi:10.1057/ip.2008.37.

Mandle, W.F., 1977. The IRB and the beginnings of the Gaelic athletic association. *Irish historical studies*, XX, 80. September.

Ministry of Community Development (MCD), 1993. *Sports excellence 2000: winning for Singapore*. Singapore: MCD and SSC Publication.

Ministry of Foreign Affairs of Singapore (MFA), 2013. *Overview: about Singapore* [online]. Available from: http://www.mfa.gov.sg/content/mfa/overseasmission/newyork/about_singapore/overview.html [Accessed 24 August 2013].

Morris, J., 2011. 'How Great is Britain', pp. 332–333.

Neumann, I.B. and Gstöhl, S., 2004 *Lilliputians in Gulliver's world? Small states in international relations*. Working Paper 1-2004, Centre for Small State Studies, University of Iceland. Reykjavik: CSSS.

Nye, J.S., 1990. Soft power. *Foreign policy*, 80, 153–171. doi:10.2307/1148580.

Nye, J.S., 2004. *Soft power. The means to success in world politics*. New York, NY: Public Affairs.

Nye, J.S., 2008. Public diplomacy and soft power. *The ANNALS of the American academy of political and social science*, 616, 94–109. doi:10.1177/0002716207311699.

Ortmann, S., 2009. Singapore: the politics of inventing national identity. *Journal of current Southeast Asian affairs*, 4, 23–46.

Preuss, H., 2004. *The economics of staging the Olympics. A comparison of the games 1972–2008*. Cheltenham: Edward Elgar.

Qie, Q., 2005. A small country's diplomacy with powers: on Singapore's establishment and evolution of the strategy of balance among the powers. *Around Southeast Asia*, 20 (1), 7–11.

Sam, M.P., 2003. What's the big idea? Reading the rhetoric of a national sport policy process. *Sociology of sport journal*, 20, 189–213.

Sherwood, H., 2012. Gaza's lone runner will carry the flag for Palestinian pride at the London Olympics. *The Guardian*, 1 March.

Singapore Sports Council (SSC), 2009. *Annual report 2008/2009*. Singapore: Singapore Sports Council.

Singapore Sports Council (SSC), 2011. *A year in the life of sporting Singapore: Annual report 2010/2011*. Singapore: Singapore Sports Council.

Smith, D., 2012. Dreams of gold in kingdom in the sky. *The Guardian*, 14 July.

Sutton, P., 2011. The concept of small states in the international political economy. *The round table: the commonwealth journal of international affairs*, 100 (413), 141–153. doi:10.1080/00358533.2011.565625.

Taylor, C., 1969. *Statistical typology of micro-states and territories: towards a definition of a micro-state. In UN Institute for Training and Research, small states and territories: status and problems*. New York, NY: Arno.

Thorhallsson, B., 2000. *The role of small states in the European union*. London: Ashgate.

Vital, D., 1967. *The inequality of states: a study of the small power in international relations*. Oxford: The Clarendon Press.

Wang, L. and Jiang, L., 2008. Balance of power and Singapore's diplomacy. *Legal system and society*, 11, 242–243.

Williams, M., 2009. The lion city and the fragrant harbor: the political economy of Singapore and Hong Kong compared. *The antitrust bulletin*, 54 (3), 517–577.

Elite sport in Scandinavian welfare states: legitimacy under pressure?

Lars Tore Ronglan

Department of Coaching and Psychology, Norwegian School of Sport Sciences, Oslo, Norway

Taking part in the global 'sports arming race' is demanding to all small nations, in terms of the efforts needed to succeed at the international stage. The Scandinavian countries are wealthy and could afford (in pure economic terms) wide-ranging elite sport investments. The question put to the foreground in this paper is the legitimacy of such efforts. More specifically, the aims are to investigate and discuss (1) the societal legitimacy essential to Scandinavian elite sport's credibility and support in general, and (2) how organizational legitimacy may be threatened by current developments aimed to strengthen international competitiveness. Based on an outline of the social democratic welfare model and the voluntary sport movements characterizing these societies, the paper emphasizes some rooted values and tensions underpinning sport in Scandinavia. Then, recent developments in the three countries' elite sport efforts are described and discussed. Over the last decades, Scandinavian elite sports have been professionalized, extended and run in line with general international tendencies. Some of these developments challenge values fundamental to the voluntary sport model. A paradox arises: aspects that at the surface seem counterproductive to modern elite sport development; voluntarism, decentralization and local ownership to sport contribute at a deeper level substantially to elite sports' legitimacy in this region. The paper is concluded by discussing conditions central to maintain elite sports' social legitimacy in Scandinavia, particularly in what ways sustainable elite sport development relies on the links to the broad voluntary movement.

Introduction

In an essay published in a special issue on sport in Scandinavian societies, Alan Bairner concluded that

> there is evidence of a specifically Nordic and/or Scandinavian approach to sport, associated above all with social solidarity. (...) Nordic sport continues to offer salutary lessons about how to play and organize sport and, in particular, about how to maintain a balance between mass participation and elite performance. (2010, p. 734)

To a certain extent, I agree with Bairner at this point. When reflecting on current elite sport developments in Scandinavia, there are indeed strong reasons to emphasize the linkage – or balance – between elite and mass sport. At the surface, the picture looks quite harmonious: compared to most other countries sport participation in the population is high (Ibsen and Seippel 2010) and, compared to their size, the countries do well in international sports (Andersen and Ronglan 2012). Mass and elite sport are, except Denmark, not organizationally separated, and a substantial part of the labour put into this field is of a non-salaried, voluntary type (Ibsen and Seippel 2010). Although differently organized at the central level, also Denmark is characterized by close ties between elite and mass sport given strong voluntary sport federations responsible for the whole variety of activities within their specific sport. This overall, quite united, structure marking the organized sport domain in Scandinavia reflects historical traditions and certain values underpinning the notion of 'what sport is' in these societies.

The demands of today's international elite sport are, however, something that even small countries as Denmark, Norway and Sweden cannot evade as long as they want to achieve results at the global scene. Over the last decades, elite sport efforts in Scandinavia have been professionalized, extended and run in line with general international tendencies. Research has shown that elite sport organizations in Western countries have become more similar during the last two decades (Green and Oakley 2001, Oakley and Green 2001, Augestad et al. 2006). Common elements include construction of elite facilities, targeted talent development programmes, support for 'full-time' athletes, provision of professional coaching and sports science and sports medicine support service (Houlihan and Green 2008). This captures a broad trend of convergence which also applies to Scandinavian countries' elite sport efforts.

A basic challenge to Scandinavian elite sport is how to deal with these 'intensification processes' – performance focusing, result optimization and resource mobilization – (Sjöblom and Fahlén 2010) in a sustainable way within a voluntary sport model associated with social solidarity (Bairner 2010). In other words, is it possible to take part in the global 'sports arming race' (De Bosscher et al. 2008) in ways that are in compliance with or strengthen, rather than undermine, social values and basic assumptions underpinning sport in these societies? Taking part in the sports arming race is indeed demanding to all small nations, in terms of the investments needed to succeed at the international stage. Now, the Scandinavian countries are wealthy and can afford (in pure economic terms) targeted elite sport efforts. The question put to the foreground in this paper is the legitimacy of such efforts; that is, what it takes to get 'value (not only medals) for money'. More specifically, the aims are to investigate and discuss (1) the societal legitimacy essential to Scandinavian elite sport's credibility and support in general, and (2) how organizational legitimacy may be threatened by efforts aimed to strengthen international competitiveness. I will restrict myself to focus on organizational tensions and questions arising from recent developments in Danish, Norwegian and Swedish elite sport efforts. As there are similarities as well as differences in the three countries' solutions and priorities, comparisons across the nations can provide a more nuanced picture of Scandinavian challenges and perspectives. After all, despite obvious similarities politically, socially and culturally, Scandinavia is not a single country but comprises three individual, small nations.

The paper unfolds as follows. First, the concept of legitimacy and its relevance to elite sport is briefly sketched out. This is followed by a rough outline of the 'social democratic' welfare model marking the Scandinavian nations and the characteristics of the voluntary sport movements in these societies. Thereafter, a more detailed description and discussion of different developments in the three countries' elite sport efforts is made, including comparison of selected cases from each country representing apparent sporting successes. This part draws on empirical material generated in a Scandinavian study on elite sport in the region (Andersen and Ronglan 2012). The paper is concluded by discussing some conditions central to elite sport's legitimacy in Scandinavia, particularly in what ways sustainable elite sport development relies on the links to the broad voluntary movement.

Elite sport and social legitimacy

Speaking of sport as 'illegitimate' draws attention towards phenomena such as cheating, doping or game fixing. Indeed, disclosure of such 'illegal unfair play' may hit involved actors hard and undermine public confidence both in individuals and in the sport organizations in which the violation occurs. Vibrant examples are the disclosures of extensive organized doping in international cycling and game fixing scandals in European football, leading the concerned international federations to put efforts into cleaning up and rebuilding trust and reputation. Now, illegal actions are not the primary focus of this paper. Legitimacy, however, goes beyond an effective enforcement of laws and regulations (legal legitimacy). Beside legal legitimacy and democratic legitimacy (traditional standards such as parliamentary oversight and representativeness), there is the broader concept of *social legitimacy*, addressing the accountability to citizens and responsiveness to the public at large.

The basis of social legitimacy is the support, and credibility societies give to an institution, agency or organization (Weiler 1999). It has been defined as 'a generalized perception or assumption that the actions of an entity are desirable, proper, or appropriate within some socially constructed system of norms, values, beliefs and definitions' (Suchman 1995, p. 574). This definition points to legitimacy as a social construction and thereby something that is embedded in culture specific conditions. Consequently, to assess the 'desirability' and 'appropriateness' of elite sport in Scandinavia the norms, values and beliefs underpinning sport in general in this region form a necessary backdrop. Furthermore, as legitimacy is a dynamic construct (Mathews 1993), it has to be continuously proved and defended under changing societal conditions.

An argument which further strengthens the need to contextualize elite sport efforts follows from the concept 'organizational legitimacy'. In building and maintaining support and credibility, organizations seek to establish congruence between the social values associated with or implied by their activities and the norms of acceptable behaviour in the larger social system in which they are a part (Mathews 1993). Dowling and Pfeffer (1975, p. 122) claim that 'insofar as these two value systems are congruent we can speak of organizational legitimacy'. Again; a consideration of Scandinavian elite sport bodies' legitimacy supposes that they are viewed in close relation to the voluntary-based organizations which constitute their basis. Organized sports constitute institutional fields (Powell and DiMaggio 1991) with values, perspectives and organizational arrangements that guide and regulate sport activities. In this respect, 'social legitimacy' and 'organizational legitimacy' are partly, but not entirely, overlapping concepts. Because several organizations constitute the organizational field, public support and credibility given to sport (social legitimacy) may be high, whereas the more specific organizational legitimacy may vary. However, there is of course reciprocity here: maintaining social legitimacy is difficult if vital actors in the institutional field suffer from lack of organizational legitimacy.

In the general policy literature, a distinction has been made between input- and output-legitimacy (Scharpf 1999). Generally spoken, 'input' concerns means and procedures in the production process, whereas 'output' refers to effectiveness and efficiency related to goal achievement (Lindgren and Persson 2010). In short, the former is associated with processes and the latter with outcomes. Applied to elite sport, input-legitimacy may be threatened if the social acceptance of resource usage or working methods of the elite sport system diminishes. Output-legitimacy may be threatened if the system fails to produce socially expected results. The two facets of legitimacy are both evident in current debates on elite sport; refer public discussions of national resource usage related to the Olympics in London and Sochi (input) and literature on elite sport systems' efficiency (De Bosscher *et al.* 2008) (output).

Reflecting upon the input–output distinction, there is obviously a relationship between the facets: there should be a reasonable correspondence. The distinction may however be useful in specifying the dimensions of (1) *how* results are produced (input) and (2) *what* the system actually produces (output). Central to input legitimacy is, in addition to resource usage, acceptance of means and procedures based on transparency and openness. Perceptions of the 'production process' as more open, representative and inclusive increase public confidence (Lindgren and Persson 2010). Related to elite sport, this aspect refers to social acceptance regarding how the results are produced, including the way elite sport efforts is organized and driven. This way, acceptance and support of the elite sport system as such can be regarded vital to input legitimacy.

When it comes to output, a decisive question is how 'output' is interpreted. In a narrow sense, output is about efficiency in producing results; in a wider sense, it concerns to what extent and in what ways the achieved results are seen as valuable to the society. Grix and Carmichael (2012) stated that the main reasons given for investment in elite sport in most Western societies appear as follows: elite sport success will lead to a better image abroad, bolster national identity and stimulate domestic mass participation; this, in turn, leads to a healthy nation and a wider pool of talents. They advanced the notion of a 'virtuous cycle' of sport to capture this philosophy which, notably, lacks empirical foundation. For instance, the elite sport–participation causality 'sounds eminently sensible, but there is little evidence to support it' (Grix and Carmichael 2012, p. 79). The same applies to the anecdotal claims that elite sport leads to social benefits such as building national pride (Sam 2009), although there is substantial research on sport (in general) and national identity (Ward 2009, Topic and Coakley 2010). However, in terms of legitimacy, as long as the reasons given to support elite sport are not thoroughly empirically refuted and clearly contested in the public discourse they seem to maintain credibility. As the relationships are complex and the assumptions underlying the 'virtuous cycle' are difficult to capture or measure at a general level, the notions of elite sport's social benefits (outcome in a wider sense) have to be assessed in local discourses.

Scandinavian welfare states and voluntarily sport movements

The Scandinavian Peninsula is a region in Northern Europe consisting of the three countries: Sweden, Denmark and Norway. In line with the topic of this special issue, they can be characterized as 'small'; today Sweden has 9.5, Denmark 5.5 and Norway 5 million inhabitants. The three neighbouring countries share a partly common history, and the languages are quite similar. In some respects, they do not represent any unity, for example, in foreign politics, Norway and Denmark (but not Sweden) are members of NATO, and Denmark and Sweden (but not Norway) are members of EU. Despite such differences, however, there are also striking similarities: politically, culturally and in relation to sport.

Social democratic welfare states

A common feature of the three countries is the welfare state model as the basis for social security and equality of rights. The justification for still labelling the Scandinavian societies 'social democracies' (Castles 2009) – even in a decade where liberal and conservative parties have strengthened their position at the expense of the social democrats – has to be found in the continuation of the Scandinavian welfare states. The notion of 'Scandinavian social democracies' rests upon the political centre of gravity in these societies during the last 50 years. Not only were social democratic politics powerful in these countries for much of the post-war period. Equally important is the distinctive welfare states that were developed in these countries, by Esping-Andersen (1990) labelled 'social democratic' welfare models.

In characterizing three typologies, Esping-Andersen (1990) distinguished between liberal, conservative and social democratic welfare regimes. The latter, quite unique to Scandinavia, is driven by an ideal of equal social benefits to all citizens and far-reaching state ambitions concerning security and well-being for all members of society. The goal is a welfare state offering an equality of high standards, and welfare production mainly takes place within the public sector. Financing of the extensive public sector requires an active labour market policy aimed at full employment and high tax revenues. Still today, in a time of shifting governing coalitions, it seems to be a reasonable degree of political consensus on these basic features. In sum, the Scandinavian countries of today are wealthy, characterized by a high level of employment, strong welfare states and an emphasis on egalitarian values.

The voluntary sport movement

Embedded in the context of the social democratic welfare state sport has developed largely within voluntary sport organizations. Despite the extensive public sector marking these societies, the domain of sport is left over to the third sector. At first sight this may seem surprising. However, this is as example of how sport fits well into another typical feature of the Scandinavian societies, namely the occurrence of large 'popular movements' (Eichberg and Loland 2010). Sport is definitively one of those.

The state keeps an arm's length distance to the voluntary sport movement. This does by no means imply that public authorities see sport as unimportant; indeed, they take a main responsibility for infrastructure and provide crucial funding to the associations (Rafoss and Troelsen 2010). But the state has left the organizing and running of sports to civil organizations, and a substantial part of the labour put into this field is unpaid voluntary work. Within the framework of the welfare state, a division of labour has arisen in which the government ensures public access to the facilities, while the sport organizations (with public support) concentrate on developing and organizing sports activities. The result is a voluntary sport movement characterized by a huge degree of autonomy and self-regulation, combined with extensive state support based on the notion of sport as an important component of the welfare society (Bergsgard and Norberg 2010). This Scandinavian model reflects a mutual dependency between the state and the sport movement marked by an 'actively neutral' state position (Norberg 1997) and sport organizations operating with 'normative autonomy regarding values and morals' (Carlsson and Lindfelt 2010, p. 719). However and particularly interesting in relation to the focus of this paper, vital for the sport movement in claiming maintained autonomy and public support at an arm's length distance, is the imperative to continuously demonstrate its significance as a cornerstone of the welfare society. As few specified political signals follow the money, the sport organizations need to show their eligibility related to the basic assumptions behind the funding. In short, the autonomy increases the need of legitimation efforts.

This leads to an account of the ideal of voluntarism, a characteristic feature of the sport movement. Local, voluntarily driven sport clubs constitute the basic units of

Scandinavian sport. In terms of resources, main sources of income in the clubs are membership fees and income from activities conducted by volunteers, while public sector funding and sponsors only account for between a third and a quarter of total income (Ibsen and Seippel 2010). In almost all sports associations, voluntary unpaid work – as a coach or a leader, on the board, in committees or to raise money – is indispensable. I agree with Ibsen and Seippel (2010) who claim that there is a positive cultural climate towards this way to organize sports in Scandinavia. Although this form of 'collective volunteer-ism' is changing concurrently with individualization processes in late modernity (Wollebæk et al. 2014), the quantity of voluntary work remains remarkably stable. Enjolras (2002) showed that increasing commercial resources did not reduce the level of voluntary work in Norwegian sport organizations. Moreover, according to Seippel (2010), proved increased amount of professional work in the organizations does not seem to threaten the level of voluntary work. In sum, although the sport model has become more differentiated due to processes such as professionalization, commercialization and globalization (Carlsson et al. 2011), voluntarism can still be regarded as one of the core values associated with organized sport in Scandinavia.

The meaning of sports

This brief sketch of the welfare state and the sport movement provide a backdrop for a main point related to social legitimacy and sport; in general, sports *matters* in these societies. Now, this is in no way unique for Scandinavia; sport matters all over the world. It would be more accurate to claim, as Bairner (2010) does viewing the region from a British point of view, that people in Scandinavian countries are more likely to be directly involved in sport as active participants and volunteer coaches than is the case in most other western societies. Because local clubs organized and run by parents and volunteers constitute the basic unit of the sport movement, it can be argued that the link between sport and local communities is stronger than elsewhere. Although literature on sport and community integration has indicated that there is a tendency to oversell sports' potential as an integrative force (Coalter 2007), empirical studies in this area have typically investigated authorities' targeted initiatives aimed to *use sport as a tool* in promoting integration (Hassan and Telford 2014). In contrast to such externally initiated top-down initiatives, it seems more reasonable to suggest such positive outcomes as an implicit consequence of a voluntary driven local club (although the relationship is hard to judge). Then, it is more likely that the relationship between the grass-roots clubs and local communities becomes internal, promoting the community's identification with and feeling of ownership of local sports.

The social organization and workings of voluntary associations contribute in defining the meaning of sport as a societal phenomenon in these countries. Beside public health, not surprisingly used as a prominent argument for supporting sport, democratic and social integration seems to be equally prominent arguments underpinning Scandinavian sports policy objectives (Bergsgard and Norberg 2010). In addition to youth and mass sport being regarded a role as provider of good health, its significance as an expression of local engagement, democratic participation and egalitarian values contributes to legitimize sport as part of the Scandinavian welfare societies (Helle-Valle 2008). This way, output legitimacy (outcomes) is more clearly related to 'participation' in a broad meaning of the term than it is to 'performance', with subsequent consequences to input legitimacy (processes). Maintained organizational legitimacy supposes clubs that remain inclusive and member driven at the local level and that federations at the central level proceed according to democratic principles such as representation of grass-roots interests by the umbrella organization. Although a recent study of the Norwegian confederation of sports (the umbrella) did not reveal evidence of oligarchic governance (Enjolras and Waldahl 2010), the study underscored that 'memberships' lack of active participation, informal network-based decision-making and issues of representativeness are likely to undermine organizational legitimacy' (p. 215). Such tendencies may be reinforced by developments in the 'elite sport system', to which we now turn.

Elite sport development in the Scandinavian context

As in the rest of the Western world, elite sport obviously plays a role also in Scandinavia, reflected in current sport policies, public interest and priorities and efforts made by the sport associations. In recent decades, elite sports have successively been given a more prominent position in policy documents (Bergsgard and Norberg 2010) and targeted elite sport bodies have supplemented the traditional organizational structure.

The organizational linkage between mass and elite sport

Before looking in more detail into recent developments in elite sport efforts, the organizational linkage between mass and elite sport need to be emphasized. Until the 1980s, no organizational unit had any sole responsibility for elite sport in neither of the Scandinavian countries. The general rule was that the same associations that promoted youth and mass sport also had the main responsibility for elite sports within their domain. The voluntary sports sector consisted of one confederation (several in Denmark) – serving as umbrella organizations – and their network of national sport organizations, regional/ district organizations, local sport councils and local sports clubs. All organized sports – children and youth sport, mass sport, talent development and elite sport – were organized and driven within the same organizational structure. This 'segmented structure' (Andersen and Ronglan 2012), meaning that each individual sport federation (e.g. skiing, cycling, swimming) holds the responsibility for all kinds of activities within their domain, still today applies as a main rule. Thus, the emergence of overarching elite sport bodies over the last decades has supplemented the segmented structure rather than radically changing it.

Establishment of elite sport bodies

In Denmark and Norway, the emergence of more distinct elite sport models can be traced back to the 1980s. Until this decade, the Olympic Committees played a modest role at the outside of the confederations, whereas the real responsibility for mass and elite sport development lied with the individual sport federations. During the 1980s, however, there was a closer cooperation between the national sport confederation (the umbrella) and the Olympic Committees in both countries, ending with a merger in the mid-1990s. A part of the cooperative efforts was the establishment of a new elite sport body in both countries: Team Denmark (TD) in Denmark (1985) and Olympiatoppen (OLT) in Norway (1988/1989).

The introduction of special elite sport organizations at the national level modified the traditional segmented model. In Denmark, the process leading to the establishment of TD involved party politicians and civil servants in key roles (Hansen 2012). Their motivation was only partly directed towards the internal efficiency of elite sport efforts, as the political discussions were framed within a welfare state perspective (Ibsen *et al.* 2010). A major concern was that elite athletes engaging in extreme efforts of modern elite sport might sacrifice health, education and opportunities in later life. As a response to this, an elite sport law was enacted which constituted a framework for TD, and TD became a state funded state agency with its own board, representing sport interests as well as broader political and societal interests (Storm 2012). This way, efforts were made to institutionalize TD in a way that secured societal and organizational legitimacy. In Norway, the establishment and further development of OLT followed a somewhat different route. In contrast to Denmark, it was leaders within the sports movement that introduced new initiatives, focusing on how to strengthen the competitiveness of elite sport (Andersen and Ronglan 2012). OLT was organized as an elite sport body integrated in the sports confederation, with no external board, supported by the state through funding but at an arm's-length distance. The autonomy of OLT, compared to TD, arguably increased the need for legitimation efforts. First, OLT has had to operate in ways that build support and credibility concerning elite sport in the population at large (social legitimacy); second, OLT's decisions are judged by the wider sport movement, and it has had to justify its eligibility within the organizational network (organizational legitimacy).

TD and OLT have over the last decades been institutionalized as core actors in elite sport production in Denmark and Norway (Augestad *et al.* 2006, Storm and Nielsen 2010). As overarching elite sport bodies, they are aimed to lead, coordinate and strengthen efforts across specific sports. In some ways, this implies a centralization of elite sport support as a response to increasing demands at the international stage. However, to stress a point touched upon earlier, the individual sport federations still have the main responsibility for developing their own sports (mass *and* elite). OLT and TD are primarily meant to work through the federations, rather than operate as isolated actors. Disagreements concerning division of responsibilities and the extent of involvement and interference are from time to time expressed and display underlying tensions embedded in this structure, particularly in Norway (who 'owns' elite sport) (Goksøyr and Hanstad 2012). For example, the cooperation between OLT and the Norwegian Ski Federation (NSF) was for a long time limited and characterized by mistrust, while the dispute concerning who (OLT or NSF) deserved credit for international skiing successes was rather hostile. NSF was among the federations that throughout the 1990s questioned (and actively worked to undermine) the organizational legitimacy of OLT (Hanstad 2002).

In Sweden, contrary to Denmark and Norway, no specific elite sport body has been established, and the traditional organizational set-up has remained remarkably stable during the last decades. This structure emphasizes the autonomy of individual sport federations and clear division of roles between the sport confederation on the one hand, and the Olympic Committee on the other. Due to increasing commercialization, the Swedish Olympic Committee (SOC) has grown and become a significant actor. Crisp tensions characterize the current relationship between the sport confederation (RF) and the SOC, stemming from long disagreement on priorities and organizational solutions (Norberg and Sjöblom 2012). Not being able to reach a cooperative solution has led both sides to claim principal ownership to elite sports and thus inhibited coordinated efforts. The tensions include a struggle for legitimacy and a rhetoric aimed at devaluating the other part: RF accuses SOC of lack of representativeness (input legitimacy), whereas SOC accuses RF of lack of competence and efficiency regarding elite sport support (output) (Norberg and Sjöblom 2012). As SOC has been professionalized and expanded, its way of supporting elite sport has become quite similar to TD and OLT: offering expertise and support to federations, teams and athletes and intervening in performance processes (but only in Olympic sports). This way, the three nations today seem quite similar concerning the ways targeted elite sport bodies (TD, OLT, SOC) operate, but quite different concerning the ways these bodies are part of/separated from the voluntary movement. Indeed, they each face their specific legitimation challenges.

Distinctive Scandinavian 'elite sport systems'?

Common to the Scandinavian countries is that a notion of a distinct 'elite sport system' seems somewhat difficult to explain or capture. In some ways, the concept makes sense in a Scandinavian context, as construction of elite sport facilities, targeted talent development programmes, support for full-time athletes, provision of professional coaching and sports medicine support service have become integrated in elite sport efforts also in these countries. The establishment and working methods of the elite sport bodies described earlier have definitely reinforced such developments. If we understand an 'elite sport system' as driving forces directed towards continuous performance enhancement and the consequences of such endeavours, this is clearly present in Scandinavia today. As *processes*, an elite sport system is evident.

More difficult, however, is to capture an elite sport system understood as an organizational structure. What complicates the picture is the intimate relationship between mass and elite sport, expressed in the ways sport as such is organized. Because where starts and where ends the 'elite sport system', understood as an organizational structure? In organizational terms, the notion of such a system has to include far more than the targeted and professionalized elite sport bodies. The sport federations, responsible for both mass and elite sport within their domain, definitely play a major role. Elite sport studies investigating for instance cross country skiing in Norway (Hansen 2014) and ice hockey in Sweden (Fahlén 2006) clearly demonstrate the federations' (including the clubs') major role related to elite sport development, particularly in huge national sports. Here, the elite sport bodies may provide important specific competence and support (Hansen 2014), but compared to the total amount of resources allocated to elite sport (money, personnel, competence, technology), the individual federations are by far the most important contributors. For example, in economic terms, the elite sport budget of the Norwegian ski association alone reaches almost the level of OLT's total budget; a budget OLT distributes between dozens of sports. Similarly, in Denmark, it is estimated that the federations' total spending on elite sport is approximately twice that of TD (Storm 2012). It is worth noting that this estimate does not include the voluntary work in the federations (at club, regional and central level), which, if included, even clearer would demonstrate the federations' role as core actors in the 'elite sport system'.

This joint responsibility for elite sport development partly explains why the Scandinavian elite sport bodies seem so modest in international comparison. Stated in a different manner, the quite limited resources (in international comparison) allocated to the elite sport bodies do not prove that elite sport efforts are as modest as this funding alone may indicate. The scale of targeted efforts initiated by the individual sport federations varies heavily from one sport to another, depending on the size of the sport, the resource base and not least political priorities made by the respective sport federation. The dual aim of the federations, promoting both elite and mass sport, constitutes a basic distinction underlying political controversies over a range of topics. A major challenge embedded in the Scandinavian sport model is that there are inherent tensions between groups which promote efficiency and performance as basic goals, and groups which promote traditional organizational values linked to democracy and representation (Steen-Johnsen and Hanstad

2008). Interwoven in the notion of Scandinavian 'elite sport systems' is continuous debates rooted in these tensions.

An implicit parallel (or opposite) to the concept of an 'elite sport system' is a 'mass sport system'. Due to the Scandinavian organizational structure, these are not separate, but to a large extent overlapping 'systems', making it harder to distinguish elite sports concerns from mass sports concerns. This interweaving has important consequences when it comes to questions related to social as well as organizational legitimacy of elite sport. A major concern is about 'ownership' of elite sport; that is, the extent to which central bodies (e.g. OLT, TD) can intervene and make decisions which bind the sport federations. By being given the 'overall responsibility' for elite sport, the central agencies seek to attach conditions to their priorities; for example, allocate resources provided that the federations meet certain requirements. Particularly to small federations with scarce resources, this can lead to 'policy drift' (Béland 2007) towards a more evident elite sport focus. This is again linked with transparency in decision-making and resource allocation, as the federations, with a dual aim of promoting elite and mass sport, may want to blur such a drift in a societal and political context where mass sport in many ways stands in a discursively privileged position (Helle-Valle 2008).

Given the interdependency between the overlapping 'mass sport system' and 'elite sport system' in Scandinavia, the region faces an increasing challenge. On the one hand; competitiveness in modern elite sport supposes an adaption to the international environ-ment; that is, comprehensive and targeted efforts aimed at producing international results. On the other hand, elite sport in Scandinavia is dependent on an adaption to the values characterizing the voluntary sport movement to maintain its legitimacy as an integrated part of the movement. So far (modest) elite sport bodies have been added to the organizational structure, modified it and strengthened the intensification processes related to elite sport. Still, however, distinct Scandinavian elite sport systems is difficult to distinguish, understood as a structure detached from organized sports as such.

Different paths to elite sport successes – three Scandinavian cases

To illustrate the interplay between 'mass' and 'elite' and the complex organizational relationships underlying Scandinavian elite sport, I now turn to three specific cases of sport successes: Swedish golf (Wijk 2012), Norwegian women's handball (Ronglan 2012) and Danish men's track cycling (Nielsen and Hoffmann 2012). The idea is to describe and compare cases that have achieved extraordinary international results over the last decade(s). The three stories provide examples of different tracks to sporting success and can thus shed light on conditions and drivers behind elite sport successes, the linkages between different parts of the sport organizations, and in which ways the portrayed stories are socially valued beyond pure athletic achievements.

Concerning international results, the 'success stories' can be summarized as follows. (1) Swedish golf: Until mid-1980s hardly any Swedish golfers qualified for world elite competitions. However, during the last two decades (until 2010), 10–15% of the world tour players were Swedes and more than 50 Swedes won tournaments at the major tours (Wijk 2012). Thus, the most remarkable aspect is the breadth of the success. (2) Norwegian women's handball: The international breakthrough happened about the same time as the Swedish golfers, when the national team in 1986 won its first medal in the World Championships. Since then, the team has dominated international handball; from 1986 to date, no other nation has won as many medals in international championships as Norway (Ronglan 2012). Thus, the sustainability of the success is striking. (3) Danish men's track cycling: This story differs somewhat from the others as track cycling has a long successful tradition as Olympic sport in Denmark. However, the 'modern' story of Danish track cycling is about how a deterioration of international competitiveness during the 1990s was turned into a new era of success from 2005 onwards (Nielsen and Hoffmann 2012). Thus, the story is mainly about regaining competitiveness.

In contextualizing these stories, I will restrict myself to elaborate on four dimensions: the relationship to mass sport participation in the respective sport, the significance of facilities/infrastructure, organizational strategies in the respective federations and the involvement of elite sport bodies. Along these dimensions, there are significant differences between the three cases, as summarized in Table 1 and described in more detail in the following sections.

'The Swedish golf miracle'

Two dimensions stand out as characteristic features of the story: first, the explosive expansion of players in general and the development of golf towards a 'folk sport' in Sweden and second, the modest role played by central sport leaders or elite sport bodies directly related to the elite sport success. Regarding the first point, it is reasonable to suggest that the huge broadening of the sport at least prepared the ground for the elite success that was to come. Massive building of golf courses throughout Sweden in the 1980s and 1990s improved training conditions for athletes and teams. The upgraded infrastructure was accompanied by an expansion of 'open' golf clubs, that is, local community-based clubs where in principle anyone was welcome to play. This contributed to transform golf from being a narrow 'upper-class sport' in Sweden to become a broad popular sport. Around 100 golf clubs and 40,000 members in the early 1970s grew to 450 clubs and 600,000 members around the millennium (Wijk 2012).

The processes leading to the broadening of golf, both geographically and socially, can be linked to the next point, namely that neither the central level of the federation nor any elite sport body operated as strong driving forces for developing world-class performance. Initially, the explosion of young players was not part of any distinct elite sport strategy;

Table 1. The development of four key dimensions during the emergence and continuation of Scandinavian success periods (adapted from Andersen and Ronglan, 2012, p. 270).

	Swedish golf	Norwegian women's handball	Danish men's track cycling
Mass sport participation	Increasing mass sport participation prior to elite sport success	Stable mass sport participation prior to/ during elite success	Diminishing mass sport participation during elite sport success
Facilities	Massive building of courts prior to elite sport success	Gradual improvement prior to/during elite sport success	The one essential track modernized and reopened
Strategies/key actors	Bottom-up process. Local/regional mobilization	Broad top-down process. Strategy to extend core competencies	Narrow top-down process. Niche strategy, strict priorities
Interaction with 'elite sport system'	Modest	Increasing	High

the agenda was to broaden the sport. However, when world-class results started to come, the relatively small 'central level' of the golf federation took some actions to nurture the continued success. Such actions included improved coach education and talent development initiatives in general, rather than any direct interventions in the club teams and regional teams which constituted the basic units of the success. As golf was no Olympic sport during this period, it did not qualify for any support from SOC.

Taken together, the story of Swedish golf fits well into the traditional notion of elite sport development within the context of the Scandinavian sports model. It pictures a powerful decentralized bottom-up process supported by state funded improvement of infrastructure leading to a remarkable increase in players as well as performance level. This story, which has been called 'the golf miracle' in Sweden (Wijk 2012), appears as a strong testimony of the close relationship between mass and elite sport. As such, it contributes to strengthen public confidence in the sport model and elite sport's value as a genuine product of the sport movement. Given the developments of current elite sport, however, it can be questioned if the golf miracle is an example of yesterday's solutions: perhaps it is literally 'miraculous' to expect elite sport success of tomorrow if a specific elite sport strategy is absent?

Institutionalized Norwegian handball success

The handball case differs from the story above. Here, the elite sport success over the last decades can be framed as a story of gradual institutionalization of basic elements necessary to be competitive internationally, primarily driven by the handball federation. Contrary to the Swedish golf case, there was neither any significant growth of players prior to or during the success, nor any massive improvements of infrastructure relevant to handball. Participation in grass-roots handball remained high and stable during the period, while there has been a steady improvement of courts and training facilities. The central dimensions of the more profound institutionalization process appeared to be a more consistent and structured talent work, an increased cooperation with the elite sport body OLT, and the implementation of a distinct and uniform holistic coaching philosophy across the youth, junior and senior national teams. These developments were facilitated by a remarkable stability in leadership position within the federation, which made it easier to develop and maintain long-term strategies (Ronglan 2012).

Compared to the Swedish golf story, which roughly can be portrayed as elite sport success emerging as a pure 'bottom-up' product of the voluntary sport model, the handball story definitively appears as a more centralized driven process. The success of the national team was not just a reflection of improved performances and efforts made at the club level. Targeted elite sport strategies were developed by key actors from the 1990s and onwards aimed at developing and extending core competences, strategies that gave priority to the national team (Ronglan 2012). However, it is important to note that the handball success, although it relied on the establishment of a more targeted elite sport model, has been underpinned by a high degree of legitimacy both within the handball federation and in the Norwegian public. One reason for this is the close link that has been maintained to community and club handball as a major national sport for girls and women (Broch 2014). Another dimension that adds societal value to the success is a public discourse linking the handball idols – who are among the most celebrated sport stars in Norway – to the image of a society marked by gender equality (Lippe 2002).

The revival of Danish track cycling

The Danish track cycling case differs from the golf and handball stories in several ways. First, track cycling is a sport with a long elite sport tradition in Denmark; the first Olympic track cycling medal was won in 1924. Next to sailing, cycling is the sport where Denmark has won most medals in the Olympic Games, and most of these have been achieved on the track. Second, the modern story of Danish track cycling is primarily about how a radical deterioration of international competitiveness during the 1990s was turned into a new era of success from 2005 and onwards. This way, this is an example of a narrow and focused strategy aimed at regain competitiveness (Nielsen and Hoffmann 2012).

The revival of Danish track cycling can be seen as an elite sport success created by the Danish cycle federation in close cooperation with TD as the central elite sport body. This alliance adopted a strict niche strategy to facilitate the development of a number of carefully selected athletes, competing in particular track cycling events. Distinguished foreign coaches was hired, who implemented targeted training models aimed at maximizing performance in the selected events. A vital part of the strategy was to get public support for re-establishing a top modern track for track cycling. Because of the broad recruitment base found in road cycling, and the centralized niche strategy employed in developing selected cyclists, only one track was needed. Leaders in the cycle federation, in close cooperation with facilitators from TD, were the entrepreneurs behind this strategy. The story illustrates how a competitive sport, in the need of a particular and defined form of support, appears as an 'ideal case' for a centralized elite sport body as TD. In such cases, specialized support and relatively small but highly targeted investments are likely to pay off. Danish track cycling is as example of how specific infrastructure and competence in combination with strict priorities can foster success despite a shrinking recruitment base. It is worth noting that the number of track cyclists, and the number of competing road cyclists, diminished during the recent elite sport success.

Top-down or bottom-up?

One should be careful to draw definite conclusions based on three cases from different time periods and founded on diverse data material. Looking at the three cases together, however, it seems clear that even within a quite homogeneous Scandinavian context, there are different paths to elite sport success. Not only did the paths to success differ, but also the context in which these developments took place. Additionally, the stories represent 'successes' in quite different meanings of the word and in quite different sports. The Danish and Swedish stories seem in many ways to be opposites in terms of strategy and scope. Nevertheless, both the centralized niche strategy adopted by central leaders in Danish cycling and TD and the evolving wave of elite golf players nurtured within a more decentralized Swedish sport model resulted in continued international success.

The three individual stories should not be seen as representative for a specific Swedish, Norwegian and Danish way of promoting elite sport development; the stories do not reflect typical national differences between the three countries. They can rather be seen as different typologies based on a continuum (bottom-up/top-down), which seem to be combined and blended in different ways across Scandinavia, leading to more or less successful processes. The divergence of the three stories might help to kill the myth that 'one size fits all'. It seems clear that societal, organizational and sport-specific contexts should be taken into account when trying to understand why particular efforts or strategies succeed or not. It is also worth noting that the three cases do not support the widespread notion ('virtuous cycle') that successful elite sport as such will generate mass sport, or the other way around. The relationship is definitely not that simple.

Common features across the stories are first of all that the three sports had a broad foundation within the population, both as mass sport activities and in terms of public interest. Second, the elite sport successes symbolized societal values beyond the achievements as such, like voluntarism (Swedish golf), gender equality (Norwegian handball) and notions of national identity (cycling in Denmark). Third, it seemed to be a relatively low level of controversies between elite sport and mass sport efforts during the success periods (Andersen and Ronglan 2012). Conflicting priorities between elite and mass sport are an ongoing concern within Scandinavian sport in general; however, this appeared not to be a central issue in these cases. This indicates that the development took place in a context of high organizational and societal legitimacy.

Scandinavian elite sport: legitimacy under pressure?

Success in elite sport can be understood in different ways. A simple way is to measure it purely as medals achieved in major international competitions. The assumption seems to be that medals as such will bring national pride. At least in a Scandinavian context, it could be argued that such an understanding of 'outcome', which seems to be an increasingly dominant perspective internationally (Grix and Carmichael 2012), is too narrow. The societal importance of sporting achievements – outcome in a wider sense – has to include reflections on whether the ways in which results were achieved are regarded valuable or not. This directs the attention towards national perspectives on what kinds of sports are important (for different reasons), and public judgments on the processes leading to the performance. To put it simple, maybe it is not the total number of medals that is crucial (at least to small countries), but *which* medals (outcome legitimacy) as well as *how* they are achieved (input legitimacy). A prime example of the latter is of course doping, clearly expressed in the current Danish debate following the scandals revealed in international cycling. The former admiration of Danish track cycling achievements is today rapidly declining as a consequence of recent Danish doping disclosures, leading to public confessions to rebuild trust (Thing and Ronglan 2014). A parallel with even wider consequences is the 'crisis of legitimacy' caused by the public's response to Finnish skiers doping violations in 2001, heavily contributing to the breakdown of the skiing federation (Lämsä 2012). Although doping may be considered among the extreme violations, such examples may illustrate the significance of input legitimacy when it comes to elite sport in Scandinavia.

As stated in the introduction, public acceptance and support to the elite sport system as such can be regarded vital to input legitimacy. Given the nature of modern elite sport, it is quite obvious that the distance between the characteristics of a voluntary sport movement on the one hand and the requirements needed to succeed in elite sport on the other is increasing. This growing gap is a global trend. However, particularly challenging within the Scandinavian model is that the tensions between 'sport for all' and international competitiveness have to be managed largely within a united organizational framework. Because the 'elite sport system' and the 'mass sport system' are heavily overlapping, there is a reciprocal influence; decisions and actions to strengthen elite sport directly influence preconditions for mass sport. In such interweaved structure, input legitimacy (related to elite sport) has to be looked upon more broadly than in sport models with a clearer division between mass and elite. In short, input legitimacy becomes more vital to social legitimacy. While the elite sport bodies tend to emphasize outcome in a narrow sense (medals) to substantiate their role and strengthen organizational legitimacy, the significance of their policies, decisions and actions (input) should not be underestimated as a main source of social legitimacy.

One example of how this interweaving between mass and elite is expressed is the ongoing debate on youth sport and talent development, a particularly hot issue because youth sport is equally important from both perspectives (participation and performance). The traditional ideal for children and youth sport in Scandinavia has been multi-sport community-based clubs promoting broad participation, sports sampling and late specialization (Støckel et al. 2010). Until recently, this has been regarded beneficial for both mass participation and talent development (Storm et al. 2012). However, from an elite sport perspective, this ideal is increasingly contested (Helle-Valle 2008, Norberg and Sjöblom 2012) because it is argued to be poorly suited to meet the demands of today's elite sport. Furthermore, it is claimed that if cultivating elite athletes is wanted, we need to take a closer look at the quality of the youth sport work: there is a need to spot talents earlier and provide professional coaches at an early stage of the preadolescents' careers (Aambø 2006).

Because such suggestions from elite sport spokesmen – earlier specialization and more centralized and professionalized talent development efforts – do not merely affects elite sport but simultaneously alter the conditions for youth sport in general, legitimation efforts have to follow two lines. It should be substantiated that the changes are productive both regarding talent development and to the sports movement in a wider sense. This is indeed a difficult exercise, because there are obvious conflict of interests and different logics at play here. In earlier specialization, there is a solid documentation pointing to the downside of early specialization, for example lack of enjoyment and drop out from sports (Baker 2003). This contradicts essential aims legitimizing the sport movement as such.

A similar ambiguity is present concerning more centralized and professionalized talent development efforts. Scandinavian sport is typically decentralized through geographical spread of clubs, ensuring a service for many youngsters and promoting multi-faceted local developmental arenas. However, centralized talent development implies that talents are encouraged to move to specific and targeted elite sport locations. Decisive human capital, athletes, professional coaches and other expertise, are clustered to enhance quality and knowledge transfer (Andersen 2012). There is little doubt that the elite sport centres have contributed in developing Scandinavian elite athletes (Andersen and Ronglan 2012), but an open question is to what extent this centralization of resources affects the local clubs. One possibility is an increased spread of competence throughout the organization; but equally possible is an emptying of local resources (talented athletes and professional expertise) as they move or are recruited to targeted centralized locations. It may be demanding to implement talent development programmes in ways that strengthen rather than deteriorate the clubs as local development arenas. If they are stretched too far, centralized efforts may undermine the foundation of talent development, youth sport in general, in a decentralized voluntary organization.

The dilemmas embedded in youth sport (participation vs. performance) are to a certain extent debated internally in Scandinavian sport organizations (Steen-Johnsen and Hanstad 2008). Such debates involve elements of legitimation efforts *within* the field (organizational legitimacy), for example when the elite sport bodies work to gain support for their engagement in youth sport. However, in the *public* discourse on sport in Scandinavia, such dilemmas are undercommunicated (Helle-Valle 2008). Instead, the link between mass and elite sport is emphasized. From the perspective of the central sport leaders, the unity is essential to maintain, because a 'united sport movement' in size and scope represents a powerful societal actor (Enjolras and Waldahl 2010). The presentation of a united front increases political influence and justifies substantial public support at an arm's length distance. In securing the organizations' monopoly in the field of organized competitive sport (Bergsgard and Norberg 2010), the image of elite sport as an integrated extension of the voluntary movement is favourable. However, this harmonized public rhetoric obscures increasing internal contradictions stemming from the growing gap discussed earlier. Today there are strong public expectations to be competitive at the international scene, massively conveyed by the media but additionally articulated in policy documents. Still, a public discourse on how this should be done in a way that safeguard elite sport as well as mass sport concerns is hardly evident. A danger of such lacking discourse is a slow and 'unnoticeable' step-by-step movement (policy drift) towards an increasingly comprehensive elite sport system with a subsequent weakening of elite sports' social legitimacy.

The Scandinavian countries are yet not there. The targeted elite sport bodies are still modest and have supplemented the traditional overall organization of sport rather than changed it in a substantial way. It is fair to claim that so far, in terms of elite sport, the competitive advantage in Scandinavia has not been a comprehensive elite sport system, but an ability to utilize the potential embedded in the popular movement to *also* create some elite sport achievements. The elite sport bodies have definitively contributed to refine this ability. Today, both the international elite sport environment and organizational interests represent strong forces towards a further expansion of targeted elite sport systems. However, maintaining and displaying a close link between local community sport and elite sport is highly valued in Scandinavia (Bairner 2010). This requires a finely tuned balance when it comes to developing elite sports in Scandinavia within the current institutional arrangements.

References

Aambø, J., 2006. *Bredde skaper ikke toppidrett* [Mass sport do not create elite sport]. Oslo: *Aftenposten*, 11 November. (*Newspaper chronicle*).

Andersen, S.S., 2012. Olypiatoppen in the Norwegian sports cluster. *In*: S.S. Andersen and L.T. Ronglan, eds. *Nordic elite sport: same ambitions – different tracks*. Oslo: Norwegian University Press, 237–256.

Andersen, S.S. and Ronglan, L.T., eds., 2012. *Nordic elite sport: same ambitions – different tracks*. Oslo: Norwegian University Press.

Augestad, P., Bergsgard, N.A., and Hansen, A., 2006. The institutionalization of an elite sport organization in Norway: the case of 'Olympiatoppen'. *Sociology of sport journal*, 23 (3), 293–313.

Bairner, A., 2010. What's Scandinavian about Scandinavian sport? *Sport in society*, 13 (4), 734–743. doi:10.1080/17430431003616555

Baker, J., 2003. Early specialization in youth sport: a requirement for adult expertise? *High ability studies*, 14 (1), 85–94. doi:10.1080/13598130304091

Béland, D., 2007. Ideas and institutional change in social security: conversion, layering and policy drift. *Social science quarterly*, 88 (1), 20–38. doi:10.1111/j.1540-6237.2007.00444.x

Bergsgard, N.A. and Norberg, J.R., 2010. Sports policy and politics – the Scandinavian way. *Sport in society*, 13 (4), 567–582. doi:10.1080/17430431003616191

Broch, T.B., 2014. 'Smiles and laughs – all teeth intact': a cultural perspective on mediated women's handball in Norway. *International journal of sport communication*, 7, 56–73. doi:10.1123/IJSC.2013-0133

Carlsson, B. and Lindfelt, M., 2010. Legal and moral pluralism: normative tensions in a Nordic sports model in transition. *Sport in society*, 13 (4), 718–733. doi:10.1080/17430431003616548

Carlsson, B., Norberg, J.R., and Persson, H.T.R., 2011. The governance of sport from a Scandinavian perspective. *International journal of sport policy and politics*, 3 (3), 305–309. doi:10.1080/19406940.2011.619827

Castles, F.G., 2009. *The social democratic image of society. A study of the achievements and origins of Scandinavian social democracy in comparative perspective*. London: Routledge.

Coalter, F., 2007. *A wider social role for sport: who's keeping the score?* London: Routledge.

De Bosscher, V., *et al.*, 2008. *The global sporting arms race. An international comparative study on sports policy factors leading to international sporting success*. Aachen: Meyer & Meyer.

Dowling, J. and Pfeffer, J., 1975. Organizational legitimacy: social values and organizational behavior. *The pacific sociological review*, 18 (1), 122–136. doi:10.2307/1388226

Eichberg, H. and Loland, S., 2010. Nordic sports – from social movements via emotional to bodily movement – and back again? *Sport in society*, 13 (4), 676–690. doi:10.1080/17430431003616431

Enjolras, B., 2002. The commercialization of voluntary sport organizations in Norway. *Nonprofit and voluntary sector quarterly*, 31, 352–376. doi:10.1177/0899764002313003

Enjolras, B. and Waldahl, R.H., 2010. Democratic governance and oligarchy in voluntary sport organizations: the case of the Norwegian Olympic Committee and Confederation of Sports. *European sport management quarterly*, 10 (2), 215–239. doi:10.1080/16184740903559909

Esping-Andersen, G., 1990. *The three worlds of welfare capitalism*. Princeton, NJ: Princeton University Press.

Fahlén, J., 2006. *Structures beyond the frameworks of the rink: on organization in Swedish ice hockey*. Thesis (PhD). Umeå University.

Goksøyr, M. and Hanstad, D.V., 2012. Elite sport development in Norway – a radical transformation. *In*: S.S. Andersen and L.T. Ronglan, eds. *Nordic elite sport: same ambitions – different tracks*. Oslo: Norwegian University Press, 27–42.

Green, M. and Oakley, B., 2001. Elite sport development systems and playing to win: uniformity and diversity in international approaches. *Leisure studies*, 20, 247–267. doi:10.1080/02614360110103598

Grix, J. and Carmichael, F., 2012. Why do governments invest in elite sport? A polemic. *International journal of sport policy and politics*, 4 (1), 73–90. doi:10.1080/19406940.2011.627358

Hansen, J., 2012. The institutionalization of Team Denmark. *In*: S.S. Andersen and L.T. Ronglan, eds. *Nordic elite sport: same ambitions – different tracks*. Oslo: Norwegian University Press, 43–61.

Hansen, P.Ø., 2014. *Making the best even better. Fine-tuning development and learning to achieve international success in cross-country skiing*. Thesis (PhD). Norwegian School of Sport Sciences.

Hanstad, D.V., 2002. *Seier'n er vår, men hvem har æren?* [We have won, but who has the honour?]. Oslo: Schibsted.

Hassan, D. and Telford, R., 2014. Sport and community integration in Northern Ireland. *Sport in society*, 17 (1), 89–101. doi:10.1080/17430437.2013.828901

Helle-Valle, J., 2008. Discourses on mass versus elite sport and pre-adult football in Norway. *International review for the sociology of sport*, 43 (4), 365–381. doi:10.1177/1012690208099872

Houlihan, B. and Green, M., eds., 2008. *Comparative elite sport development. Systems, structures and public policy*. Oxford: Butterworth-Heinemann.

Ibsen, B., Hansen, J., and Storm, R., 2010. Elite sport development in Denmark. *In*: B. Houlihan and M. Green, eds. *Routledge handbook of sport development*. London: Routledge, 381–393.

Ibsen, B. and Seippel, Ø., 2010. Voluntary organized sport in Denmark and Norway. *Sport in society*, 13 (4), 593–608. doi:10.1080/17430431003616266

Lämsä, J., 2012. Finnish elite sport – from class-based tensions to pluralist complexity. *In*: S.S. Andersen and L.T. Ronglan, eds. *Nordic elite sport: same ambitions – different tracks*. Oslo: Norwegian University Press, 83–106.

Lindgren, K.-O. and Persson, T., 2010. Input and output legitimacy: synergy or trade-off? Empirical evidence from an EU survey. *Journal of European public policy*, 17 (4), 449–467. doi:10.1080/13501761003673591

Lippe, G.v.d., 2002. Media image: sport, gender and national identities in five European countries. *International review for the sociology of sport*, 37 (3–4), 371–395. doi:10.1177/101269020203700306

Mathews, M.R., 1993. *Socially responsible accounting*. London: Chapman & Hall.

Nielsen, K. and Hoffmann, A., 2012. The revival of Danish track cycling. *In*: S.S. Andersen and L.T. Ronglan, eds. *Nordic elite sport: same ambitions – different tracks*. Oslo: Norwegian University Press, 168–189.

Norberg, J.R., 1997. A mutual dependency: Nordic sports organizations and the state. *The international journal of the history of sport*, 14 (3), 115–135. doi:10.1080/09523369708714003

Norberg, J.R. and Sjöblom, P., 2012. The Swedish elite sport system – or the lack of it? *In*: S.S. Andersen and L.T. Ronglan, eds. *Nordic elite sport: same ambitions – different tracks*. Oslo: Norwegian University Press, 62–82.

Oakley, B. and Green, M., 2001. The productions of Olympic champions: international perspectives on elite sport development systems. *European journal of sport management*, 8 (1), 83–105.

Powell, W.W. and DiMaggio, P.J., eds., 1991. *The new institutionalism in organizational analysis*. Chicago, IL: University of Chicago Press.

Rafoss, K. and Troelsen, J., 2010. Sports facilities for all? The financing, distribution and use of sports facilities in Scandinavian countries. *Sport in society*, 13 (4), 643–656. doi:10.1080/17430431003616399

Ronglan, L.T., 2012. Norwegian women's handball – organizing for sustainable success. *In*: S.S. Andersen and L.T. Ronglan, eds. *Nordic elite sport: same ambitions – different tracks*. Oslo: Norwegian University Press, 131–151.

Sam, M., 2009. The public management of sport. Wicked problems, challenges and dilemmas. *Public management review*, 11 (4), 499–514. doi:10.1080/14719030902989565

Scharpf, F.W., 1999. *Governing in Europe: effective and democratic?* Oxford: Oxford University Press.

Seippel, Ø., 2010. Professionals and volunteers: on the future of a Scandinavian sport model. *Sport in society*, 13 (2), 199–211. doi:10.1080/17430430903522921

Sjöblom, P. and Fahlén, J., 2010. The survival of the fittest: intensification, totalization and homogenization in Swedish competitive sport. *Sport in society*, 13 (4), 704–717. doi:10.1080/17430431003616514

Steen-Johnsen, K. and Hanstad, D.V., 2008. Change and power in complex democratic organizations. The Case of Norwegian elite sports. *European sport management quarterly*, 8 (2), 123–143. doi:10.1080/16184740802024393

Støckel, J.T., *et al.*, 2010. Sport for children and youth in the Scandinavian countries. *Sport in society*, 13 (4), 625–642. doi:10.1080/17430431003616332

Storm, L.K., Henriksen, K., and Krogh, M.K., 2012. Specialization pathways among elite Danish athletes: a look at the developmental model of sport participation from a cultural perspective. *International journal of sport psychology*, 43 (3), 199–222.

Storm, R.K., 2012. Danish elite sport and Team Denmark: new trends? *In*: S.S. Andersen and L.T. Ronglan, eds. *Nordic elite sport: same ambitions – different tracks*. Oslo: Norwegian University Press, 224–236.

Storm, R.K. and Nielsen, K., 2010. In a peak fitness condition? The Danish elite sports model in an international perspective: managerial efficiency and best practice in achieving international sporting success. *International journal of sport management and marketing*, 7, 104–118. doi:10.1504/IJSMM.2010.029715

Suchman, M.C., 1995. Managing legitimacy: strategic and institutional approaches. *Academy of management journal*, 20 (3), 571–610.

Thing, L. and Ronglan, L.T., 2014. Athletes' confessions: the sports biography as an interaction ritual. *Scandinavian journal of medicine and science in sports*. doi:10.1111/sms.12198

Topic, M.D. and Coakley, J., 2010. Complicating the relationship between sport and national identity: the case of post-socialist Slovenia. *Sociology of sport journal*, 27, 371–389.

Ward, T., 2009. Sport and national identity. *Soccer & society*, 10 (5), 518–531. doi:10.1080/14660970902955455

Weiler, J.H.H., 1999. *The constitution of Europe: "do the new clothes have an emperor?" and other essays on European integration.* Cambridge: Cambridge University Press.

Wijk, J., 2012. The Swedish 'golf and tennis miracle' – two parallel stories. *In*: S.S. Andersen and L.T. Ronglan, eds. *Nordic elite sport: same ambitions – different tracks.* Oslo: Norwegian University Press, 109–130.

Wincott, D., 2002. National States, European Union and changing dynamics in the quest for legitimacy. *In*: A. Arnull and D. Wincott., eds. *Accountability and legitimacy in the European Union.* Oxford: Oxford University Press, 487–496.

Wollebæk, D., Skirstad, B., and Hanstad, D.V., 2014. Between two volunteer cultures: social composition and motivation among volunteers at the 2010 test event for the FIS Nordic World Ski Championships. *International review for the sociology of sport*, 49 (1), 22–41. doi:10.1177/1012690212453355

Challenges and constraints in developing and implementing sports policy and provision in Antigua and Barbuda: which way now for a small island state?

Natalie Darko[a] and Christopher Mackintosh[b]

[a]School of Science and Technology Sports Science, Nottingham Trent University, Nottingham UK; [b]The School of Education of Leisure and Sports Studies, Liverpool, UK

This paper examines the challenges and constraints of sport policy agenda setting and policy development in a small nation context of Antigua and Barbuda. It also aims to understand and explore existing limitations, issues and trajectories in sport policy implementation. The project draws upon a mixed-methods approach encompassing documentary analysis, 30 in-depth interviews and visual methodology in the form of photo observations. Through this methodology, the purpose of the paper is to open up sport policy agendas allowing the 'voices' of those local populations, policymakers, coaches and volunteers to be heard within the context of this study and wider sport policy research. Initial findings indicate sport and physical activity as a contested policy priority, barriers in cross-departmental collaboration, elite sport and performance agenda dilemmas and considerable limitations in third sector human infrastructure and physical facilities. Implications from this small nation sport policy context highlight the need for improved public policy problem definition and the need for clarity in agenda setting within tiers of the evolving sport policy community. Finally, the tentative potential positive policy spaces for future implementation and lessons in policy design involving national, regional and local actors and agencies are identified.

Introduction

There has been a growth of academic interest in the analysis of sport policy as developed by governments in global settings (Houlihan 2005, Bergsgard et al. 2007). Equally, there has been a growing range of interest in the various aspects of government machinery and its influence on sports policy including 'the public value' of sport (Brookes and Wiggan 2009, Sam 2011), modernization agendas (Houlihan and Green 2009), wider social policy goals linked to sport (Coalter 2007, Palmer 2013) and systems and factors in the development of elite sports talent (De Bosscher et al. 2006, Stotlar and Wonders 2006, Houlihan 2009). However, most of this literature has been on the larger, 'western' or Global North state economies (Palmer 2013). This imbalance is in part addressed through the research undertaken in this paper that considers the challenges and constraints of agenda setting and implementation of sports policy development in the small nation case of Antigua and Barbuda.

Currently studies of sports policy in the Caribbean region are minimal. Exceptions to this include an analysis of new public management (NPM) in Trinidad and Tobago's sports delivery system (McCree 2009) and the minimal role of sport in economic development policy (McCree 2008). Crucially, though, Trinidad and Tobago has a *White paper on Sport* dating back as far as 1988 (Government of Trinidad and Tobago (GOTT) 1988), and a first government sport policy rolled out in 2002 (Government of Trinidad and Tobago (GOTT) 2002). A further study considered the potential role for World Cup cricket tourism as a catalyst for economic development in the West Indies (Tyson *et al.* 2005). Whilst these studies set the scene for a field of study in the region, understanding of sports policy development in the region is emergent at best.

Analysis of smaller nation states is not to be confused with states in developing countries or what has increasingly been referred to as sport-for-development, sport-for peace and/or sport-in-development (Coalter 2007, Lindsey and Grattan 2012). In this sense this paper is not an analysis of whether policy goals have been achieved in a developing economy to pursue wider social policy goals around public health, education and specific fields such as HIV and community medicine. This is not to say that lessons cannot be learnt from the sport-for-development literature in this context. Indeed there are distinct parallels with this context, where there appears to be features of sport-for-development fields such as top-down policy and programme development, power imbalances between policy actors (Lindsey and Banda 2011, Lindsey and Grattan 2012) and a need to recognize and reposition local actors within the research process (Kay 2009). In part the case of Antigua and Barbuda in this paper offers an evaluation of a country that is comparatively small in size, 'emergent' and aspirational in terms of its sports policy and provides particular insights into the challenges/difficulties of policy development. Whilst past research that has taken a comparative analysis is helpful as a starting point for unpicking central potential themes to address (Henry 2007), the starting point for this project was a dialogue between research team, the National Olympic Committee (NOC) and the Ministry of Sport (MoS). This was underpinned by a strong commitment to the need for knowledge, fresh insights and the establishment of a starting point for sports policy development, and to open dialogue between those involved in its design and implementation. Thus the central aims of this research paper are:

- to explore the challenges of a sport policy agenda setting and policy development in a small nation context;
- to understand and examine existing challenges, issues and constraints in sport policy implementation in Antigua and Barbuda;
- to open up sport policy agendas allowing the 'voices' of those local populations, policymakers, coaches and volunteers to be heard within the context of this study and wider sport policy research;
- to identify and evaluate the key policy priorities and tensions present within the emergent sport policy community of Antigua and Barbuda.

Existing robust research data and strategic documentation in this national context was informally noted down in hard copy paper. Therefore, as has been stated in relation to the parallel and related field of education, 'educational research on the Caribbean focuses upon the larger islands and there is little tradition of ... research in the smaller eastern Caribbean states' (Younger and George 2012, p. 7). However, this potential gap in knowledge, understanding and baseline level of policy evidence and infrastructure has been a core rationale for developing the project and the relationship between the research team and government. A core theme within the academic literature has been the emergence of the need for evidence-based policymaking and associated systems (Houlihan and Green 2009, Piggin *et al.* 2009, Smith *et al.* 2010). Such small states with emergent policy structures do not have sufficient policy and programme maturity that fit such mantras easily. Likewise, Collins (2010) clearly establishes the policy and theoretical dilemmas inherent in aspiring to follow other country's mass participation levels and associated programme development. We are also mindful to align to the research perspective of Palmer (2013) by not imposing western 'Orientalist' perspectives and policy understandings, frameworks and conceptual discourses onto the research project, data and subjectivities. Likewise Kay (2009) and Lindsey and Grattan (2012) argue for a decolonization of knowledge, research and methodologies in developmental contexts. This assertion applies to our research philosophy given our explicit focus on opening up and prioritizing the voices of local actors in this small nation context.

This project was informed by the collaboration and research dialogue between two UK universities research teams, the NOC and MoS for Antigua and Barbuda underpinned by the philosophical position of Lindsey and Grattan (2012). Here, the authors argue for closer relationships led by local agencies as opposed to Global North imposed agendas. It was not a commissioned piece of work as such but was established as part of a longer-term vision to develop better practices and policies by building an ongoing research relationship (Darko and Mackintosh 2012). One of the key drivers behind this approach was the need to draw lessons from past experiences from other countries that have had limited infrastructure in developing contexts.[1] Indeed a lack of data on sports participation and programmes from government sources has been identified as a core theme in African developing nations (Souchaud 1995, Andreff 2001), and this scarcity was the starting point for the present study.

Here we have attempted to allow the 'voices' of those local populations, policy-makers, coaches and volunteers to be heard within our study as opposed to imposing a westernized, false dichotomy of choices (Shehu and Mokgwathi 2007). But, an ability to open up such research in small, developing nations and allowing them to be 'heard' can be seen in the honest account from a sport policy research blog account by Lindsay (2012):

> Whilst undertaking research with organisations from the Global South…[I have felt] seriously conflicted. As someone from the 'richer' Global North, interviewees have …made many eminently reasonable requests for support from me. Balancing a desire to contribute …to in-country development against the impossibility of meeting all of the requests for support, of not encouraging dependency and of maintaining the neutrality that is often expected of a researcher has frequently been challenging

The research team faced this central dilemma from the outset of the project in this small state.

Theoretical considerations

Small nations

The highly contested domain of theoretically or practically defining what constitutes a small state (Hey 2003, Colomer 2007, Marleku 2013) provides an unhelpful starting point for establishing a clear analytical tool in this study. Hey (2003) goes as far as to suggest that 'smallness' itself is a problematic analytical tool. Clearly there are blurred dividing lines between what a small state represents whether defined by demographic, economic or geographic size. In this paper we use the term small state as a starting point for locating our empirical study within a wider discourse of sports policy analysis. Hey (2003, p. 2) identifies the following three main conceptualizations of the small state:

> *Microstate* – states with a population less than one million inhabitants such as the former British Colonies in the Caribbean; *small states in the developed world* – especially Austria, Belgium, Luxembourg, the Netherlands and Switzerland; and *small states in the so-called third world*, including former colonies in Africa, Asia and Latin America.

Precise definition around size of population is problematic and subjective, although countries with less than one million inhabitants are often classified as 'micro' states (Colomer 2007). Others have classified micro-states as those countries with less than one million inhabitants (World Bank 2004). Therefore, the overall classification system or schema for such states has no established consensus (Hower 2008). Of relevance to this paper we also recognize the approach suggested by Keohane (1969) who highlights the importance of subjectivity and power relations in such conceptualizations, in the sense that small states are defined how they see themselves and how others go about defining them. Certainly it appears Antigua would 'fit' with an understanding of the micro-state in this literature, yet at under 90,000 inhabitants it is far from near the upper limit of 1 million participants suggested by some (Easterly and Kraay 1999, Hey 2003) and even further from the 1.5 million population figure quoted by others (Marleku 2013). What is clearer is that nearly two-thirds of the world's population reside in either small countries or those under the legislative control of small non-state governments (Colomer 2007). Antigua and Barbuda is one such country that sits nearer the micro-state conceptualization, of which it has been suggested there are around 40 such countries. A specific research focus of this article was to assess the challenges of sport policy development and implementation in such a small nation context. Colomer (2007) identifies that there are three characteristic benefits of small nation democratic government, first, that of *deliberation* where citizens have more opportunity to deal directly with political actors and institutions. Second, *aggregation* where citizens inhabit a more homogenous community and have more harmonious values, culture and collectively find it easier to identify priorities for public goods. Finally, *enforcement* meaning citizens are more likely to comply with collective rules and leaders may be more responsive in terms of their own independent decision making. Similarly, in Antigua and Barbuda the small nation educational policy research context was identified as having the benefits of high actor interconnectivity, a geographically small scale and strong collaborative synergies within the school zoning system (Younger and George 2012). Whether such considerations apply in this case of sport policy will be considered within this paper.

Antigua and Barbuda

The twin islands of Antigua and Barbuda lie between the Atlantic Ocean to the east and the Caribbean Sea to the west. It has a population of approximately 89,000 (Indexmundi 2013). In total '91% of the inhabitants are black... 4.4% are mixed, 1.7% White and 2.9% [are classified as] other' (Clancy 2012, p. 6). The majority of Antiguans are of African lineage, descendants of slaves brought to the island to work. The population also consists of Hispanic immigrants, mainly from the Dominican Republic. There are a higher proportion of males than females, with the sex ratio for the total population being 0.9 male(s)/female (2011 est, Indexmundi 2013).

The islands are economically undeveloped. Historically, the sugar cane industry has been a central means for supporting the islands' income (O'Loughlin 1961). However, tourism now dominates the economy, accounting for approximately 60% of GDP and 40% of investment (Indexmundi 2013). Sport has never been an integral part of Caribbean economic revenue and development (McCree 2009).

Antigua and Barbuda's governance and culture have largely been influenced by the British Empire, of which the country was formally part of until 1981. A parliamentary democracy under a federal constitutional monarchy exists, with two levels of government, central and local (Clancy 2012). The bicameral legislature comprises a 17-member House of Representatives (the lower house) elected every 5 years and a Senate (upper house) of 17 appointed members. Political parties that currently exist include the United Progressive Party (UPP), currently holding the majority of seats, the Antigua Labour Party (ALP) and Barbuda People's Movement (BPM).

Whilst sports are part of the culture in Antigua and Barbuda, it is predominantly travel writers (Kras 2008) who have commented on levels of sports participation and physical activity. Our research revealed that sports associations, the NOC and government schools have unofficial figures of sports participation, evident in paper and non-digitized format However, these statistics are not readily available and their reliability is questionable. There is also limited research that provides a description of sports policy and examines the challenges of its development. The paucity of such data is apparent across many of the developing Caribbean islands (McCree 2009).

Public policy problems, agenda setting and implementation

In the context of this small state this paper focuses on the theoretical sphere of the sport policy agenda, political priorities, challenges and constraints around implementation. In analytical terms wider questions of whether it is structure or agency dominate (Parsons 1995, Colebatch 1998, Cairney 2012). The balance between institutional structural influences that have shaped and influenced Antiguan and Barbudan sport policy aligns closely with the interactions of powerful political, policy and community actors. Indeed, it seems particularly pertinent to consider such issues in this unique political setting of islands of under 89,000 inhabitants. In many cases government committees, departments and policy networks are more likely to rest with the decision making of a small set of individual actors. As a theoretical starting point we have taken the view of policy analysis suggested by Sabatier (2007, p. 4) that 'given the staggering complexity of the policy process, the analyst must find some way of simplifying the situation in order to have any chance of understanding it'. Following this call we make no attempt to use an overarching theoretical frame to guide our research. As has been argued in relation to sport-for-development contexts in the Global South, research driven by a particular theoretical framework can reify singular abstract accounts (Moore 1999, Long 2001). Here we draw a parallel with the work of Lindsey and Grattan (2012) and Kay (2010) in our attempt to protect against western colonizing theoretical knowledge in this research setting. However, we do use sensitizing theoretical ideas (Sibeon 1998) that can be utilized as resources for developing understanding in this empirical study. In the context of public sport policy analysis in this paper we take the definition of agency as 'the ability of an actor to act to realise its goals. The implication of this is that this is the intentional action based on an actor's thought process' (Cairney 2012, p. 10). Actors are assumed to be entities that can make decisions, formulate views and act upon such decisions. We draw a distinction between *individual* human actors and *social* actors such as committees, micro groups and organizations

(Sibeon 1998). Here, we also share the view that 'organisational policy decisions and organisational actions are sometimes the indeterminate and contingent outcome of conflict and struggle among the individuals, groups or departments that constitute the organisation' (Clegg 1989, p. 197). In following on from this standpoint Cobb and Coughlin (1998) make a useful distinction between two different types of policy actors, the policy agenda 'expander' and 'container'. Here, it is delineated that some policy-expanding actors redefine, reshape and represent issues that are not under current consideration. In contrast to this, the policy-containing actors are those that seek to prevent issues from reaching an agenda. In the case of Antigua and Barbuda, and that of a specifically small or micro-state we have found this a particularly useful conceptual distinction to make. We make the further conceptual clarification that the state is therefore not an actor in itself. In this sense, 'it is not the state that acts, but state actors within particular parts of the state' (Smith 1993, p. 50). A detailed discussion of this is beyond the scope of the paper, but it provides clarity of a theoretical standpoint to underpin the research.

Policy analysis is broadly concerned with 'problems' and the linked relationships of public policies to these problems, the content of policy and what policymakers do or do not do in delivering against the outcomes of policy (Parsons 1995). Numerous authors have outlined approaches to studying phases, stages and cycles of the policy process that the policy analyst is concerned with (Hogwood and Gunn 1984, Parsons 1995, Hill 2005). However, others have argued this is an oversimplification of a complex process (Sabatier and Jenkins-Smith 2003, Cairney 2012). In contrast other sport policy researchers such as Keat and Sam (2013) have used a three-way conceptualization of the policy process proposed by Rist (1998) in terms of policy problem, policy instrument and policy target to provide a lens on the regional sport policy process in New Zealand. This framework could provide a neat sensitizing conceptual 'triad' to unpick the realm of policy analysis in Antigua and Barbuda. However, part of the challenge of the small nation context of this paper is the incomplete policy infrastructure, limited problem definition, often hidden instruments and vague notions of targeting through policy. We are also sensitive to not enact westernized false dichotomy of choices on the study of policy in such settings (Shehu and Mokgwathi 2007). However, this literature provides a wider conceptual context to this research paper as the focus for this study of a small nation is sport policy agenda setting, policy development constraints, challenges and emergent issues in implementation.

Defining and prioritizing policy problems in the field of sport and physical activity are highly contested in most government settings (Houlihan 2005, Houlihan and Green 2009). For example, Sam and Jackson (2004) have identified issues around policy coherence and coordination alongside other authors exploring the need for greater 'evidence-based' sport policy (Piggin et al. 2009). Priorities between the dichotomy of elite sport success and mass sports participation also play out amidst complex sets of actors and institutional historical contexts (Grix and Carmichael 2012). Sport policy development and analysis in Antigua and Barbuda is emergent at best with a considerable lack of current internal research, baseline statistical data and academic material (Darko and Mackintosh 2012). As stated above, the academic and empirical starting point for this project was incomplete data, limited policy baseline information and fragmented knowledge from the local sport policy community. This paper is in part about agenda setting and problem definition, which Knill and Tosun (2012) argue is about identifying 'initial moments' and a range of policy and 'problem' perceptions that usually operate within a highly contested domain. In considering a theoretical starting point for the problem definition in the case of Antigua and Barbuda, we also draw upon Knill and Tosun's (2012) framework that identifies two core features of problem definition. First, the level of objective data that is available on a problem and, second, the degree to which this data are acknowledged and utilized. In the case of Antigua and Barbuda there is minimal data on sports policy, provision and participation and even less so any apparent use of this relevant evidence. This suggests actor values can be centrally important, as Knill and Tosun (2012, p. 101) propose 'the more uncertain the information environment surrounding an issue, the more likely it is that an individual will rely on these established values'.

Resultantly, the lack of attention this policy sub-field has received in terms of the existing and historical agendas, priorities and initial development of policy instruments provides fertile ground for gaining insight to the sport policy process in a small nation context. Equally, the highly incomplete, information-limited and value-driven policy actor environment supports our conceptualization of this specific small island context as one that demands a grounded inductive empirical investigation. We instead acknowledge the complexity of the policy process (Sabatier and Jenkins 2003, Houlihan 2005, Sabatier 2007, Cairney 2012). Following Sabatier's (2007) call for the need to pinpoint a starting point, we 'recognise how complexity, change and following the consciousness of the actors we are studying, limit our scope for the establishment of generalisations' (Hill 2005, p. 15).

Government, sports policy infrastructure and background

A brief history of government involvement in sport

Private and voluntary investment centring on individual activities and their needs has dominated sports provision. The various political parties and individual actors have played a role in supporting provision in sports since the 1940s; however, changes in government, political conflicts and lack of economic resources have halted sustained practice and successful formulation of provision. There is no existing academic research into the voluntary sector, its resources, challenges and infrastructure.

Whilst the government has assisted in provision, non-governmental organizations (such as the Antigua and Barbuda National Olympic Committee) have also assisted. The NOC was established in 1996, after the demise of the West Indies Federation (Mordecai 1968). In accordance with the Olympic Charter, the NOC progresses and protects the Olympic Movement in Antigua and Barbuda and liaises with governmental and non-governmental bodies, to accomplish this (International Olympic Committee 2013). Numerous sports and sporting events are supported by the NOC. They seek to support the development of sport for all programmes and high performance. They also participate in the training of sports administrators and economically facilitate participation in international games, such as The Pan Am Games using the earlier framework proposed by Cobb and Coughlin (1998). The NOC could be seen as a key social actor conceptualized as an issue expander in how it attempted to bring sport policy issues to the fore and prioritized related 'problems' and agendas since 1996.

Within the existing Antigua and Barbuda ministry, The Ministry of Education, Sports, Youth and Gender Affairs (MESYGA) has oversight of the Local Government Department. Within this, the Local Government Department falls within the Office of the Minister of State with responsibility for Sports, Local Government and Special Projects (OMS SLS). The OMS SLS is responsible for providing technical support to the Department in the form of a consultant dedicated to conducting a review of the local government system and to making recommendations for its future development.

Following the General Elections of 2009, Dr. Leandro was appointed as the Minister of Education, Youth, Sports and Gender Affairs. Senator Winston Williams was also appointed to serve in this Ministry as the Minister of State. The Department of Sports & Recreational Management comprises the Sports & Recreational Events Management Division, Youth Sports & Community Development Unit, National Executive Council on Sports and the National Institute of Sports & Recreation (NISR) and the Sports & Recreational Product Development Division. The NISR was established to provide 'education and training for sports administrators, technicians and high performance athletes. [It] … also serve[s] to provide sports related services to include research and professional development and enrichment courses' (Antigua and Barbuda National Sport and Recreation Policy 2011–14, p. 10).

The Ministry of Education also has a designated Sports Unit to develop sports at all levels and the Office of the Minister of State in the Ministry of Education, Sports, Gender & Youth Affairs is responsible for Sports, Boys Training School, Local Government & Special Projects including the National School Meals Service (NSMS).[2] Please see Figure 1 below for the organization chart of the Secretariat, Minister of State: Sports, National School Meals Service & Special Projects.

Provision for participation in physical education is apparent at Pre-Primary (3–5), Primary (5–12), Secondary (12–17) and Tertiary (17 and over) levels within schools. Despite this provision, physical education and *activity* are culturally accorded low academic or intellectual value. Furthermore, physical education in government schools is limited at all levels, unless students take it as a subject for CXC (Caribbean Examinations

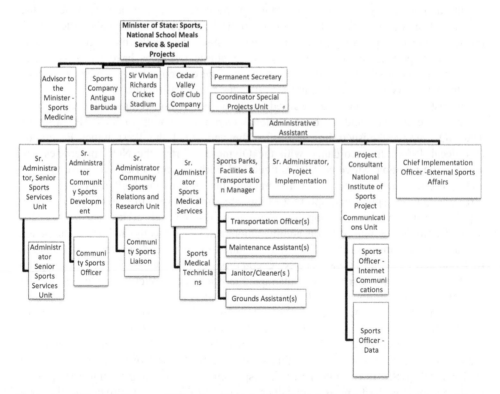

Figure 1. Office of Ministry of Education (2013a). 2013 Organizational chart: Secretariat, Minister of State: Sports, National School Meals Service & Special Projects. Source Business Plan for 2013 MOSNSMS SUBMISSION TO CABINET 6 11 12, Ministry of Education, Sports, Youth and Gender Affairs: 5.

Council) exams (2012). The association between sport and employment is minimal within the Caribbean islands (McCree 2009). The lack of commercialization of sport and professionalism contributes to these cultural perceptions. These traditions have potentially led to a lack of political and cultural interest in stimulating the economy through sports-related activity.

Due to the low levels of economic development in Caribbean small states, the amount of ministerial funding for sports and recreation is minimal. In the Antigua and Barbuda 2012 Budget Statement published on 5/12/2011 (p. 8), it is stated that an allocation of $76,337,364 Eastern Caribbean Dollars (approximately US$ 28.2 million) is made to implement the programmes and activities for the Ministry of Education, Sports, Youth and Gender Affairs. The difficulty this raises for sports provision, development and policy implementation is that financial support is heavily reliant on private funding and voluntary provision. Table 1 outlines the financial allocation and expenditure of the various departments within this Office. It also illustrates the proposed budget for 2013.

Development of National Sports and Recreation Policy

Implementation of national sports and recreation policies for Caribbean islands is slowly developing, but they are regularly halted by changes of government, lack of economic resources and the restrictive traditions regarding the low value attached to the activity of sport. Some of the policies that exist, such as those in Grenada, are recently formulated. Subsequently, academic examination of sports policy in Caribbean is an emerging research area (McCree 2009). Over the years attempts have been made to implement a successful National Sports and Recreation Policy for Antigua and Barbuda; however, it was not until 2011 that a national policy materialized.

The Minister of State, responsible for Sports, established a Sports and Recreational Advisory Council (SRAC) to review the previous proposal for a national policy. This council, comprising key sports and recreational stakeholders, conducted a review of the policy, research in the sports and recreation and developed a document entitled 'the National Policy on Sports and Recreation ... [to] be further developed into legislation entitled the National Sports and Recreational Act' (A&B NSRP 2011–14, p. 4).

The second (UPP) administration drafted and enacted a National Sports Policy for Antigua and Barbuda in 2011. In several phases key individual actors have had significant influence on the shape, direction and pace of change. With a focus on putting sports in the core of communities and empowering them, they sought to promote the development of sports and participation. This draft 'was presented to the Cabinet for Approval in August 2011, with subsequent submission to the Ministry of Legal Affairs for drafting of a Bill entitled the National Sports and Recreation Bill, tabled in the Parliament for its considera-tion' (A&B NSRP 2011–14, p. 24).

Under this policy it is envisaged that the National Executive Council for Sports (NECS) is established to facilitate a holistic approach to sports provision. As a social actor or 'micro group' (Sibeon 1998) it comprises representatives from the Ministry of Sports, sporting associations and corporate organizations. Likewise, in principle, the NECS is a potential sport policy issue, problem and agenda 'expander' (Cobb and Coughlin 1998). The NECS promotes the partnering of key stakeholders in sports, stimulates growth and development in sports through sponsorship of community sporting clubs and provides financing for national sporting events and programmes. It will super-vise and administer contributions to sports with the necessary inspections. It is also 'responsible for monitoring and reporting on the state of compliance with the policies

Table 1. Office of Ministry of Education (2013b). 2013 Business Plan (Including 2012 Financial Report), Budget Forum 2–17 September 2012, Office of the Minister of State in the Ministry of Education, Sports, Youth and Gender Affairs. Figures are represented in both the local currency Eastern Caribbean Dollars (XCD$) and US Dollars.[3]

| DEPTS | Approved 2012 Estimates | | 2012 | | | | 2013 | |
| | | | January–August Expended | | September–December | | Proposed | |
	XCD $	US $	XCD $	US$	XCD $	US$	XCD $	US$
Sports PE	4,495,754	1,665,094 07	2,937,210.23	1,087,855.64	1,558,543.77	577,238.43	4,570,034	1,692,605.19
Sports Activities	505,060	187,059.26	214,991.27	79,626.40	291,268.73	107,877.31	1,349,000	499,629.63
NSMS PE	3,741,480	1,385,733.33	2,394,815.29	886,968.63	1,328,368.27	491,988.25	4,039,290	1,496,033.33
NSMS Activities	2,739,282	1,014,548.89	1,012,743.02	375,090.01	878,627.22	325,417.49	2,909,282	1,077,511.85
Total	11,481,576.00	4,252,435.56	6,559,759.81	2,429,540.67	4,054,807.99	1,501,780.74	12,867,606.00	4,765,780.00

... and will have authorisation to recommend, ... appropriate sanctions... as deemed necessary to bring non-compliant parties back into line'(A&B NSRP 2011–14, p. 5).

Aligned with international and Caribbean National Sports policies for Jamaica, Trinidad and Tobago and St Lucia, the A&B NSRP covers two broad dimensions of contemporary sports, Total Participation in Sports and High performance sports. In accordance with international definitions Total Participation in Sports is conceptualized as focusing on sports for all (Bergsgard *et al.* 2007). This policy seeks to encourage activities for all individuals irrespective of age, race, gender, ethnicity, religion and those who are 'specially challenged' (A&B NSRP 2011–14, p. 5). High Performance Sport is understood as focusing on elite athletes, allowing for successful development and international competition. Provision for both elite and mass sport is addressed simultaneously and must be linked to a 'developed Physical Education programme from pre-school to primary, secondary and vocational schools to the tertiary education level' (A&B NSRP 2011–14, p. 8). This dichotomy reflects that of nearly every state-run sport system (Shehu and Mokgwathi 2007). Whether this is appropriate in the context of small island states is a significant issue (see below).

The purpose, objectives and concomitant language of the policy are identical to the National Sport Policy of Trinidad and Tobago (2002), informed by the Australian National Sport Policy (McCree 2009). For example, the mission statement: 'Total Participation, Quality Training and Excellence in Sports' within the A&B NSRP (2011–14, p. 1) is a slight variation of the Trinidad and Tobago statement: 'To enrich our lives through Total Participation, Quality Training and Excellence in Sport'. Furthermore, seven of the major related objectives that make provisions for total participation and high performance are identical to the Trinidad and Tobago policy (p. 8) and the eighth is comparable. Interestingly, the A&B NSRP clearly states, on page 6, that it has eight (8) major related objectives, yet nine are listed.

As CARICOM's sub-committee on sport is instrumental in developing policy guidelines for sport, it is understandable why there is a level of convergence and comparability between the themes and language. Furthermore, with the global movement of policy and the concomitant ideologies, it is unsurprising that there is a level of resemblance (Palmer 2013). However, implementation of the policy is potentially problematic if differences in economic, social, cultural and political contexts between the small states are not recognized at the ministerial level, by the SRAC and emerging NECS (Collins 2010).

Methodology

This research was initiated by the senior researcher following recent visits to the islands through contacting the acting president of the NOC. The research aims were designed by the research team and facilitation was negotiated primarily with the NOC. The NOC facilitated access to the Ministry. However, this affected the way in which the research was carried out as the two organizations often worked independently with regard to the existence of sports provision. Accommodation expenses and office space were provided for the senior researcher by the NOC. Additional travel and subsistence expenses were supported by the researcher's university and self-funded. The MoS provided transport for access to ministry facilities and staff. The senior researcher also sought additional transport to access facilities and meet interviewees. Due to the limited level of funds, the research data was collected over an intense three-week period in September 2012.

The study utilized a mixed-method approach guided by the interpretivist policy analysis perspective (Denzin 2001, Wagenaar 2012). The methods included analysis of secondary sources including government and sports policy documents, existing paperwork in the MoS and NOC. Secondary data sources included a limited survey of 200 people examining sports participation, physical activity levels, participation in physical education and perceptions of provision amongst the local population[4]. Furthermore, 30 semi-structured interviews and observation utilizing visual research methods (resulting in 100 photographs) for facility observation were also employed. Mixed-methods research designs have become more established in studies of physical activity and sports, and importantly sports policy evaluation (Gibson 2012). The focus of this study is on the qualitative interview and visual observational data collected to inform the research aims and the central purpose of this paper. Secondary data (due to their limitations) provide contextual policy information considerations for the research team and government, but are not the focus of this paper.

The series of semi-structured interviews was conducted with senior and junior members of the Ministry of Sport, National Olympic Committee and National Sports Association members. Participants were questioned using an interview guide as to whether they were aware of the existing sport policy, their perceptions of it and their role, if any, in its design, development and implementation. Visual research methods (photographic observation) (Pink 2009) were also utilized to document and interpret the provision of sports facilities and implementation of sport policy. The philosophy underpinning this methodology is to access the views and attitudes of key actors and individuals operating within the policy process to support the purpose of the project (Wagenaar 2012). The data collected allowed us to evaluate whether the sports policy had met its intended objectives regarding facility provision and improvement. A reflexive approach was adopted to illustrate *and* interpret the provision of sports facilities. Whilst descriptive content alone illustrates the existence and condition of facilities, the idealistic discourse that surrounds the Caribbean islands could potentially cloud audience interpretations and limit representation of sports provision beyond the westernized tourist gaze (Urry 2002).

Our reflexive awareness (Pink 2009) has been important in our collection of photographs to document facilities. However, the level of disrepair unintentionally draws attention to the urgent need for assistance, support and development. It is therefore important to recognize that as western researchers, located in a large nation state in the Global North, our cultural understandings of sports provision could impact the choice of photographs to take and our interpretations (Palmer 2013). Kay (2009) has drawn attention to the challenges that Global North researchers face in understanding the complexity of local context. As western researchers located in an economically developed society with an established sports policy and extensive sports facilities, our interpretations are inherent in our understanding of this. Thus our interpretations and analysis are potentially developed through comparisons to our own social context.

In accordance with the British Sociological Association's Statement of Ethical Practice (2002, 2004), ethical issues and considerations were addressed in the design, facilitation and dissemination of the study. Notably, informed consent was accessed and the anonymity of participants was assured where possible. The project was granted ethical approval by the host organization, Nottingham Trent University Ethical Committee, and agreed with the NoC in association with the MoS.

Utilizing a thematic approach, the interview data were analysed to identify emerging and relevant key themes. These were labelled and categorized, entailing the use of diagrammatic maps, with colour codes for illustrating interrelated and secondary themes (Butler-Kisber 2010). These were aligned to themes that emerged in the visual material and secondary data analysis.

Findings

The findings section of this paper explores the challenges and constraints in sport policy agenda setting and implementation in Antigua and Barbuda presenting the key themes that emerged from this research project. In particular it identifies the specific constraining issues, implementation tensions and areas of contested priorities around this sphere of policy analysis.

Physical activity and sport as a contested policy priority

Whilst the NECS and MoS are identified in the policy as playing a role in the agenda setting and implementation of the policy and the design of the key objectives, the Ministry of Education (MoE) and the National Institute of Sports and Recreation (NISR) also play a pivotal role. The synergy between these actors is the central fulcrum of problem-defining roles and has influenced how the agenda has been expanded and constrained (Cobb and Coughlin 1998). Our analysis reveals that developments were being made to work with the MoE and develop the institute. However, the low academic value attached to sport and physical activity in schools at the ministerial level has been one of the biggest challenges in implementing these strategies. Within the policy, The MoE is allocated seven responsibilities to facilitate in achieving the designated 'Total Participation' and 'High Performance' agendas. In accordance with the holistic approach to provision, they are required to work with the MoS to ensure 'that Physical Education and Sports is part of the curriculum at all levels' (A&B NSRP 2011–14, p. 13). They will also work together to provide the 'training of teachers in the teaching of Physical Education and Sports' (A&B NSRP 2011–14, p. 13). For preschool and secondary education it is stated that the Ministry will be solely responsible for providing support to ensure that physical education programmes, inclusive of catering services, is available 'twice a week' (A&B NSRP 2011–14, p. 13). Furthermore, to address the low values attached to sport and participation amongst the population, the Ministry is also required to 'create an environment where participation and achievement in sports shall be encouraged alongside academic achieve-ment' (A&B NSRP 2011–14, p. 13).

Whilst the policy document states that MoS is responsible for improving provision of PE and sport within curriculum, our data and analysis of secondary sources (Darko and Mackintosh 2012) illustrate that participation in physical *activity* was minimal at primary and secondary levels and the majority of young people want additional physical *activities* within the school day. The secondary data survey of 200 people identified that the majority of school children and young people (under 18 years of age) felt that there should be more time in the school day for PE, including physical activity. The majority wanted additional hours of PE in school, an additional 2 hours of PE per day. This was also a central theme that arose in qualitative responses amongst young people. One pupil stated: 'I would like to join the VB team but I have a lot of homework after school and I have to study, if there were more hours of PE in the day then I could but there isn't'.

The secondary data in the government internal survey also revealed that the majority of adult participants expressed similar views regarding the allocation of time in the school day for physical education and activity (Darko and Mackintosh 2012). Due to the tropical climate and high temperatures (Kras 2008), the school day at all levels is much shorter than in the UK. This potentially limits the opportunity for the MoE to extend the school day for the provision of sport. However, improvement in sport facilities, with provision for covered and shaded courts and pitches, is important for assisting in this provision. For example, one of our interviewees, a secondary physical education and qualified football coach, stated:

> The facilities we have in government schools are poor. In my school there is a field for cricket and football and a cemented uncovered area for basketball and netball. There are no basketball or netball rings... this is a huge problem...this still makes it difficult for me to teach the basic skills. Sometimes I just can't teach it all.

Furthermore, one ministerial school sport coach stated:

> The facilities are minimal and it's too hot to coach basketball outside. In my area [parish] you might see a ring, but it's broken and the ground is not good. We also don't have indoor courts and you just can't provide the skills sessions.

Rhetoric of the sport policy vision compared against the reality for participants, coaches and the local community delivery partners is a common theme. Likewise, whether the government sport policy agenda and instruments need to be focused on the dualistic elite participation and mass participation goals of western nations is problematic in this context. This indicates a need to more clearly define the 'policy problem' (Parsons 1995, Colebatch 1998) and begin to shape the political and programme agendas around potential instrument design more effectively. Given the incomplete knowledge, limited understanding and emergent nature of sport policy infrastructure on the islands, the identification and formulation of a 'policy problem' at all could be questioned or deemed premature. Similarly, the very specific nature of the multiple island nation state make delivery and implementation potentially geographically disjointed by physical conditions and varied island facilities.

Barriers in cross-departmental collaboration in sports policy

One of the additional issues that the MoS and non-government organizations faced was an apparent lack of support and collaboration with the MoE. A senior member of the MoS stated: 'The education department ... is not going to change at policy level the physical education provision... They are not interested in more sports, simply more education'.

This relates to the earlier conceptual notion of a policy agenda 'container' (Cobb and Coughlin 1998) with the MoE seeking to restrain and restrict sport policy problems and issues from reaching the design and implementation agenda. Interviews with members of the sports associations, the NOC and the MoS coaches also revealed these views. The majority felt that that cooperation and collaboration between the MoS, MoE, NOC, associations and public can be established for the improvement in participation. Unfortunately, whilst it was indicated above that the formulation of the policy was developed in consultation with the sports associations and the NOC, all our interviews with these members revealed that they were not involved in these consultations. One senior member of the NOC stated: 'A policy document should be developed between the MoS and the MoE where sports are compulsory in all schools from kindergarten to 12th grade'.

One of the sports association members, who held a former senior ministerial post within the MoE, stated: 'We need to extend school day, but government seem keen to get rid of sport in school and put it on the shoulders of the National Associations, but they do not have the money to fund and support sport'.

Our qualitative data revealed that the majority of members of the association and athletes had no knowledge of the existing policy and strategies regarding provision of sport and physical activity in schools. There were requests from sports coaches, PE teachers and sports association members for inter-policy documents at the ministerial level to dictate provision of PE and improvement in standards. It was indicated by these interviewees that powerful individuals/personalities (such as sports ambassadors and sports role models) should dictate sports policy development but they stated that should also be accompanied by the ministry and its members. They requested non-ministerial members for the first stage of this policy development, because a level of distrust in the ministry existed due to previous failures in policy development and successful and sustained implementation. Whilst some members of the MoS, PE staff and ministerial sports coaches presented a dedicated approach to the provision of increased physical activity in school, some school staff members were apathetic and this was not addressed at the institutional level through policy. A senior member of the ministerial school sports department stated:

> We need an inter-policy document where we have that extra hour and a half from one thirty until three o' clock in the secondary school, and those times would be allocated to sports, culture and the arts and we can get more production from existing sporting personnel in the school once that is implemented.

Whilst there were these calls for policy development and new agenda setting, our data revealed that provision of PE staff and ministerial sports coaches was minimal[5]. Secondary data revealed findings from a small survey of 200 people that indicated that the majority of young people (under 18) were only taking part in school physical activity once or twice a week (Darko and Mackintosh 2012). Males reported taking part in 3 hours per week and females in 1.9 hours per week. Furthermore, sedentary behaviour[6] amongst young people is relatively high, with the current average figure at 5 hours 30 minutes per day. The highest recorded figures were 8.5 hours for males and 15 hours for females. Improving levels of sedentary behaviour must be a central priority for addressing the health of the Antigua population as research indicates that adult obesity levels in the Caribbean are increasing, with current figures indicating that 18.1% males and 33.3% of females (over the age of 20 years) are currently overweight (WHO 2013). Furthermore, childhood obesity is also an emerging concern, due to a lack of nutritional education regarding high sugar juice drinks and junk food (Williams and Daniels 2008).

Pupils also stated that the central reasons for not participating in PE included a lack of PE staff and/or sports coaches to facilitate frequent and consistent sessions, PE classes clashed with other subjects and the school did not provide sports that the pupils were interested in. PE staff also found it difficult to facilitate participation in inter-school competitions because there were few ministerial sports coaches to provide this role. One physical education teacher stated, 'there are limited coaches. One is often responsible for three and four schools, so in some cases PE has to take on this role to assist in… competitions but it's not really their responsibility according to the policy here'.

The elite sport and performance infrastructure dilemma

Given the limited provision in schools, community facilities and grassroots infrastructure it is an inherent policy dilemma to then consider the high cost and investment priority of elite sporting performance systems. It could even be suggested that the policy debates around elite sport positioned from a western lens (Grix and Carmichael 2012), which are often cited, hold little meaning in this context. However, it is apparent that to develop total participation and high performance, the Ministry intends to establish the NISR that shall be responsible primarily for coaching education. This will entail organization, review and renewal of more local training programmes and enhanced international publicity for local coaches. Furthermore, 'minimum coaching standards will be established across three major levels' (A&B NSRP 2011–14, p. 12). The focus on high performance is central to the formation of this institute, as it seeks to also provide training and education to high-performance athletes. It is stated that it will provide 'sports related services to include research and professional development and sports enrichment courses [and] will be fully equipped with the necessary amenities and equipment' (A&B NSRP 2011–14, p. 10).

Interviews with members of the MoS revealed that at the time of the research the NISR was their central priority and deemed the key agenda issue they were keen to expand within government. This contrasts with the voices and standpoints of those participants interviewed and that clearly identify local facility and infrastructure needs as a priority. Recognition had been given to the role of holistic provision and lack of finances, as meetings had been held with the Antigua Medical University (The American University) to facilitate the development of this institute. According to a senior member of the MoS this institute would include 'Pharmacy, Paramedic, Sports Tourism, Sports Management and Sports Medicine courses such as Physiotherapy, and Sport Psychology' (Interviewee: MoS). To develop the academic value of sport, the ministry planned to have 'an officer who will introduce to schools, sports medicine services [and to be ale] to train athletes in theoretical levels' (A&B NSRP 2011–14, p. 13). However, at the time of the research, it was unclear what the basis for such a role would be and the rationale for such a limited investment across the whole nation.

This approach does recognize the limited economic funds for building development through its collaboration with the university. However, our interview data and examination of sport building facilities for athlete participation and housing of sports clubs and association revealed limited provision. With a focus on promoting and improving high performance, the ministry sought to allow athletes to access this facility and the trained sports medics. It was envisaged that this provision would be heavily subsidised by them. They would provide 'sports medical services, diagnostic services for Sports Associations to access and this will be covered (financially) by the government' (Senior MoS staff).

Recognition was given by the Minister and members to the lack of sports medical knowledge and academic expertise within this field within the MoS. To address this they 'employed a person whose background is in public health and pharmacy to facilitate in this' (MoS staff). However, interviews with presidents of two sports associations and medical staff within this field revealed that no consultation process had taken place at this stage with them in the process of facilitating and implementing this. One president, a qualified doctor of sports medicine,[7] stated: 'What they define as a medical school is problematic. I've not been consulted at all. Who will provide sports management, tourism and psychology courses?'

The Antigua University is a medical university and at present it does not offer additional disciplines in Sports Science, Sports Tourism, Management or Psychology. The Ministry may envisage this provision in Sports Science, Sports Tourism, Management or Psychology. The Ministry may also envisage the provision of future development, but it is unclear who will fund the provision of these courses and PE, with little evidence to illustrate that young people will enrol. Equally, if the cultural perception of sport and its academic value is not promoted through school its future viability could be further questioned. Our data analysis revealed that both young people and adults wanted to see improvements in the support for athletes and sports participation.

The proposed Antigua Sports Village, due to be built for January 2015, also aims to assist in addressing the lack of suitable facilities. An interview with the project coordinators and an architect from the design company revealed that this stadium is intended to improve mass participation and high performance. The village will possess two multipurpose stadiums hosting approximately 12,000 people. Provision will be made for international baseball, swimming, athletics, basketball and rowing. A convention centre, sports entertainment centre, sports medicine clinic and multipurpose gymnasium will also be built. In accordance with the aims of the sports policy, this facility will allow for mass participation as free access would be granted to the population. Furthermore, the provision of elite and international competition facilities will allow for high-performance training and participation in events. One of the designers stated: 'We want to attract international events... the likes of Usain Bolt. We want to do regional events giving local athletes access the facilities for the training, but also improve a healthy lifestyle amongst the general population'.

Funding for the village is to be raised via government and private investment and through the allocation of naming rights. Whilst this approach recognizes the lack of economic resources within the ministry for facility development, scepticism was apparent amongst the population and sports associations. Members of the public felt that the ministry did not have the funds to build this facility independently or contribute to its development due to their previous uncompleted sports development provision. Furthermore, the recent evidence of political corruption and fraud surrounding Sir Alan Stanford's[8] provision of sports facilities had led to uncertainty about the interest from potential investors. Whilst not a focus of this research, it is crucial to recognize in terms of agency and individual actor behaviour that the influence of this high-profile corruption case had created a significant shift in terms of levels of trust around government sport policy.

Developing a community and third sector infrastructure

The A&B NSRP (2011) stated the need for a holistic approach to sport policy development with the empowerment of communities at its core. Findings form this study illustrate distinct challenges at the local level in the country in terms of physical provision, facilities, human resources in coaching and opportunities to develop sport from a grassroots base. Whilst the NOC, the associations and members can and are assisting in the facilitation of this policy through after-school sports provision, it must be recognized that current sport provision is driven predominantly by voluntary members of the associations.

A further recommendation for the proposed NISR is to address the provision of sports development programmes as a means to promote participation. Secondary survey data illustrated that the majority of young people and adults were unaware of any sports development programmes but also programmes for school leavers (Darko and Mackintosh 2012). Whilst now slightly dated, further research conducted by CARICOM in 2003 supports these findings with limited awareness in local populations of sport development opportunities (Caribbean Community Secretariat, CARICOM 2013). CARICOM researchers contacted personnel in the ministerial Department responsible for Youth Affairs and/or Sport in Antigua and Barbuda and discovered that they were aware of the concept of development through sport, but unable to identify such programmes at the country level. Whilst the Ministry were able

to identify a number of small development programmes, further measures to implement sports development programmes at grassroots levels to target young people were
limited.

Although policy implementation was a focus of this research, once in the field it
appeared that the between-policy rhetoric and actual instruments of delivery was considerable. This in itself is a crucial finding, but also one that illustrates the existing agenda
'skew' from the priorities of local infrastructure, coaches and participation opportunities
that lie far from the national policy visionary statements. Furthermore, the empirical
evidence to illustrate whether the community needs, design, coordination planning and
programme implementation achieved their intended impact and objectives was limited.
The minimal project/programme design, development, implementation, evaluation and
impact was not developed in consultation with relevant sport clubs associations, national
and international agencies, academic experts and most importantly the general public.
This also was not facilitated through the use of questionnaires, focus groups, interviews
and data analysis. However, as suggested by the national policy, the lack of central skills
to undertake such a process that will genuinely empower the communities and voluntary
associations is significantly limited.

Due to the lack of economic funds provided by the ministry, private investment
and voluntary practice have allowed for the existence, planning and organization of
sports. At the time of the research, provision had been made by the government
(MoS) to improve total participation through community and sports association
engagement. With focus on management lying with the community clubs, the MoS
has begun to implement a programme that offers clubs and associations a lease of
existing facilities owned by the ministry. Examination of many of the existing sports
facilities revealed that there is a significant level of inadequate provision for safe
participation in sport. The majority of facilities visited lacked clean running water and
access to any toilets. Many of the surfaces of the courts, pitches and track facilities
needed to be significantly improved to allow for safe participation. Whilst the
marking of boundaries and cutting of grass were provided by ministerial grounds-
staff and volunteers during the data collection, very few facilities provided shaded or
covered areas to participate or spectate. In addition, some areas of the facilities were
identified as condemned and unsafe. A sample of the photographs is presented in
Figure 2, below.

Interviews with senior members of the ministry revealed that a leasing system at that
time was being reviewed and agreed by the legal department. The ministry found that
whilst some clubs were interested and had taken up this opportunity, some completely
opposed it and viewed it as a ministerial responsibility. One member of the MoS stated:
'We have faced opposition; one club does not want the building until it is completed, all
improved and finished. They cannot see that they will be given to the building to generate
income, but they don't want it unless we improve it'.

In addition to these oppositions, the politics of policy implementation affected the
progression of this strategy. Interviews revealed that ministerial staff possessed traditional
ideologies about the value of sport and the financial role of the ministry. Whilst the NOC
provided opportunities to apply for a contribution to costs and stipends, our data revealed
that all of the sports associations rely heavily on voluntary provisions provided by
coaching staff and those with knowledge or previous involvement in the sport. This
inevitably impacts the level of funds available for facility development and event organization. For example, a member of the NOC and president of one of the sports associations stated:

Figure 2.   Photo sample sheet of ministerial sports facilities.

> Whilst we can raise 3000EC we can never raise enough to generate 50% of the funds. One association applied for 50% of the funds from us which we approved, but they couldn't get the remainder and thus could not go to the ... championships. In such a small country it is difficult to raise that kind of money for facility development- it would take us 3 years even more.

Despite this, traditional views within the ministry halted further assistance and support for facility provision. One senior member of the MoS stated:

> There are people within the ministry who feel that associations have the capacity and money. *BUT* (emphasis added) he is simply pointing out the problems without recognising they are volunteers. You need to work with them, sit down with them not simply advise and not assist them.

During the first week of the data collection, the interviews with the MoS revealed that they were planning fund improvement in facilities (sport venues) and all school sports coaches would attend those sites and create after-school provision. However, towards the end of the research process this strategy was abandoned, a member of the MoS stated:

> The education department (MoE) opposed it. [Furthermore] we also realised that the associations get paid by schools for some of their work. If we implement this process we will be taking the money out of the associations' hands. What has happened is that certain coaches have picked one or two schools, not all, that are reliable (pay). So this strategy might not work. The ... (ministerial staff member) pointed out that this should be driven by leaders in sport- associations-, not the government.

Despite this divergence, our findings show that facility development was a central priority for all of the association members, athletes and sports ambassadors interviewed.

Furthermore, as discussed above, the majority of adults and young people felt the need for more sport and physical activities and opportunities for people in Antigua to take part, and improvements in facilities were essential to this provision. Furthermore, a vice president for one of the sports associations stated

> Transport of athletes is a real problem...we need a mini-bus as we all spend time picking athletes up and taking them home. The bus system does not facilitate access to training and parents cannot get here from work, furthermore talented athletes do not have the money to access transport.

Further measures need to be taken to address the higher level of sedentary behaviour amongst young girls and their lack of interest. Our interviews with female sports coaches and female sports association members revealed further measures must be taken to address the shortage of females assisting in school and non-school sports provision. One female coach stated:

> I'm the only female ... coach working with athletes from our association within schools and in the sport, and. Parents don't see an adequate structure, because there are few female coaches and even toilets for the girls. This discourages girls and parents bringing children to participate.

In light of these findings, further measures need to be adopted to promote female role models, and to provide financial support for the attainment of coaching qualifications amongst women. Whilst the NOC, association and federations such as FIFA are assisting in this provision for athletics and football, further assistance and promotion are required at the ministerial level to support these organizations and generate interest in attaining qualifications as the grassroots level.

Limitations of the study

Whilst this study has made a significant contribution to the lack of research examining Caribbean sports policy and provision, the research is not without its limitations. One of the central difficulties faced was the lack of academic material to develop an understanding of the historical, policy and political involvement in sports and recreation. We also found that young people were keen to participate in the research. However, we often provided free coaching, training and supplement advice sessions to facilitate willingness and to promote a level of trust between ourselves and the participants. We also found that the majority of adults were sceptical about participating. Many initially assumed that the research was being conducted by the ministry and that their input would not facilitate future sports development. This scepticism was due to historical lack of provision and the previous withdrawal of sports programmes/activities by the ministry. However, once participants were informed that the research was being conducted by an independent academic institution and supported primarily through the NOC, participants were more willing. Whilst the ministry played a minor role, they assisted in key aspects of the research, notably providing transportation, assistance in the administration of secondary data questionnaires and the provision of a number of important documents. We also found that whilst a significant amount of data was collected over the 3-week time frame, members of the ministry of education and the prime minister were difficult to access. Such lack of access to key actors is indicative perhaps of the active process of 'containing' the sport policy agenda (Cobb and Coughlin 1998). Furthermore, planned visits arranged by the ministry to the island of Barbuda had to be rescheduled by the ministry and thus could not be facilitated within the research data collection time.

Discussion and conclusion

As stated at the outset of this paper small or micro-states with emergent sport policy structures may not have sufficient policy and programme maturity to fit well with many of the typical evidence-based mantras (Piggin *et al.* 2009, Smith *et al.* 2010) and western priority agendas in the wider policy literature (Houlihan and Green 2009, Grix and Carmichael 2012). It appears that local actors in the form of ministerial and committee elite individuals through to the relatively small collective of local association activists and volunteers play a significant role in delivery and implementation outcomes. It is our view that this is amplified in the context of the micro-state. As Clegg (1989) proposes, the decisions of organizations and public policy outcomes are born out of the struggle between committees, individuals and departments. Using the Cobb and Coughlin (1998) sensitizing framework of policy actors as 'expanders' and 'containers', various key social actors and individual actors have been highlighted as central to the policy process. This project has been the first attempt to build insights and understanding into agenda setting, policy development and policy implementation and inform the future direction of the Antiguan and Barbuda Sport and Recreation policy.

Key themes of developing local-level infrastructure, improving access to core physical education, gaining clarity over centralized elite performance sport policy and improving sports development programme development and infrastructure have been identified through this study. A core challenge of undertaking the project has been the lack of a robust starting point for the study and the shifting sands of the policy landscape in this small state. Furthermore, robust research with young people at primary, secondary and tertiary levels that examines their views of this provision, participation levels and their interests sport would also assist with further implementation and reformulation of the policy. Jeanes (2011) advocates such engagement and consultation with young people are important to assist in shaping the policy and practice of development in Global South settings. Both Jeanes (2011) and Kay (2009) advocate that partnerships with local NGO staff and academics may be a way of developing appropriate strategies to include young people in research. However, the micro-state nature of the Caribbean islands means that resources and skills to develop knowledge in evidence-based policy are highly limited, as is the capacity to undertake such advocacy and partnership working.

An inherent challenge as identified by Lindsay (2012) and Kay (2013) is the potential issue facing researchers from the Global North that contributes towards such projects and then are faced with the position of then moving on from the data collection, delivering recommendations and leaving the 'field'. In the case of this study it is hoped that this project has been the start of a longer-term research dialogue and relationship between the NOC, the government and research team that is sustainable and supportive. The limitations of the study have been clearly identified, but it is also resoundingly clear that shaping the next steps for sport policy and associated programmes and initiatives needs to be taken with great care. The desired outcome of the project, i.e., to open up agenda setting dialogue, has been successful in what is a complex political policy climate. As a small state with limited physical and human infrastructure, imposing the values, aspirations and policy trajectory of western states may not be in the interest of the government or the communities it represents. Further research into existing provision and participation to inform government understanding of these complex twin islands and diverse sporting populations is fundamental to shaping a clearer evidence base for shaping a more sustainable and achievable sports policy in the future.

Colomer's (2007) argument that there are three characteristic benefits of small nation democratic government around improvements in deliberation, aggregation and enforcement seems to be challenged in the case of Antigua and Barbuda. Here citizens and local actors appear to have a considerable disconnect from policymakers and those in positions of decision-making power. Likewise in the case of sport policy we saw little of harmonization and agreement and considerable tiers of disaggregation between local communities and national policy rhetoric. It seems that the policy problems might have begun to be brought to the fore through this project; however, the complex tasks centred upon policy design, instrument development and clear agenda setting seem very distant at this stage. This also aligns to the central paradox of an evolving elite policy community of actors that sit in stark contrast to the minimal provision, coaching and physical activity development opportunities at the local level. This research has highlighted the lack of skills in place to support the empowerment of the voluntary association network. Philosophically we also have recognized the reflexive challenge in exiting a research setting with limited resources and the inherent limits facing this research team in our attempt to decolonize our methodology (Kay 2009). Voices and perspectives of local actors have been prioritized and agenda have been crystallized, but the resource issues and fragmented implementation remain once the team has left this phase of the research process.

In gaining access to high-level ministerial staff, it has also exposed how many possess traditional ideologies about the value of sport, the assumed 'top down' advisory role of policymakers and the lack of input to the sporting system of those local and regional agencies and volunteers that support it. It is evident that MoE and MoS actor personalities, viewpoints, philosophies and individual standpoints play a very dominant role in shaping agendas, influencing partnership working and making coherent policy priorities. As suggested at the outset, the micro-state context, physical interconnectedness and the small geographical size of Antigua and Barbuda in particular do open clear possibilities such as already seen in the parallel national policy field of school teacher education programme development in Antigua and Barbuda (Younger and George 2012). It is hoped that local populations will get similar opportunities to shape their own opportunities in dialogue around sport provision, participation and policies in the future. Avoiding the imposition of western visions and dualisms between elite medal winning and mass participation and assumed systems of policy design and instruments will be fundamental in preventing future problematic sport policy.

Notes

1. This is the first phase of the project and it is intended to be part of a next phase of research, consultation and training between the project partners
2. Senator Winston Williams is responsible for this provision.
3. Figures converted to US dollars on 23 September 2013, 1 USD = 2.70000
4. Secondary data was limited in scope but did provide some useful contextual information on sports participation attitudes, levels of self-reported participation and hours of engagement. Further details of these findings can be found in Darko and Mackintosh (2012).
5. It should be noted that we were unable to interview staff within the Ministry of Education due to their time constraints.
6. Sedentary behaviour is defined as a group of behaviours that occur whilst sitting or lying down while awake and typically require very low energy expenditure, characterized by an energy expenditure ≤ 1.5 METs (Sedentary Behaviour Research Network 2012)

7   Our research revealed that there were only two qualified doctors of sports medicine currently living on the islands

8. Sir Allen Stanford privately developed aspects of Antigua and Barbuda's infrastructure and contributed significantly to the development and existence of professional sport. He was prosecuted of being involved in (7bn) investment fraud (*The Telegraph*, Friday 19 June 2009)

References

Andreff, W., 2001. The correlation between economic underdevelopment and sport. *European sport management quarterly*, 1 (4), 251–279. doi:10.1080/16184740108721902

Anon, 2009. Cricket entrepreneur Sir Allen Stanford charged over alleged $7billion fraud. *The telegraph*, Friday 19 June 2009 [online]. Available from: http://www.telegraph.co.uk/finance/financetopics/sir-allen-stanford/5581927/Cricket-entrepreneur-Sir-Allen-Stanford-charged-over-alleged-7billion-fraud.html [Accessed 25 October 2013].

Bergsgard, N., *et al.*, 2007. *Sports policy: a comparative analysis of stability and change.* Oxford: Elsevier.

Brookes, S. and Wiggan, J., 2009. Reflecting the public value of sport: a game of two halves. *Public management review*, 11 (4), 401–420. doi:10.1080/14719030902989490

Butler-Kisber, L., 2010. *Qualitative inquiry: thematic, narrative and arts-informed perspectives.* London: Sage.

Cairney, P., 2012. *Understanding public policy: theories and issues.* New York: Palgrave MacMillan.

Caribbean Community Secretariat, CARICOM, 2013. *Regional survey of development through sport programmes implemented at the country level (2003)* [online]. Available from: http://www.caricom.org/jsp/community_organs/regionalsurvey_sportsprogrammes.jsp?menu=cob [Accessed 17 January 2013].

Caribbean Examinations Council, Caricom 2012. Available from: http://www.caricom.org/jsp/community/cxc.jsp?menu=community [Accessed 17 January 2012].

Clancy, T., 2012. *Countries of the world: Antigua and Barbuda.* Seattle, WA: CreateSpace Independent Publishing Platform.

Clegg, S., 1989. *Frameworks of power.* London: Sage.

Coalter, F., 2007. *A wider social role for sport: who's keeping the score?* London: Routledge.

Cobb, R.W. and Coughlin, J.F., 1998. Are elderly drivers a road hazard? Problem definition and political impact. *Journal of aging studies*, 12 (4), 411–427. doi:10.1016/S0890-4065(98)90027-5

Colebatch, H.K., 1998. *Policy.* Buckingham: Open University Press.

Collins, M., 2010. From 'sport for good' to 'sport for sport's sake – not a good move for sports development in England? *International journal of sport policy and politics*, 2 (3), 367–379. doi:10.1080/19406940.2010.519342

Colomer, J.M., 2007. *Great empires, small nations: the uncertain future of the sovereign state.* London: Routledge.

Darko, N. and Mackintosh, C., 2012. *Sports participation and provision: Antigua and Barbuda 2012–13 research report.* Nottingham: Nottingham Trent University.

De Bosscher, V., *et al.*, 2006. A conceptual framework for analysing sports policy factors leading to international sporting success. *European sport management quarterly*, 6 (2), 185–215. doi:10.1080/16184740600955087

Denzin, N.K., 2001. *Interpretive interactionism.* London: Sage.

Easterly, W. and Kraay, A., 1999. *Small states, small problems?* Policy Research Working Paper 2139. Washington, DC: The World Bank.

Gibson, K., 2012. Two (or more) feet are better than one: mixed methods research in sport and physical culture. *In*: K. Young and M. Atkinson, eds. *Qualitative research on sport and physical culture (research in the sociology of sport).* Vol. 6. Bingley: Emerald Group Publishing Limited, 213–232.

Government of Antigua and Barbuda, Ministry of Sport, 2011. *National policy on sports & recreation (Antigua and arbuda) 2011–14, "Total participation, quality training & excellence in sports, Antigua and Barbuda".* Antigua: Antigua and Barbuda, Ministry of Sport. [Online] Available from: http://www.365antigua.com/sports/985AntiguaBarbudaSportsRecreationPolicy2011-2014.pdf [Accessed 7 May 2014].

Government of Trinidad and Tobago (GOTT), 1988. *White paper: the establishment of a national sporting authority for the republic of Trinidad and Tobago.* Port of Spain: Government for the Republic for Trinidad and Tobago.

Government of Trinidad and Tobago (GOTT), 2002. *The national sport policy of Trinidad and Tobago* [online]. Port of Spain: Government for the Republic for Trinidad and Tobago. Available from: http://sport.gov.tt/resources/sport-policies [Accessed 23 October 2010].

Grix, J. and Carmichael, F., 2012. Why do governments invest in elite sport? A polemic. *International journal of sport policy and politics*, 4 (1), 73–90. doi:10.1080/19406940.2011.627358

Henry, I., 2007. *Transnational and comparative research in sport: globalisation, governance and comparative sports policy.* London: Routledge.

Hey, A.K., ed., 2003. *Small states in world politics: explaining foreign policy behaviour.* Boulder, CO: Lynne Rienner.

Hill, M., 2005. *The public policy process.* 4th ed. Harlow: Pearson Education Limited.

Hogwood, B.W. and Gunn, L., 1984. *Policy analysis for the real world.* London: Oxford University Press.

Houlihan, B., 2005. Public sector sport policy: developing a framework for analysis. *International Review for the Sociology of Sport*, 40 (2), 163–185. doi:10.1177/1012690205057193

Houlihan, B., 2009. Mechanisms of international influence on domestic elite sport policy. *International journal of sport policy and politics*, 1 (1), 51–69. doi:10.1080/19406940902739090

Houlihan, B. and Green, M., 2009. Modernization and sport: the reform of sport England and UK sport. *Public administration*, 87 (3), 678–698. doi:10.1111/j.1467-9299.2008.01733.x

Hower, S.B., 2008. *Do small states make bad allies?* Washington, DC: School of Arts and Science of the Catholic University of America.

Indexmundi, (2013). *Antigua and Barbuda Factbook 2013* [online]. Available from: http://www.indexmundi.com/antigua_and_barbuda/ [Accessed 17 January 2013].

International Olympic Committee, 2013. *The national Olympic committee* [online]. Lausanne: International Olympic Committee. Available from: http://www.olympic.org/ioc-governance-national-olympic-committees [Accessed 17January 2013].

Jeanes, R., 2011. Educating through sport? Examining HIV/AIDS education and sport-for-development through the perspectives of Zambian young people. *Sport, education society*, 1 (19). doi:10.1080/13573322.2011.579093

Kay, T., 2009. Developing through sport: evidencing sport impacts on young people. *Sport in society*, 12 (9), 1177–1191. doi:10.1080/17430430903137837

Kay, T., 2010. Developing through sport and leisure? … Sport in support of female empowerment in Delhi, India. *In*: B. Houlihan and M. Green, eds. *Handbook of sports development.* London: Routledge, 308–322.

Kay, T., 2013. The politics & ethics of sport & international development research. *In: 7th Annual PSA Conference*, 1–2 February 2012. Bath: Bath University.

Keat, R.A. and Sam, M.P., 2013. Regional implementation of New Zealand sport policy: new instrument, new challenges. *International journal of sport policy and politics*, 5 (1), 39–54. doi:10.1080/19406940.2012.656684

Keohane, R.O., 1969. Lilliputians' dilemmas: small states in international politics. *International organization*, 23 (2), 291–310. doi:10.1017/S002081830003160X

Knill, C. and Tosun, J., 2012. *Public policy: a new introduction.* Basingstoke: Palgrave Macmillan.

Kras, S.L., 2008. *Cultures of the world, Antigua and Barbuda.* Tarrytown, NY: Marshall Cavendish Limited, Times Publishing Limited. Available from: http://books.google.co.uk/books?id=TnItHSAgevMC&printsec=frontcover&source=gbs_ge_summary_r&cad=0#v=onepage&q&f=false

Lindsay, I., 2012. *Ethically challenged? Researching sport and development in the global South* [online]. Posted on 9 August 2012. Available from: http://blogs.edgehill.ac.uk/ssg [Accessed 17 April 2013].

Lindsey, I. and Banda, D., 2011. Sport and the fight against HIV/AIDS in Zambia: a 'partnership' approach? *International review for the sociology of sport*, 46 (1), 90–107. doi:10.1177/1012690210376020

Lindsey, I. and Grattan, A., 2012. An 'international movement'? Decentring sport-for-development within Zambian communities. *International journal of sport policy and politics*, 4 (1), 91–110. doi:10.1080/19406940.2011.627360

Long, N., 2001. *Development sociology: actor perspectives*. London: Routledge.

Marleku, A., 2013. Small states foreign policy: the case of Kosovo. *Mediterranean journal of social sciences*, 4 (2), 287–300.

McCree, R., 2008. The social bases for the exclusion of sport from Caribbean economic development. *Iberoamericana: Nordic journal of latin American studies*, 38 (1–2), 154–176.

McCree, R., 2009. Sport policy and the new public management in the Caribbean: convergence or resurgence? *Public management review*, 11 (4), 461–476. doi:10.1080/14719030902989532

Moore, D.S., 1999. The crucible of cultural politics: reworking 'development' in Zimbabwe's eastern highlands. *American Ethnologist*, 26 (3), 654–689. doi:10.1525/ae.1999.26.3.654

Mordecai, J., 1968. *Federation of the West Indies*. Evanston: Northwestern University Press.

National Sport Policy of Trinidad and Tobago, 2002. *To enrich our lives through total participation, quality training and excellence in sport*, October. Trinidad and Tobago: Ministry of Sport, The Government of the Republic of Trinidad and Tobago.

O'Loughlin, C., 1961. Problems in the economic development of Antigua. *Social and economic studies*, 10 (3), 237–277.

Office of Ministry of Education, 2013a. *Organizational chart: secretariat, minister of state: sports, national school meals service & special projects, in business plan for 2013 MOSNSMS SUBMISSION TO CABINET 6 11 12*. Antigua: Office of Ministry of Education, Sports, Youth and Gender Affairs.

Office of Ministry of Education, 2013b. *Office of ministry of education business plan (INCL 2012 Financial report) budget forum 2 – September 17 2012*. Antigua: Office of Ministry of Education, Sports, Youth and Gender Affairs.

Palmer, C., 2013. *Global sports policy*. London: Sage.

Parsons, W., 1995. *Public policy: an introduction to the theory and practice of policy analysis*. Aldershot: Edward Elgar Publishing Limited.

Piggin, J., Jackson, S.J., and Lewis, M., 2009. Knowledge, power and politics: contesting 'evidence-based' national sport policy. *International review for the sociology of sport*, 44 (1), 87–101. doi:10.1177/1012690209102825

Pink, S., 2009. *Visual ethnography*. London: Sage.

Rist, R.C., 1998. Choosing the right policy instrument at the right time: the contextual challenges of selection and implementation. *In*: I.M. Bemelmans-Videc, R.C. Rist, and E. Vedung, eds. *Carrots, sticks & sermons: policy instruments & their evaluations*. New Brunswick, NJ: Transaction Publishers, 149–164.

Sabatier, P.A., ed., 2007. *Theories of the policy process*. Oxford: Westview Press.

Sabatier, P.A. and Jenkins-Smith, H., 2003. *Policy change and learning: an advocacy coalition approach*. Boulder, CO: Westview Press.

Sam, M.P., 2011. Building legitimacy at sport Canada: pitfalls of public value creation? *International review of administrative sciences*, 77 (4), 757–778. doi:10.1177/0020852311419389

Sam, M.P. and Jackson, S.J., 2004. Sport policy development in New Zealand: paradoxes of an integrative paradigm. *International review for the sociology of sport*, 39, 205–222. doi:10.1177/1012690204043463

Sedentary Behaviour Research Network, 2012. *Standardized use of the terms 'sedentary' and 'sedentary behaviours'* [online]. Available from: http://www.sedentarybehaviour.org/what-is-sedentary-behaviour [Accessed 28 March 2013].

Shehu, J. and Mokgwathi, M.M., 2007. A discourse analysis of the national sport and recreation policy for Botswana. *Sport, education and society*, 12 (2), 193–210. doi:10.1080/13573320701287544

Sibeon, R., 1998. *Contemporary sociology and policy analysis: the new sociology of public policy*. Eastham: Tudor Business Publishing.

Smith, A. and Leech, R., 2010. 'Evidence what evidence?': evidence-based policy making and school sport partnerships in north west England. *International journal of sport policy and politics*, 2 (3), 327–345. doi:10.1080/19406940.2010.519341

Smith, M.J., 1993. *Pressure, power and policy*. Hemel Hemstead: Harvester Wheatsheaf.

Souchaud, Y., 1995. *Situation sportive dans les pays moins avancés d'Afrique: bilan*. Juillet: Division de la Jeunesse et des Activités Sportives, UNESCO.

Stotlar, D.K. and Wonders, A., 2006. Developing elite athletes: a content analysis of US national governing body systems. *International journal of applied sports sciences*, 18 (2), 121–144.

Tyson, B., *et al.*, 2005. West Indies world cup cricket: hallmark events as catalysts for community tourism development. *Journal of sport and TOURISM*, 10 (4), 323–334. doi:10.1080/14775080600806653

Urry, J., 2002. *Tourist gaze*. London: Sage.

Wagenaar, H., 2012. *Meaning in action. Interpretation and dialogue in policy analysis*. Armonk, NY: M.E. Sharpe.

Williams, C.A. and Daniels, C.L., 2008. Antigua and Barbuda. *In*: I. Epstein and S.L. Lutjens, eds. *The greenwood encyclopedia of children's issues worldwide: North America and the Caribbean*. Westport, CT: Greenwood Press, 1–24.

World Bank, 2004. *Supporting small and vulnerable states*. IDA14 Discussion paper. Washington, DC: The World Bank.

World Health Organisation, 2013. *Antigua and Barbuda: health profile 2013* [online]. Geneva: World Health Organisation. Available from: http://www.who.int/countries/atg/en/ [Accessed 23 October 2010].

Younger, M. and George, P., 2012. Developing communities of practice in practice: overcoming suspicion and establishing dialogue amongst primary school teachers in Antigua and Barbuda. *Professional development in education*, 1–18. doi:10.1080/19415257.2012.724440

Resisting self-regulation: an analysis of sport policy programme making and implementation in Sweden

Josef Fahlén, Inger Eliasson and Kim Wickman

Department of Education, Umeå University, Umeå, Sweden

Political programming of sport has become the new orthodoxy in many countries where the strive for a more healthy and civically engaged population is intertwined with an ambition to encourage and make responsible individuals and organizations for meeting societal goals. Although much effort has been put into studying this phenomenon, there is still a shortage of understanding of how, why and with what results sport policy programmes are made and implemented. To address this shortage this article reports on a study of the largest government intervention in sport in Sweden with the purpose of exploring processes of responsibilization and self-regulation at play in the relationship between the government and sport as well as between sport organizations on different levels. Results show how sport has received a more salient position on the government agenda, where more instrumental goals have been accompanied by increased resources to aid in their attainment. This process has assisted in the ambitions to modernize sports organizations by encouraging development through self-regulation. The sports organizations involved have embraced the new goals and resources. However, instead of self-regulating in the desired direction, each organizational level in the sports system has forwarded the responsibility for development to the next level below. This process has left the sports clubs with the full responsibility of meeting the government goals, a responsibility they have not accepted. Understandings of these phenomena and processes are discussed by pointing to the specific institutional landscape and tradition of Swedish sport.

Introduction

An increase of government involvement (Houlihan and Green 2008) and use of New Public Management technologies in the governance of sport have been well documented by scholars studying sport governance in Australia (Sotiriadou 2009), New Zeeland (Sam and Jackson 2004), Canada (Green and Houlihan 2004) and the United Kingdom (Green 2004). It has also been contended that these technologies and the policy ideas behind them are spreading throughout the western industrialized world (Green and Oakley 2001) by mechanisms of policy learning (Green and Houlihan 2005), policy transfer and lesson drawing (Green 2007). But, as Houlihan notes, 'the impact of non-domestic influences consequently depends not just on their specific characteristics, but also on the particular pattern of institutional arrangements, both organisational and cultural, at the domestic level' (Houlihan 2009, p. 7).

Since little is known about possible increased government interest in sport and its consequences outside the English-speaking contexts, this paper aims to provide an empirical example of a pattern of institutional arrangements differing in organization and culture from those that have been explored in the literature thus far by exploring processes of responsibilization and self-regulation at play in the relationship between the government and sport as well as between sports organizations on different levels. The need for such knowledge is reflected in another quote by Houlihan: 'For a number of countries, especially the more neo-liberal, the international ideological environment will appear far less alien than for countries where the commodification of services is more limited, as in the Scandinavian countries...' (2009, p. 7). Therefore, it is our intention to show how neoliberal ideas on the governance of sport are carried out in one of the Scandinavian countries, Sweden.

What makes Sweden especially interesting is recent data presented by The Heritage Foundation, which placed Sweden in first place on a list ranking the liberalization speed of OECD countries (The Heritage Foundation 2012). Since 1995, no other OECD country has experienced more rapid processes of liberalization, deregulation and privatization, which makes an interesting case against the background of the increased government involvement in sport observed internationally. This development has taken Sweden from being, perhaps, one of the most typical social democratic regimes in Esping-Andersen's (1990) typology to a country that is now internationally renowned for its deregulated school, railway and pensions systems, television and radio broadcasting, domestic aviation, postal service, telecom market, employment agencies, motor vehicle inspections and pharmacy market.

This development of the general political landscape makes Swedish sport particularly interesting. Especially in relation to a more neoliberal international environment since Swedish sport is often described as being part of the Scandinavian sports model, with its particular patterns of institutional arrangements, hallmarked by large national voluntary sports organizations with almost a monopoly on competitive sports (Bergsgard *et al.* 2007, Bairner 2010, Bergsgard and Norberg 2010, Fahlén and Karp 2010, Seippel 2010, Norberg 2011). These specific characteristics and recent developments form the background of our aim to increase understanding of how government interest in sport impacts on the delivery of sport policy by exploring processes of responsibilization and self-regulation at play in the relationship between the government and sport as well as between sports organizations on different levels.

In order to reach this aim, this article utilizes data from a large-scale evaluation (performed by the authors and colleagues) of the latest sport-for-all programme, The Lift for Sport, launched by the Swedish Government in 2007 (similar ventures have also been launched in the neighbouring countries Denmark and Norway as reported on by Ibsen (2002) and Skille (2009)). In the programme, the Government commissioned the umbrella organization for sport, the Swedish Sports Confederation (RF), to develop activities for more children and youth and develop activities so they choose to be active in sport longer. The programme was funded with an investment of € 200 million from 2007 to 2011. The basic idea of the programme was to stimulate development work in national sports organizations (NSOs) and to let sports clubs apply for funding for projects aimed at working towards the ambitions in the programme manifesto corresponding to the guidelines in the RF-policy programme (Riksidrottsförbundet n.d.a). In this text, we take this programme as a token of an internationally noted increase in government involvement (e.g., Norberg 2011), in an approach resembling the one taken in the work of Keat and Sam (2013).

Government actions in sport, similar to the one described above, have been scrutinized by sport policy writers, such as Green and Houlihan (2006), Green (2009), Keat and Sam

(2013) and Phillpots *et al.* (2011). Their contributions have furthered our understanding of how sport issues have gained higher priority on government agendas, how sport has come to be used increasingly as a political means to achieve sports-external (and also sports-internal) ends and how these processes have worked in modernizing sports organizations through impositions of business practices. They have also taught us that the means for modernization is self-regulation, meaning organizations involved in the delivery of policy are encouraged to, and made responsible for developing their organization, management and practice in order to be better equipped to meet government demands connected to the funding they receive. In contrast to previous hierarchical governing mechanisms, governing by self-regulation aims to empower recipients (sport organizations, schools and individuals) by providing them with autonomy to decide how they should develop. However, as previously mentioned authors have shown, self-regulation is but an illusory freedom since goals and the monitoring of results are as effective regulations as any of the previous hierarchical governing mechanisms. In contrast, we have come to know that such governing mechanisms also imply several contradictions in the relationship between the governors and recipients, one being the promotion of entrepreneurial and autonomous recipients on the one hand and the ambition to control, coordinate and align recipients on the other hand.

Furthermore, and specifically useful for the purpose of this paper, these contributions have shown how sport policy development, sport policymaking and sport policy implementation can, at first sight, take on a unified appearance, but after in-depth study, take on another (see also the review of approaches for studying policy implementation in general by deLeon and deLeon (2002)). It is specifically in this regard, our analysis can add to existing knowledge. By studying a policy process from start to finish (figuratively speaking), we can contribute knowledge on policymaking and policy implementation. Before presenting the details of this process, we begin with an outline of the institutional arrangement of Swedish sport.

The institutional arrangement of Swedish sport

As mentioned in the introduction, the institutional landscape of Swedish sport is hallmarked by one large national voluntary sports organization, RF, which has enjoyed annual government support since 1913 (€ 170 million in 2010, Norberg 2011) and has, since 1970, a government mandate to 'act on behalf of the government' in distributing government funds to sports organizations (Norberg 2002). Acting on behalf of the government, RF is trusted to administer Swedish sport towards the objectives of public health, civic education, growth and entertainment (Sjöblom and Fahlén 2010). This arrangement has remained stable for more than a century. The basic organizing idea builds on the notion of the sporting individual partaking in sport as a member (some 3 million in total out of a population of 9.5 million) of a local sports club (some 20,000 in total).

Politically, Sweden has traditionally been seen as being characterized by a strong belief in the welfare state, built on social democratic tradition where public authorities have strong positions and widespread support (Seippel *et al.* 2010). For sport, the Scandinavian welfare policy model has been paramount to its growth and development since the Scandinavian idea of welfare has not been limited to health care and schools, but has also included citizens' access to recreation and leisure activities in which sport has been given a leading role (Bergsgard and Norberg 2010). This role, together with the government mandate to 'act on behalf of the government', has assigned RF a double function in the Swedish society – the highest authority in voluntary organized sport and a public authority in sport policy (Norberg 2011). The role of government has traditionally been limited to decisions on the extent of the funding and its overarching goals, while RF has had the mandate to decide on the means for reaching goals. This state–RF relationship, which the Swedish sports historian Johan Norberg (2004) has termed 'the implicit contract', has enabled the government to control its expenditure and RF to preserve its self-determination in a corporative collaboration.

But during recent decades, the long-standing practice of letting sport look after its own business, as long as it acts in the service of the state, has changed (Bergsgard and Norberg 2010). Norberg (2011) even asks if the implicit contract is on its way to being terminated or at least renegotiated to the benefit of more government control. Norberg (2011) points to recent societal reformations as explanations for this renegotiation, such as EU membership, economic recession, non-social democratic governments and increasing liberalization in the state administration focusing on target-setting, audits and evaluations in both its own administrative units and external organizations. For sport, the increase in government control has taken forms of reformulated policy goals focusing on inclusion and integration during the late 1980s, a national sports commission suggesting closer control of the funding to sport in the 1990s and another sports commission in the 2000s suggesting an annual external audit of the government support for sport (Österlind and Wright 2012).

More specifically, and in the focus of this paper, the increase in government intervention has taken the form of an increase in sport funding through the first government-funded sport-for-all programme, The Handshake, in 2002. In this programme, € 100 million was added to the annual government support with the explicit aims of opening doors to sport for more children and youth, keeping fees low, investing more in girls' participation, preventing drug use and intensifying cooperation with schools (Riksidrottsförbundet n.d.b). The programme was followed by another in 2006, alluded to in the introduction of this paper, adding an additional € 200 million of support, which further strengthened the impression of an increase in government intervention in sport. In the results, we will look at this development and its consequences more in detail. But before doing so, we will outline the theoretical arguments framing our understanding of Swedish policymaking and delivery.

Theoretical framework

Theoretically, our understanding is framed by the combination of concepts put forward by Goodwin and Grix (2011). They suggest a greater role for structures and institutions alongside the ideas, culture and belief of actors in explanations of societal developments. They take their departure in critiquing the governance narrative, which, they argue, with due support from other political science scholars (e.g., Marsh *et al.* 2003), exaggerates the decline of state power. Their support for bringing the structures back stems, theoretically, from the ideas of Chris Skelcher (2000), who argues that network governance – self-organizing networks of mutually resource-dependent actors – is in fact centrally governed by the state in its capacity to establish, sustain and finance networks and partnerships. In doing so, central governments can retain authority over other actors and limit the authority of rival sources of power while still instilling actors with a sense of freedom. The value of taking influence from the decentred approach (Bevir and Richards 2009), which Goodwin and Grix support, lays in its attention to diverse and conflicting beliefs among agents in all political processes. However, as Goodwin and Grix also point out, a decentred approach can be combined with an acknowledgement of structures and institutions as emphasized by Marsh *et al.* (2003).

However, involving ourselves in the governance debate is not primarily about positioning ourselves between 'those that seek to emphasise the role of institutions and structures... and those that attempt to focus attention on the beliefs and ideas of the actors' (Grix 2010, p. 160) on an ontological level. It is, from our perspective, more of an epistemological issue of going beneath 'surface observation [which] is usually enough evidence to confirm a shift from big "government" to more autonomous governance by networks and partnerships involved in policy-making and delivery' (Grix 2010, p. 160). In other words, the understanding of policymaking and implementation offered in this text is not primarily dependent on where we position ourselves on the structure-agency continuum, but more on our ability to capture what appears on the surface and uncover what happens beneath (no linear account intended). While this surface-beneath distinction may lead thoughts towards the notion of policy being made at the top and implemented at the bottom, we have in, our approach, tried to be sensitive to the argument put forth by scholars involved in policy-implementation analysis that policymaking and policy implementation are difficult to separate and that policy (both making and implementation) is constantly being made and remade (Kay 1996). On that particular note, we have paid attention to the policy-implementation debate referred to by O'Gorman (2011). In that debate, the merits of synthesizing elements of top-down and bottom-up approaches, focusing on both the structure of a policy and the actions of implementers, are advocated (see also the synthesis of the two approaches for studying policy implementation in general by Sabatier (1986)). We will, in the following, expand on how this approach has been taken in our study.

Methodology

This article utilizes data from a large-scale evaluation (performed by the authors and colleagues) of the latest sport-for-all programme, The Lift for Sport, launched by the Swedish Government in 2007. In the evaluation, the authors and colleagues were commissioned to review the programme in terms of how NSOs perceive the commission from RF and the government, how NSOs relate the commission to their regular activities, which strategies and methods NSOs use to reach the government's aims (and whether those aims change over time), how NSOs' goals, strategies, methods and results correspond to the guidelines in the RF-policy programme and to the ambitions of increasing gender and class equality, and the results of the programme. For these purposes, data were collected from four main sources:

(1) The government missive to RF formulating a supplementary policy for Swedish sport; the programme manifesto formulated by RF as guidelines to NSOs, Regional Sports Organisations (RSOs) and sports clubs for the implementation of the policy programme; and the NSO development plans RF commissioned as more detailed implementation plans where each NSO should document a situation analysis, vision for the policy programme, strategies for and priorities in the programme implementation, plans for increasing gender and class equality, plans for cooperating with regional organizations, an analysis of perceived bottlenecks and barriers for a successful delivery of the policy programme and a description of how success would be measured.
(2) Interviews with 27 key personnel involved in distributing the programme funds in five NSOs (Swedish Budo & Martial Arts Federation, Swedish Floorball Federation, Swedish Gymnastics Federation, Swedish Ski Association and

Swedish Sports Organisation for the Disabled and the Swedish Paralympic Committee). The selection of NSOs was made by RF for the purpose of programme evaluation. The five NSOs assemble 642,300 out of 3,291,000 members in Swedish sport (Riksidrottsförbundet 2010). Interviewees were selected on the basis of their assessed ability to provide facts and experiences from both strategic and operative levels in the NSOs. For that purpose, we chose to interview the NSO chairperson or another member of the board, the secretary general, the programme administrative official and a few other administrative officers deemed central (by each NSO) to the execution of the programme (such as programme directors, chief accountants and administrative directors). The interviews were semi-structured (Friis Thing and Ottesen 2013) in nature and consisted of questions about the commission from RF and the government, the relationship between regular day-to-day operations and programme operations, goals, development plan, strategies and methods, results, follow-up and change.

(3) Project applications made by sports clubs for programme funding ($n = 2563$). The programme was designed so the total programme budget was distributed to the NSOs according to the size of their activities. A large portion of these funds was earmarked to let sports clubs apply for funding for projects aimed at working towards the ambitions in the programme manifesto. In the evaluation, all accepted applications from sports clubs in the five NSOs during the programme's first (2007–2008) and third (2009–2010) years were collected in order to examine the applying clubs' and granting NSOs' general ideas about development, how programme aims were to be reached and how project ideas corresponded to the guidelines in the RF-policy programme. Using an instrument developed by Karp *et al.* (2007), project applications were categorized in five aspects: scope, main content, methods, approach and focus.

(4) Questionnaires filled out by representatives of the sports clubs applying for funding (n 486). In the programme evaluation, an electronic questionnaire was sent out to representatives of the sports clubs who had applied for funding in 2011 (n 1026, response rate 47%). Through the questionnaires, we gathered the applying clubs' experiences of taking part in the programme. The questionnaire consisted of 56 questions with five themes: (a) general experiences of the programme, specific experiences of the distribution of programme funds and the project design chosen as means for reaching the programme aims; (b) experiences of the NSO development plan, criteria for granting funds to projects, support and follow-up; (c) facts on implemented projects; (d) results of implemented projects; and (e) experiences of the projects as means for development.

For the purpose of this article, we have treated the first two data sources (government missives, programme manifesto, NSO development plans and interviews) as structures, institutions and surface observations. Consequently, the last two data sources (project applications and questionnaires) were treated as ideas, culture, beliefs and actions of implementers. With this approach, we have recognized both 'structural and institutional path dependency whilst accounting for the beliefs and ideas of the actors...' (Grix 2010, p. 165). We have also paid attention to O'Gorman's (2011) encouragement to explicitly address the phenomenon of sport policy and programme implementation. O'Gorman calls for more thorough analyses of implementation in general, but, specifically, for more theoretically informed analyses that can enhance the understanding of 'how and why sport policies and programmes have been implemented in the way they have, but also how we come to make assumptions and propositions as to their impacts and relative successes and failures' (O'Gorman 2011, p. 87). In heeding O'Gorman's concomitant analysis of the shortcomings in existing sport policy implementation research, we have utilized the framework laid out previously to offer understandings of how and, more specifically, why increased government interest in sport impacts the delivery of sport policy as it does. While acknowledging that our design might give the impression of a top-down approach, our argument for beginning this description of methods used and the later following presentation of results is that 'the sport policy system is essentially top-down in practice' (Kay 1996, p. 242).

Findings

The findings are arranged as follows. First, we outline the structures and institutions underpinning the policy programme as expressed in government missives, programme manifesto, NSO development plans and interviews. Second, we use data from project applications and sports clubs questionnaires to sketch the contours of ideas, culture, beliefs and actions of implementers.

The surface of the policy programme

Our analyses of the evaluation data from the surface show how an increase of government involvement has taken form. In Government Decision 1 (Regeringen 2007), the government decided how the surplus from AB Svenska Spel (the state gambling company) should be allocated and to what ends. The decision stated that € 50 million per year over a period of four years was to be divided between (a) developing NSO and RSO operations (€ 4 million); (b) developing NSO and RSO organizations (€ 8,2 million); (c) special projects (€ 9 million); (d) evaluation of effects (€ 0.8 million); and (e) sports club development projects (€ 28 million). The overarching aim for the programme was put forth as the following:

> Support and encourage NSOs and sports clubs to open the doors to sport for more children and youth and to develop their activities so that they chose to participate longer. NSOs are given resources to develop their sports, for intensifying their work by developing strategies, identify needs, assist with facts and competence, evaluate and spread good examples. Further efforts are to be made to increase recruitment and development of leaders and cooperation with schools. All work should consider gender and class equality. (Regeringen 2007)

It is evident that the government ambition is to govern sport in a specific direction, both in terms of content (widened recruitment) and in terms of governing per se (NSOs are provided with resources to develop themselves). In addition, the government formulated key performance indicators:

> An account shall be made assessing how many more girls and boys have begun to engage in sport and exercise as a result of the programme and how many have continued to participate. The account shall also describe efforts made to strengthen NSO activities and management. Finally, the account shall describe efforts made to intensify the cooperation with schools, improve access to sport and to develop leaders. (Regeringen 2007)

This quotation shows that accountability is key to the process and that evidence, in terms of numbers, is the way of keeping scores. For the more detailed steering of the programme, RF formulated some additional guidelines for NSOs, RSOs and clubs:

> An annual report shall be made to RF in three parts: Reporting the total amount of activities, divided by gender and age. These numbers are to be collected from NSOs, RSOs and clubs. In addition, the report shall contain a description of NSO work based on the development plan and an account of how key performance indicators have been met. Regarding cooperation with schools, the number of schools and the school years participating shall be accounted for. The annual report is a condition for the continuation of the regular support. (Riksidrottsförbundet n.d.a)

The responsibilization of the recipient, evident in the relationship between the government and sport, is clearly expressed also in the relationship between RF and the NSOs. NSOs are expected to provide data to an overall programme evaluation and to account for how they plan to follow up on their development plan. NSOs are responsible for the appropriate use of allotted resources and for monitoring club activities by establishing contracts with clubs receiving project funds. The contracts shall regulate project conformity with programme aims and accounts from receiving clubs. Should contracts be broken, funds are to be returned to the NSO. NSOs shall also report to RF how funds are used for the development of NSO and RSO management and operations.

In a memo from RF to the NSOs dated 8 April 2009 (Riksidrottsförbundet 2009), the disciplining and self-regulation of NSOs are further explained and more guidelines are added. In the guidelines, the NSOs' responsibility for monitoring club project conformity with programme aims is further highlighted. This monitoring should focus on ensuring that funds are not distributed to clubs without children or youth as members, prohibiting clubs from securing project funds from more than one source, ensuring that funds for projects involving more than one club are evenly distributed, collecting qualitative (not only quantitative) information about projects and reclaiming funds from projects that have not been realized.

Our analyses of evaluation data from the surface, in terms of NSO development plans, show that the NSOs have also taken up the governing principles in the above-mentioned relationships – pushing the responsibility for development further down the chain of command. However, they have not regulated themselves as desired by the government and RF, i.e., identifying their own specific needs and developing their own specific strategies to address those needs. Instead, aims are mirror images of the general ambitions formulated by the government and RF (expansion, i.e., more leaders, facilities and clubs, which, in turn, are expected to result in more participants that will participate longer), even if the issue of facilities for instance is not a problem for the NSO in question. A quote from one NSO's development plan is provided as an example:

> NSO affiliated clubs shall be able to initiate special ventures in accordance with the basic ideas of 'The Lift for Sport', and thereby: (a) expand, especially in pressing areas – such as in locations with short supply of attractive activities for teenagers or in locations with special needs and important target groups such as youth in general and girls in particular, and groups within these groups which are especially hard to reach with club activities; (b) develop, especially with regard to competence among the club's most active and promising young members – both regarding their sport specific skills and their ability to contribute to club activities with instruction and leadership in the future. (Swedish Budo & Martial Arts Federation 2007)

The NSO development plans show how the NSOs reproduce the model used by the government in its governing of RF and, in turn, by RF in its governing of the NSOs, implying that the governing body relinquishes the responsibility for the design of the programme to the governed one. This is illustrated by a quotation taken from the Swedish Floorball Federation's development plan:

> Decisions concerning 'The Lift for Sport' are to be made by the NSO-administration, but we want commitment and development locally. This will be reached by stimulating RSOs to develop clubs. Quality assured development and growth are keywords in our development. Therefore, [local] leaders' competence is key, both coaches' and board members.' (Swedish Floorball Federation 2007)

In the development plans, it is noticeable how the processes of autonomization and responsibilization continue with the NSOs as senders and the sports clubs as recipients. Club commitment and development, together with local leaders, are the means by which programme aims are to be reached.

Signs of these processes also become visible in the analyses of the 27 interviews with key personnel involved in distributing the programme funds in the five NSOs. In these analyses, it appears that the programme is a much welcomed initiative despite the fact that it might be conceived as a break with the implicit contract referred to earlier (Norberg 2004). The NSO representatives are receptive to the demands, direction and follow-ups inherent in the programme:

> On the contrary [to being conceived as a break with the implicit contract], it is all good. In the same way as it is an exclusive prerogative for the sender of grants to distribute them [as they please], it is their exclusive prerogative to attach a system for control and follow-up as they see fit. (Secretary General, Swedish Ski Association 2010)

This quotation shows that governing in terms of checks and balances is perceived by the NSOs as a natural part of the development and something that must be expected as part of these types of directed grants. Their own explanation of that is the experienced concordance between programme aims and the NSOs' aims for regular activities, here symbolized in a quotation by the chairman of the board of the Swedish Gymnastics Federation:

> We have made it our cause to see it ['The Lift for Sport'] as a part of the development work we ought to do anyway. With these resources we can do more and better...It ['The Lift for Sport'] is part of the commission we already have...This is what is tricky with our statistics, you cannot isolate this specific effect from another. (Chairman of the board, Swedish Gymnastics Federation 2011)

The quotation simultaneously shows how programme aims are merged with the NSOs' aims for regular activities, thereby making it possible for NSOs to tone down expectations and relieve themselves of some of the responsibility laid upon them for reaching key performance indicators. A similar way of negotiating this responsibility is to view programme funds as extended regular state support as expressed by the Secretary General of the Swedish Sports Organisation for the Disabled and the Swedish Paralympic Committee:

> It would not have mattered [whether funds had been part of the regular state support or earmarked as 'The Lift for Sport']. We had already begun a development process...where we prioritized our most important development areas...We were fortunate to start that process

simultaneously as 'The Lift for Sport' was launched...It has provided us with resources to work with issues we were already working with. (Secretary General, Swedish Sports Organisation for the Disabled and the Swedish Paralympic Committee 2010)

In sum, our main impression, in terms of governing from the analyses of government missives, programme manifesto, NSO development plans and interviews, is that government steering has increased, new modes of governing have been imposed (explicit goals, responsibilization and evaluation of key performance indicators) and these new modes of governing work in passing the responsibility for reaching programme goals to the next organization in line.

The underneath of the policy programme

Our analyses of evaluation data from beneath, in terms of project applications for programme funds, reveal a slightly different picture. Certainly, the projects that clubs seek funds for are in the broad outlines aligned with overall government aims, RF guidelines and NSO development plans. However, many of the guidelines in the RF-policy programme are conspicuous by their absence in the analysed project applications. When categorizing the contents of the project applications in relation to the RF-policy programme guidelines, we find very few applications explicitly expressing ambitions relating to *promoting respect for others* (0.3% in year one and 0% in year three), *considering participants' views* (0.3% in year one and 0% in year three) and *promoting fair play* (0.6% in year one and 0.1% in year three). These proportions can be compared to those of *developing leaders* (20.2% in year one and 24.6% in year three, *developing facilities* (12.6% in year one and 11.4% in year three) and *developing rules and policies* (22.8% in year one and 22.1% in year three).

The processes of self-regulation and responsibilization observed between the government and RF and between RF and the NSOs are also in play between the NSOs and the sports clubs. However, the processes have not resulted in the self-regulation and accepted responsibility aimed for, at least not by judging from the content in the applications for programme funds. When left free to formulate project ideas, sports clubs conform to the main ideas of the programme (expansion, i.e., more leaders, facilities and clubs, which, in turn, are expected to result in more participants participating longer) rather than tailoring projects to their specific needs. As a result, some aspects of development agreed on in the RF-policy programme are unattended. Another example of that is visible in our analysis of the focus in the applications in relation to the overall aim of increasing gender and class equality. Very few applications explicitly express ambitions to *increase gender equality* (3.3% in year one and 1.2% in year three), *increase class equality* (3.6% in year one and 2.0% in year three) or *increase gender and class equality* (0.4% in year one and 8.3% in year three).

Our analyses of evaluation data from beneath in terms of the 486 questionnaires filled out by the sports clubs representatives applying for funding also show how the alignment with overall government aims, RF guidelines and NSO development plans is high, at least in broad outlines. But only half of the respondents actually know about the content of the NSO development plan (53% fairly poor knowledge/very poor knowledge/no knowledge [$n = 486$]). This result suggests that half of the programme activities arranged are designed without regard to the programme aims even if many activities show concordance per se. The result also lends further support to the previous analysis, suggesting that the self-regulation and responsibility handed down from the NSOs are not acted upon by the sports clubs.

In our analysis of target groups for project activities, the impression gained from the analysis of the applications' focus is strengthened. *Children and youth in general* represent the main target group for 68% of the studied projects while *children with immigrant backgrounds* (19%), *children with disabilities* (19%) and *children from low income households* (13%) are targeted less (*n* = 486). This result shows that the overarching aim of the programme, that 'all work should consider gender and class equality', is not a high priority for the sports clubs. The sports clubs' priorities are also visible in the analysis of their experiences regarding the programme as a means for club development, which was another overarching aim of the programme. This analysis shows that the programme has, to the least extent, contributed to *increased class equality* and *increased gender equality*. A similar impression is gained from the analysis of perceived results of project activities. This analysis shows that sports clubs representatives perceive *recruitment of children from low-income households* and *recruitment of leaders from low-income households* to be the least visible results of arranged programme activities. Taken together, these analyses of questionnaire data show, albeit with small differences, how sports clubs prioritize and how they have not accepted responsibility for some of the specific features in the programme ambitions, handed down from the government via RF and the NSOs.

While these results might not be surprising, they can be understood through our analysis of questionnaire data showing sports clubs' notions on who should have influence on the development of sport. Club representatives rated their own influence highest and in decreasing order thereafter NSO, RF and the government. This result implies that, in the sports clubs' notions, the question about how sport is best developed is not a matter for the government, but for the sports clubs themselves to decide on. Our analysis suggests that the ambitions in this programme are hazardous to expect as long as they are formulated at the top of the system.

Discussion and conclusions

Returning to our original ambition, which is to show how neoliberal ideas on the governance of sport are carried out in Sweden, our analyses show how the making of sport policy in Sweden bears many features similar to those observed in the English-speaking contexts. Our analysis of government missives, the programme manifesto, NSO development plans and interviews with 27 key personnel involved in distributing the programme funds in five NSOs show how The Lift for Sport as the latest and largest government intervention in sport has brought with it more specific and more instrumental goals for sport to attain. This development has been observed also in Denmark and Norway (Ibsen 2002, Skille 2009). It has also involved new governing instruments such as the introduction of key performance indicators. Key features in this process have been responsibilization, demands on accountability and self-regulation. These features are visible in the communication between the government and RF, RF and the NSOs, and the NSOs and the sports clubs. However, only small signs of wanted self-regulation are as of yet visible. Instead, each organization in the chain of command is forwarding the responsibility for development, accountability for results and demands on self-regulation to the next organization in line. These are our conclusions when looking at the surface.

When looking beneath the surface, our analysis of project applications and questionnaires shows how this forwarded responsibility for development, accountability and demands on self-regulation is, to a large extent, disregarded also at the club level. The Lift for Sport has made little impression on club activities. Although applications adhere to some of the main ideas of the programme, many of them are left unattended. Ironically enough, many of the guidelines left unattended are the ones considered most important by the Swedish research community (SOU 2008), government (Regeringen 2011) and RF (Riksidrottsförbundet 2005) in addressing many of the problems Swedish sport is facing, such as unhealthy pressure from coaches, peers and parents; drop-out in early years; and poor recruitment from underrepresented groups. Questionnaire results reinforce that impression. Project results are, when looking at them from a distance, reported to be in line with programme aims. However, from closer examination, it is apparent that when it comes to recruitment, children and youth with immigrant backgrounds, disabilities and/or from low-income households are neglected, so is the focus on increasing gender equality. Our analysis of project applications and questionnaires shows how central governance issued by the government and mediated by RF and the NSOs fails to exert authority over the implementing actors, the sports clubs, in terms of stimulating development through self-regulation. It is evident that neither government missives, programme guidelines and NSO development plans, nor additional and earmarked resources have been able to stimulate development through self-regulation and, in the end, to secure envisioned effects. On the contrary, it seems the power and informal authority to govern the grass roots activities in sport remain in the hands of the implementers: the sports clubs. Our main conclusion of the beneath-surface analysis is that policy fails to survive the journey from top to bottom because the sports clubs have been unwilling or unable to self-regulate in the desired direction. But, as some data indicate, it can also be a result of the poor knowledge about the desired direction in detail.

Returning to our initial aim to increase the understanding of how government interest in sport impacts the delivery of sport policy, we want to move beneath surface explanations, such as 'policy implementation in the end comes down to the people who actually implement it' (Lipsky 1980, p. 8) and 'sport policy [is] a "weak" policy area' (Grix 2010, p. 169). Instead, we propose that RF and the NSOs, on the one hand, are, in their capacity as representative organs, more concerned with acting in accordance with official politics and dependent on the legitimacy connected with that compliance. The sports clubs, on the other hand, are, in their capacity as membership-based organizations, more concerned with the needs and wishes of their existing members (and dependent on their resources), rather than with answering to political expectations regarding recruitment of new participants and equality (Stenling 2014). We argue that it is easier to align oneself with organizations higher up in the hierarchy when the costs for alignments are low (i.e., RF and the NSOs can align their operations by simply rephrasing policy documents and guidelines) compared to when they are high (i.e., sports clubs actually have to change the basic idea of their activities from we-for-us to us-for-them). Similar to the findings reported by Keat and Sam (2013), we claim that if costs appear too high, the risk of sports clubs opting out increases.

A similar understanding of these findings is that the implicit contract referred to in the context description (Norberg 2004) becomes more implicit the further it travels from the actual agreeing parties. Stated another way, by pushing responsibility further down the chain of command, RF and NSOs can shield the implicit contract and still protect sports clubs' autonomy and self-determination, which more hierarchical governing mechanisms would not allow (Stenling 2014).

Agreeing with Grix (2009), we see that the direction of accountability is altered by the modernization agenda, but the alteration is not uniform across all organizations in the system. This proposition is lent weight from the sports clubs' own understanding of their role in the policy process: They should have the main influence on the development of sport. The main obstacle for effective programme implementation seems to be that the implementers pay attention to the main underlying notion of the programme, recruiting more members, but they do not observe, understand or concur with the method for reaching that aim, to self-regulate.

When relating these findings to recent developments in the general political Swedish landscape noted in the introduction, we see that instead of a deregulation of sport, state regulation increases. At the same time, though, influence from grassroots agents (implementing sports clubs) over core activities seems unaffected (cf., Grix 2009, discussion on the opposite effects of increased state intervention). We suggest that this deviance (see Goodwin and Grix 2011, discussion on the deviant sport and education policy sectors in the UK) is associated with the Scandinavian and Swedish pattern of institutional arrangements, organizational and cultural, hallmarked by large national voluntary sports organizations with almost a monopoly on competitive sports. In contrast to Norberg's (2011) suggestion that the implicit contract is on its way to being renegotiated to the benefit of more government control, we argue that the component of voluntariness inherent in RF's part of the contract trumps the government's stake in providing resources. As long as the government depends on voluntary efforts for reaching more instrumental goals, power will remain with sport. This argument also resonates with the findings reported in the studies of the Danish (The Sport Policy Idea Programme) and Norwegian (The Sports City Programme) counterparts to The Lift for Sport, showing that the voluntary-based institutional arrangement in the Scandinavian countries still provides a stronghold against top-down initiatives with external goals differing too much from sports clubs' core activities (Ibsen 2002, Skille 2009).

To conclude, in addition to providing an understanding of the gap between policy-making and policy implementation, the observations made in this text provide support for the notion held by Goodwin and Grix (2011) that understanding of development processes is dependent on both structures and institutions on the one hand, and on ideas, cultures and beliefs on the other. It also lends backing to the arguments posited by Grix (2010), Kay (1996) and O'Gorman (2011), albeit in other words, that policy analysis should focus on both surface and underlying power relations and resource dependencies, both structural and institutional path dependency and beliefs, and ideas of involved actors, both elements of top-down and bottom-up approaches, and both the structure of a policy and the actions of implementers simultaneously. In order to further this understanding of sport policy development, sport policymaking and sport policy implementation, we call for more research that focuses on the whole sequence of events, from policymaking to policy implementation, in order to avail both surface and beneath observations. Such ventures would also need to be sensitive to the fact that project activities are not necessarily the same as regular activities. In order to reach a more fine-grained understanding of policy implementation we need research focusing not only on specific policy initiatives but also on the daily activities in sports clubs. We would also like to call for more studies to be carried out in other countries outside the English-speaking contexts, with different institutional landscapes to continue the contextual modulation of current knowledge.

References

Bairner, A., 2010. What's Scandinavian about Scandinavian sport? *Sport in society – cultures, commerce, media, politics*, 4 (13), 734–743.

Bergsgard, N.A. and Norberg, J.R., 2010. Sports policy and politics – the Scandinavian way. *Sport in society – cultures, commerce, media, politics*, 4 (13), 567–582.

Bergsgard, N.A., *et al.*, 2007. *Sport policy: a comparative analysis of stability and change*. New York: Elsevier.

Bevir, M. and Richards, D., 2009. Decentring policy networks: a theoretical agenda. *Public administration*, 87 (1), 3–14. doi:10.1111/j.1467-9299.2008.01736.x

deLeon, P. and deLeon, L., 2002. What ever happened to policy implementation? An alternative approach. *Journal of public administration research and theory*, 12 (4), 467–492. doi:10.1093/oxfordjournals.jpart.a003544

Esping-Andersen, G., 1990. *The three worlds of welfare capitalism*. Cambridge: Polity Press.

Fahlén, J. and Karp, S., 2010. Access denied: the new sports for all – programme in sweden and the reinforcement of the sports performance logic. *Sport & EU review*, 2 (1), 3–22.

Friis Thing, L. and Ottesen, L., 2013. Det individuelle kvalitative interview [The individual qualitative interview]. *In*: L. Friis Thing and L. Ottesen, eds. *Metoder i idraetsforskning*. Köpenhamn: Munksgaard, 74–89.

Goodwin, M. and Grix, J., 2011. Bringing structures back in: the 'governance narrative', the 'decentred approach' and 'asymmetrical network governance' in the education and sport policy communities. *Public administration*, 89 (2), 537–556. doi:10.1111/j.1467-9299.2011.01921.x

Green, M., 2004. Power, policy, and political priorities: elite sport development in Canada and the United Kingdom. *Sociology of sport journal*, 21 (4), 376–396.

Green, M., 2007. Policy transfer, lesson drawing and perspectives on elite sport development systems. *International journal of sport management and marketing*, 2 (4), 426–441. doi:10.1504/IJSMM.2007.013715

Green, M., 2009. Podium or participation? Analysing policy priorities under changing modes of sport governance in the United Kingdom. *International journal of sport policy and politics*, 1 (2), 121–144. doi:10.1080/19406940902950697

Green, M. and Houlihan, B., 2004. Advocacy coalitions and elite sport policy change in Canada and the United Kingdom. *International review for the sociology of sport*, 39, 387–403. doi:10.1177/1012690204049066

Green, M. and Houlihan, B., 2005. *Elite sport development: policy learning and political priorities*. London: Routledge.

Green, M. and Houlihan, B., 2006. Governmentality, modernization and the 'disciplining' of national sporting organizations: athletics in Australia and United Kingdom. *Sociology of sport journal*, 23 (1), 47–71.

Green, M. and Oakley, B., 2001. Elite sport development systems and playing to win: uniformity and diversity in international approaches. *Leisure studies*, 20 (4), 247–267. doi:10.1080/02614360110103598

Grix, J., 2009. The impact of UK sport policy on the governance of athletics. *International journal of sport policy and politics*, 1 (1), 31–49. doi:10.1080/19406940802681202

Grix, J., 2010. The 'governance debate' and the study of sport policy. *International journal of sport policy and politics*, 2 (2), 159–171. doi:10.1080/19406940.2010.488061

The Heritage Foundation, 2012. *Index of economic freedom: graph the data – Sweden* [online]. Available from: http://www.heritage.org/index/visualize [Accessed 5 November 2012].

Houlihan, B., 2009. Mechanisms of international influence on domestic elite sport policy. *International journal of sport policy and politics*, 1 (1), 51–69. doi:10.1080/19406940902739090

Houlihan, B. and Green, M., 2008. *Comparative elite sport development – systems, structures and public policy*. Oxford: Elsevier.

Ibsen, B., 2002. *Evaluering af det idrætspolitiske idéprogram* [Evaluation of the sport policy idea programme]. Københavns Universitet and Institut for forskning i Idræt og Folkelig Oplysning.

Karp, S., Olofsson, E., and Söderström, T., 2007. *I skuggan av fotbollen. handslagsprojektens betydelse för de mindre idrotterna* [In the shadows of football. The significance of the Handshake projects for smaller sports]. Stockholm: Riksidrottsförbundet.

Kay, T., 1996. Just do it? Turning sports policy into sports practice. *Managing leisure*, 1 (4), 233–247. doi:10.1080/136067196376339

Keat, R.A. and Sam, M.P., 2013. Regional implementation of new zealand sport policy: new instrument, new challenges. *International journal of sport policy and politics*, 5 (1), 39–54. doi:10.1080/19406940.2012.656684

Lipsky, M., 1980. *Street-level bureaucracy: dilemmas of the individual in public services*. New York: Russell Sage Foundation.

Marsh, D., Richards, D., and Smith, M., 2003. Unequal plurality: towards an asymmetric power model of British politics. *Government and opposition*, 38 (3), 306–332. doi:10.1111/1477-7053. t01-1-00017

Norberg, J.R., 2002. Idrottsrörelsen och staten. *In*: J. Lindroth and J.R. Norberg, eds. *Riksidrottsförbundet 1903–2003* [The Swedish Sports Confederation 1903–2003]. Stockholm: Informationsförlaget, 181–231.

Norberg, J.R., 2004. *Idrottens väg till folkhemmet: studier i statlig idrottspolitik 1913–1970* [Sport's road to the welfare state: studies in Swedish government policy towards sport, 1913–1970]. Stockholm: SISU Idrottsböcker.

Norberg, J.R., 2011. A contract reconsidered? Changes in the Swedish state's relation to the sports movement. *International journal of sport policy and politics*, 3 (3), 311–325. doi:10.1080/19406940.2011.596157

O'Gorman, J., 2011. Where is the implementation in sport policy and programme analysis? The english football association's charter standard as an illustration. *International journal of sport policy and politics*, 3 (1), 85–108. doi:10.1080/19406940.2010.548339

Österlind, M. and Wright, J., 2012. If sport's the solution then what's the problem? The social significance of sport in the moral governing of 'good' and 'healthy' citizens in Sweden, 1922–1998. *Sport, education and society*. doi:10.1080/13573322.2012.726217

Phillpots, L., Grix, J., and Quarmby, T., 2011. Centralized grassroots sport policy and 'new governance': a case study of county sports partnerships in the UK - unpacking the paradox. *International review for the sociology of sport*, 46 (3), 265–281. doi:10.1177/1012690210378461

Regeringen, 2007. *Regeringsbeslut 1* [Government decision 1]. Stockholm: Kulturdepartementet.

Regeringen, 2011. *Regeringsbeslut 15* [Government decision 15]. Stockholm: Kulturdepartementet.

Riksidrottsförbundet, 2005. *Idrotten vill* [What sports wants]. Stockholm: Riksidrottsförbundet.

Riksidrottsförbundet, 2009. *PM angående förhållningssätt samt plan för internkontroll* [Memorandum on approach to and plan for internal control]. Stockholm: Riksidrottsförbundet.

Riksidrottsförbundet, 2010. *Idrotten i siffror* [Sports in numbers]. Stockholm: Riksidrottsförbundet.

Riksidrottsförbundet, n.d.b. *Handslagets programförklaring* [The Handshake – sports for all programme manifesto]. Available from: http://www.rf.se/t3.asp?p=77127 [Accessed 20 April 2007].

Riksidrottsförbundet, n.d.a. *Idrottslyftet – riktlinjer* [The Lift for Sport – guidelines]. Stockholm: Riksidrottsförbundet. Available from: http://www.rf.se/Vi-arbetar-med/Politiskafragor/Idrottslyftet/ [Accessed 12 May 2009].

Sabatier, P.A., 1986. Top-down and bottom-up approaches to implementation research: a critical analysis and suggested synthesis. *Journal of public policy*, 6 (1), 21–48. doi:10.1017/S0143814X00003846

Sam, M.P. and Jackson, S.J., 2004. Sport policy development in New Zealand: paradoxes of an integrative paradigm. *International review for the sociology of sport*, 39 (2), 205–222. doi:10.1177/1012690204043463

Seippel, Ø., 2010. Professionals and volunteers: on the future of a Scandinavian sport model. *Sport in Society: cultures, commerce, media, politics*, 13 (2), 199–211. doi:10.1080/17430430903522921

Seippel, Ø., Ibsen, B., and Norberg, J.R., 2010. Introduction: sport in Scandinavian societies. *Sport in society: cultures, commerce, media, politics*, 13 (4), 563–566. doi:10.1080/17430431003616167

Sjöblom, P. and Fahlén, J., 2010. The survival of the fittest: intensification, totalization and homogenization in Swedish competitive sport. *Sport in society: cultures, commerce, media, politics*, 13 (4), 704–717. doi:10.1080/17430431003616514

Skelcher, C., 2000. Changing images of the state: overloaded, hollowed-out, congested. *Public policy and administration*, 15 (3), 3–19. doi:10.1177/095207670001500302

Skille, E.Å., 2009. State sport policy and voluntary sport clubs: the case of the Norwegian sports city program as social policy. *European sport management quarterly*, 9 (1), 63–79. doi:10.1080/16184740802461736

Sotiriadou, K., 2009. The Australian sport system and its stakeholders: development of cooperative relationships. *Sport in society – cultures, commerce, media, politics*, 12 (7), 842–860.

SOU 2008:59. *Föreningsfostran och tävlingsfostran en utvärdering av statens stöd till idrotten* [Democratic fostering and competition fostering. An evaluation of the government support to sport]. *Betänkande från Idrottsstödsutredningen.* Stockholm: Fritzes.

Stenling, C., 2014. Sport programme implementation as translation and organizational identity construction: the implementation of drive-in sport in Swedish sports as an illustration. *International journal of sport policy and politics*, 6 (1), 55–69. doi:10.1080/19406940.2013.766900

Sport policy and transformation in small states: New Zealand's struggle between vulnerability and resilience

Michael P. Sam

School of Physical Education, Sport and Exercise Sciences, University of Otago, Dunedin, New Zealand

Small states are broadly distinguished on economic, political and cultural grounds and more particularly in relation to their vulnerability and resilience. This paper examines how legitimations around a country's small size can induce compromises to buttress particular sport policies. Drawing from the New Zealand context, it explores how domestic cooperation can be prompted by the discursive frames of smallness itself. It further suggests that New Zealand's corresponding ambition to 'punch above its weight' has enabled policy transformations to make the sport system appear more legitimate but no less vulnerable. Because scale invites consolidation, targeting and rationing, central sport agencies in small states may have to paradoxically invoke strategies to break the very communal bonds that provide them with the 'fertile' conditions for growth and competitive advantage. The study of small states may help scholars and policy-makers to better understand the significance of 'managed intimacy' as a counterbalance to neoliberal doctrines.

The value of sport in achieving state objectives is a topic that prefaces nearly all books touching on sport policy and politics, and for good reason. At various times, western governments tinker with the balance of justifications – for example between sport's utility as national unifier, as economic driver and/or as catalyst for public health. In turn, such legitimations (Chalip 1996) shape policies and programmes, with tangible effects and consequences on the lived experiences of individuals and their organisations. The recasting of physical education in schools for example, or the linking of sport with tourism are common policy transformations that substantively alter a nation's sporting landscape. However, just as we know from the growing body of research – that sport policies demonstrate convergence internationally (Houlihan and Green 2008, De Bosscher *et al.* 2008) – we also know that their effects and outcomes are context specific, empirically reflecting Hall's (1986) thesis of hegemony with no 'guarantees'. In this light, it is worth considering whether the sport policy trajectories of small nations might be shaped by their context-specific legitimations. Indeed how does 'smallness' feature as a legitimation in sport policy and with what consequences?

From the outset, it is acknowledged that sport has been important in the historical formation of national identity (Bairner 2001). Indeed, small states are not unique in having shared mythologies around sport and thus a more specific dimension of this identity relates to a nation's perceptions of vulnerability to global forces. The purpose of this paper is to examine how legitimations around a country's size can induce compromises to buttress particular sport policies. Drawing from the New Zealand context, it explores how domestic cooperation can be prompted by the discursive frames of smallness itself. In particular, this paper suggests that New Zealand's corresponding ambition to 'punch above its weight' has enabled policy transformations to make the sport system appear more legitimate but no less vulnerable.

The study of small states

Studies about small nations typically devote considerable space to defining what a small state is, and it is likewise seen to be a necessary part of identifying this study's parameters. While population and geographic size are often used as criteria, in very broad terms, small nations are distinguished on economic, political and cultural grounds (Katzenstein 1985). Economically, they are said to have smaller domestic markets, making international trade essential for growth. In this view, the vast majority of smaller states lack economic influence and are therefore 'price takers' (Tõnurist 2010), suggesting that foreign investment and global commodity prices may have a proportionately greater potential to create distortions. This is not to say however that small states are uniform in their economic makeup. Relative to the Balkan states for example, Norway's oil reserves put this Scandinavian nation at the economically strong end of the spectrum. Such is the diversity that various economic indices attempt to quantify the susceptibility of small states to economic shocks (see Briguglio *et al.* 2006). In terms of sport, several economic features might be relevant such as the smaller economies of scale that may affect domestic competition structures, and the comparatively limited pool of talented human resources (e.g. coaches, athletes, officials) in countries with smaller populations.

A second feature of small nations is that in international politics, they are often said to lack political 'clout', as they tend to be absent in the Group of Eight (G8), the United Nations Security Council and so forth.[1] Where this once justified the exclusion of small states in international relations research (Gstöhl 2002), the geo-political power of small states is now recognised as an important consideration in contemporary analyses (Wivel and Steinmetz 2013). Indeed, the study of small states is salient because of their issue-specific influence in international affairs; the Maldives for example, hold a moral influence vis-á-vis sea-level rise (Thorhallsson and Wivel 2006). So rather than identifying small states as 'weak', they may be equally recognised as having at times, a disproportionate amount of power in particular international arenas. International sport arguably constitutes one such arena in which small states can wield power, particularly vis-á-vis organisations like FIFA that still operate via one nation, one vote systems (Forster 2006).

Culturally, the smallness of a nation is often associated with ethnic, religious and linguistic homogeneity (Campbell and Hall 2009). In this view, smallness/homogeneity is seen to be advantageous variables to achieving economic or political ends. There are of course striking exceptions to the link between smallness and uniformity such as Switzerland, a country having more than 20% foreign-born residents and four official languages. Furthermore, claims of cultural homogeneity are difficult to sustain owing to changing migration patterns, the borderless labour laws of the European Union (EU) and the existence of bicultural or divided societies (e.g. Fiji and Ireland). Nevertheless, it would be difficult to challenge the notion that small nations are also small societies (Benedict 1967) with highly personalised role relationships (Farrugia 1993) and therefore distinct from larger states.

Although most scholars agree that scale makes a difference, the demarcation of small states remains imprecise (Sutton 2011). Aside from objective criteria that might include some combination of population, territory size, military expenditure and gross domestic product (GDP), the treatment of small states is therefore subject to matters of disciplinary scope and epistemology. Generally however, they are understood in relation to a specific 'spatio-temporal context' (Wivel and Steinmetz 2013) reflecting two broad approaches. The first approach defines smallness in relation to power or the capacity to influence international affairs. Based in the neorealist paradigm, small nations are analysed against the background of their ties with a 'superpower', or supra-national institutions such as the EU. The subject of study varies widely (between influence in trade talks or regional security) but the starting point is generally that small states are comparatively weak, and must therefore align themselves according to the institutional signals of larger state actors (Armstrong and Read 1998). A second approach, and the one with which this paper is more closely aligned, is that smallness is constructed by the nation itself. In this view, size is internally or domestically imagined, forming part of its cultural makeup and by extension, informing its choice of actions. This constructivist view is less pessimistic than the neorealist starting point, and instead suggests that smallness is potentially 'harnessable' as a resource (Browning 2006). In the case of international relations, small states can capitalise on appearing 'non-threatening', less ambitious or independent (Browning 2006). Likewise domestically, a country's small size may function as a rallying point for the concentration of resources, or the creation of collaborative institutions, as in the case of Finland's success in technology (Schienstock 2007).

Vulnerability and resilience

A prominent bridging dimension between neorealist and constructivist perspectives on small states revolves around their vulnerability (Katzenstein 2003). For economists vulnerability relates to a state's exposure to 'external shocks' because of particular intrinsic features of their economies, most notably a reliance on imports, a narrow range of exports, geographic distance to markets, etc. States are considered vulnerable to the degree that they are at the mercy of global economic and political forces beyond their control (Thorhallsson 2006). Following this line, one could argue that global sport has features that render small nations susceptible to shocks. One source of susceptibility is simply the scale of their development programmes, whereas another relates to the potential for athletes and coaches to move to larger, more financially lucrative countries (Gerrard 2002). In more constructionist terms, a small state's exposure to 'shock' in international sport comes from the small number of total medals they might typically expect. Indeed, any small deviation from the expected target (due to injury, sickness or luck) represents a proportionately greater blow to their medal count, and by extension a vulnerability to the legitimacy of their systems.

If vulnerability provides a useful starting point, it follows that a closely related premise is that small states pursue strategies to build resilience (Briguglio *et al.* 2006). For Katzenstein (1985, 2003), small states have developed resilience over time to counter their vulnerability during particular historical periods such as economic depressions or world wars. The adaptive effects of these experiences are thus evident in small states adopting corporatist institutions (i.e. close partnerships between government and interest groups), policies aimed at social integration and a coordinated response to problems. Reflecting a more 'intentional design' perspective, Briguglio *et al.* (2006) suggest that the main strategies to build resilience (or cope with shocks) lie with instituting sound governance, macro-economic management and social cohesion policies. From this standpoint, sport resonates well as a kind of social cohesion policy for small states, with sport event hosting particularly adept at demonstrating both sound governance and 'good' management of a state's economy. Notably, the markers of resilience are heavily imbued with neoliberal principles such as upholding the primacy of deregulated markets and business-friendly labour laws (Briguglio *et al.* 2006). And while the assumptions may be problematic for small states (Thorhallsson and Kattel 2013), they are nevertheless significant from the perspective that these are similar prescriptions supported by global institutions such as the UN and International Monetary Fund. Hence, small countries like New Zealand who have already heavily adopted neoliberal strategies are, in historical institutionalist terms, encouraged to continue on the same path (Pierson 2000).

In recognising that the vulnerability and capacity of small states is issue specific (Neumann and Gstöhl 2004), the following sections explore the dynamics between a nation's smallness (both perceived and 'real') and its sport policy trajectories. New Zealand is perhaps one of the most analysed small nations in terms of sport. This is perhaps not surprising given it is: (a) a relatively wealthy nation in the British Commonwealth; (b) a country in which its national sport (rugby) is clearly identifiable; (c) a state having a notable political history around sport owing to rugby's ties with South African Apartheid; and (d) a country that has historically succeeded in international sport (see Sport and New Zealand Identity section). Sport in New Zealand has thus been researched in terms of its centrality to social movements (Richards 1999), national identity (Jackson and Andrews 1999, Cosgrove and Bruce 2005), the prioritisation of high-performance sport (Piggin *et al.* 2009a), participation structures (Keat and Sam 2013), physical education (Pope 2014) and broadcasting (Scherer and Sam 2012).

What follows is a work of synthesis. The case illustrates the interconnections, interdependencies and influences between constructions of a nation's size, ambitions and sport policies. We outline examples in which the nature of the country's sporting institutions enable state action in prioritising elite sport while rendering muted opposition to more forceful interventions. If we understand that states enact policies to minimise the consequences of 'smallness' for the economy, it follows that similar strategies would appear in relation to sport. The section below thus attempts to make some inroads to addressing whether there are any sport-specific consequences to being small.

The case of New Zealand

New Zealand (population 4.3 million) is a nation at the 'global' periphery. Far removed from the large markets of Europe, Asia and North America, it is susceptible to changing global commodity prices particularly in dairy and meat industries. Its relative 'smallness' is apparent in economic terms, having a GDP of $140 billion USD compared with the $1.5 trillion USD of its South Pacific neighbour, Australia.

The country's economy reached a tipping point in the 1980s. High foreign debt, unemployment and rising inflation resulted in New Zealand becoming the model neoliberal reformer, privatising public assets, floating its currency, removing tariffs and recasting its state sector structures (Norman 2004). Despite the initial pain of economic change, the

Labour Government took pride in the New Zealand 'experiment' and the attention it received from international supporters of the Washington consensus (Wallis 1997, Buchanan 2010).

Culturally, New Zealand's national identity has remained very much tied to its colonial past; as recently as the 1970s, Britain was still considered the 'mother country'. But aided by the neoliberal reforms of the 1980s as well as rugby politics (in relation to the country's sporting ties with Apartheid South Africa), the 1990s witnessed a changing national identity and confidence. Although New Zealand had often portrayed itself as the underdog in international affairs (Bridgman and Barry 2002), the country managed to resist the will of powerful states on issues of regional security and nuclear proliferation in the South Pacific. At the turn of the new century, a new Labour Government (1999–2008) would undertake to 'brand' the nation and build a competitive national identity through arts, culture and sport (Scherer and Jackson 2010, Skilling 2010).

Sport and New Zealand identity

New Zealand has been described as the 'great little sporting nation' and there is no doubt sport is a defining feature of its national identity (Jackson and Andrews 1999). The country's iconic rugby team, the All Blacks, has historically idealized the nation as a classless, egalitarian and racially harmonious society (Scherer and Jackson 2010). Rugby has also featured heavily in the nation's positioning as an independent, prosperous state. These themes along with an emerging concern for global competitiveness in the late 1980s would be reflected in the government's new approach to sport.

> The sporting prowess of New Zealanders has made a major contribution to putting New Zealand 'on the map'. From the beginning of the century, our sportsmen and women have continued to produce high-quality sporting performances which have helped to establish an international reputation and healthy respect for New Zealand's sporting potential. (Sports Development Inquiry Committee 1985, p. 23)

Today, the idea that New Zealand 'punches above its weight' relative to other countries persists in a variety of fields including climate change, education, music and entertainment. But sport remains the most intuitive and most frequently touted object of this metaphor, owing to New Zealand's fairly extensive record of performances in rugby and Olympic sport (Sport NZ 2007). Typifying this narrative, one Government-commissioned review began with:

> New Zealand, despite a small population and geographical isolation, has done extraordinarily well in international competition in a range of sports, both team and individual, and is rightly regarded as a sporting nation. Within the sporting and wider community, it is accepted that sport is important to most New Zealanders' image of themselves and to the image that New Zealand presents to the rest of the world. (Whineray 1995, p. 4)

The country's successes in middle-distance running remain as a particular source of national pride. Peter Snell and Murray Halberg both won gold at the Rome Olympic Games in 1960, with Snell winning two further medals at the subsequent Tokyo Games. Despite New Zealand sporting ties with Apartheid South Africa resulting in boycotts at the Montreal Olympics in 1976, it is John Walker's 1500 m gold medal that New Zealanders perhaps most remember from these Games, owing to its frequent reference in media. That New Zealand would go on to 'beat' Australia at the 1984 Olympics and succeeded in securing 13 medals in 1988 (Seoul) simply affirmed its perception as a 'sporting nation'. Indeed as Prime Minister Jim Bolger would later claim, New Zealand's 'sports men and women have established a reputation out of all proportion to our size' (Bolger 1993, p. 33).

Over the past two decades, sport has become an ever more important feature in the country's political landscape. For example, two consecutive wins (1995 and 2000) in the America's Cup (an international sailing regatta) gave rise to the Team New Zealand syndicate receiving grants of between $8 million and $36 million from the government for subsequent challenges (Jackson 2004, John and Jackson 2011). New Zealand's recent hosting of the 2011 Rugby World Cup and its shared hosting (with Australia) of the 2015 Cricket World Cup are also testament to sport's continuing political importance. In addition, the Rugby World Cup 2011 organisers' concept of a 'stadium of 4 million people' has become emblematic of the country's ability to leverage its small size for economic and social cohesion objectives (Jackson and Scherer 2013).

Sport policy reforms

New Zealand has had a reasonably short history of state intervention in sport. After brief involvement in the 1930s, sport reappeared on the government agenda in the 1970s as part of the expanding welfare state package of social policies. It gained traction in the 1980s on the heels of an incoming Labour Government, ironically at the time where the state apparatus was being de-regulated, privatised and marketised. The Hillary Commission for Sport and Recreation (HC) was established in 1987 following a government-commissioned inquiry. While focusing on domestic provision, the inquiry (entitled 'Sport on the Move') would draw comparisons with Britain and Australia, stating New Zealand was 'far behind' other Western industrialised nations (Sports Development Inquiry Committee 1985, p. 48).

Following new legislation, the HC would be supported through a combination of lottery and government appropriations, the bulk of which was earmarked for community sport. The HC became a Crown agency in 1992, replacing 'recreation' in its legislative mandate with fitness and physical leisure (Collins and Downey 2000). Throughout the 1980s and 1990s, the agency contracted out its support of elite sport to an independent public trust called the *New Zealand Sports Foundation*, with relative success (as already noted). Perceived failure at the 2000 Olympic Games (Knight *et al.* 2005) held in Sydney, Australia, however became a watershed for sport policy. Fulfilling a pre-election promise to examine the sport sector, the Labour Government's *Ministerial Taskforce on Sport, Fitness and Leisure* carried out its inquiry in the months prior to, and immediately after, the games. The taskforce heard much around New Zealand's nostalgic standing as a proud sporting nation. Losses the year before by the All Blacks at the Rugby World Cup and the Silver Ferns at the Netball World Championships, contributed to the taskforce's construction of a crisis in sport (Sam and Jackson 2004). New Zealand's lack of competitiveness thus became a prominent policy narrative, with frequent reference to the successes of neighbouring Australia (Sam 2003, Knight *et al.* 2005). In its recommendations, the taskforce suggested that New Zealand's small size provided little choice but to streamline, stating that 'population is not sufficient to justify the proliferation of uncoordinated institutions purporting to support or develop elite sports' (Ministerial Taskforce 2001).

The taskforce's report resulted in the establishment of a new central sport agency, dubbed SPARC (for Sport and Recreation NZ). Accepting its role as sector leader, SPARC began by legitimising sport's place in the national psyche. In its first strategic plan, it highlighted that sport and recreation 'are a big part of New Zealand culture', citing research that '95% of New Zealanders get more satisfaction from world-class performances by New Zealand sports teams or individuals than from similar achievements by other Kiwi achievers' (SPARC 2002). Embracing the doctrines of 'contestability' espoused by the taskforce, SPARC also announced its priority sport strategy that would eventually turn into its system of performance-based budgeting through targeted investments (Piggin *et al.* 2009b, Sam 2012).

After another disappointing Olympic Games in 2004, SPARC adopted a more forceful role in sport, promising that it would: 'concentrate on monitoring performance and acting decisively where failure is evident' (SPARC 2005, p. 5). It prefaced its high-performance strategy by noting that: 'we cannot compete on the basis of size and funding because we cannot match the resources of larger countries.... New Zealand has to adopt a new and updated strategy of investing smarter if we want to be competitive on the world stage' (p. 3). SPARC's chief executive went on to declare that:

> Our challenge is to encourage New Zealanders not to accept that we are small and under-resourced, rather that we are small, smart and innovative. We need to foster an attitude that says we will do everything possible in order to extract maximum value from our investment and develop a culture that acknowledges that winning is a worthy goal. Meeting this challenge will be worth its weight in gold. (NZAS and SPARC 2005, p. 4)

The government agency thus argued that smallness should be translated into an ambition to become 'wiser' and 'savvier' (SPARC 2006b, 2007). Resilience by extension was to be built upon fostering a change in attitude around sport. By 2006, the 'small, smart and innovative' by-line appeared as the key mobilising doctrine in strategy documents and other reviews on elite sport (SPARC and NZAS 2006, 2010). SPARC thus began to enact its priority-sport approach in earnest, justified largely in relation to the country's small size. In its briefing to the minister of sport, the agency declared:

> We need to foster an attitude throughout sport that says we and they will do everything possible in order to extract maximum value from high-performance investment and develop a culture that strives to win. New Zealand cannot compete on the basis of size and funding. It is futile to try to emulate the seemingly endless resources of the larger major sporting countries. We do not have the resources to outspend our rivals, but we certainly can be smarter, more nimble and more innovative. (SPARC 2006a, p. 10–11)

In this way, the central agency's pleas for unity and compromise would lead to further targeting and a more direct involvement in the affairs of national sport organisations. This is not to say however, that everyone agreed to the new approach. Piggin's (2010) analysis traced several sources of resistance and identified the ways in which the reforms and rhetoric would be subsequently challenged and disputed. Notably, and attesting to the link between small states and compromise, the study found that sport administrators felt threatened to speak out against changes because as one informant suggested, 'New Zealand is a very, very small place' (Piggin 2010, p. 90). Beyond lending credence to New Zealand as a small society, this statement also reflects the small size of the sport sector itself.

In this environment, the government has sought to insulate elite sport to further establish a culture of excellence that would enable the making of 'difficult' decisions. SPARC thus changed its name in 2012 to Sport New Zealand (Sport NZ) and created a separate subsidiary called High Performance Sport New Zealand (HPSNZ). The chief executive of Sport NZ would later claim that 'nothing had changed – just the brand', and that 'we were not being recognised internationally' (Miskimmin 2012). At the same time, Sport NZ began intervening more frequently in the affairs of particular NSOs (such as those governing rugby league, swimming) by either appointing individuals directly to their boards, commissioning reviews or instituting governance reforms as a condition to funding (Sam 2012). Thus, while 'punching above its weight' may well have required nimbleness and flexibility, it has equally demanded a collective (and perhaps at times, coerced) acceptance that targeting resources and being more interventionist were justifiable strategies. Indeed such compromises are now viewed with pride by the newly established agency responsible for elite sport (HPSNZ). As one official put it: 'We are small. We know each other.... We build trust, which enables us to make difficult decisions' (Bullen 2013). In this statement, we see that New Zealand's smallness is paradoxically claimed as a source of resilience.

Discussion

The New Zealand case points to the possibility that shared constructions of smallness, vulnerability and resilience play a role in sport policy discourse. The connection between national identity and elite sport development is nearly universal, but New Zealand clearly exhibits what Richards (1982, p. 170) would describe as the tendency for small countries to display collective identities 'asserted against the outside world'. Indeed, the belief that New Zealand 'punches above its weight' has been a key marker of the nation's identity, and reinforced time and again. Faced with an apparent decline in Olympic performance, the government thus accepted responsibility for elite sport, first indirectly through legislation that would divert lottery profits and then directly via 'vote' investment. Of course, New Zealand is not the only country to respond in this way (the Australian Institute of Sport was created under similar circumstances), but the way in which elite sport has developed is arguably also linked to the country's small economies of scale (i.e. weaker domestic competition, distance to 'markets'), lack of 'resource endowments' (i.e. athletes and coaches) and potentially higher degrees of fluctuations in performance (where a decrease of one to two medals is proportionately larger in a small state). In sum, New Zealand's trajectory has been shaped by elements of real and perceived vulnerability.

Indeed smallness, taken as a kind of comparative resource scarcity, has invited consolidation, a narrowing of objectives, targeting and rationing. This is not surprising given the broader tendency of small states to both pursue a narrower range of foreign policy objectives while also prioritising particular sectors of their economies (Armstrong and Read 1998). Although specialising and prioritising selected sports has been a feature in other, larger countries (De Bosscher et al. 2008), the doctrines around rationing have been pursued both forcefully and systematically down to frontline services.

Beyond reducing the number of priority sports, the agency responsible for elite sport, HPSNZ, has halved the number of athletes it supports from 950 in 2006 to 440 athletes in 2013. Likewise it decreased the number of carded (grant funded) coaches from 200 to 90

Table 1. Targeted investment (Bullen 2013).

	2006	2013
Investment	29 million NZD	60 million NZD
Sports	24	14
Carded athletes	950	440
Carded coaches	200	90

(see Table 1). This rationing has paradoxically occurred in an environment of steadily increasing budgets, where HPSNZ's allocation doubled in the same period. The commitment to such targeted investment at both a policy and operational level is persistently defended in relation to the limited resources of the country and New Zealand's inability to keep up with larger nations. In defending HPSNZ's decision to cut funding to Basketball NZ for example, the chief executive recently reiterated that 'New Zealand is a small country, with significantly less funding available than many of our competitors', that 'no-one will win' if resources are spread too thinly, and that if basketball were funded, 'it wouldn't be fair' to another sport 'that had a better chance of winning on the world stage' (High Performance Sport New Zealand 2013). To a degree, the narrative of 'punching above our weight' has enabled the logic of 'no alternative' and its corollary, 'no compromise' to gain traction. Consequently, the comparative emphasis on elite sport has grown, from initially occupying approximately 40% of the total sport expenditure (in 2002) to exceeding 60% of the total sport budget (in 2013). Budgeted expenditure on elite sport in 2013/14 is now NZD $58.2 million, against the NZD $19.2 million allocated to community sport.

If smallness and constructions of vulnerability (i.e. having limited resources compared with other nations) enabled this shift, it could also be suggested that New Zealand's size might have played a part in the muted resistance to such reforms. Indeed Piggin's (2010) analysis points to a 'widely held belief that speaking out against SPARC policies was not necessarily beneficial and could be detrimental to either critics themselves or their sport' (p. 89–90). This may reflect Lowenthal's (1987, p. 39) thesis of a 'managed intimacy' in small states, where:

> Small-state inhabitants learn to get along, like it or not, with folk they will know in myriad contexts over their whole lives. To enable the social mechanism to function without undue stress, they minimise or mitigate overt conflict. They become expert at muting hostility, deferring their own views, containing disagreement, avoiding dispute, in the interest of stability and compromise.

This is not to suggest that the sport sector is without its detractors but rather that its small size perhaps necessitates 'sophisticated modes of accommodation' (Lowenthal 1987, p. 39).

Leveraging smallness in the face of growth

The literature on small states largely focuses on the economic problems they face as a result of globalisation. If one accepts that vulnerability is as much constructed as it is real, the opportunities and threats from 'being small' are a matter of perspective. Being small is no doubt a disadvantage in the area of international elite sport – fewer people means fewer resources, and a comparatively smaller pool of athletes, coaches and support personnel. And yet we have seen that smallness also allows for the mobilisation and distribution of resources that might not otherwise be acceptable. As Campbell and Hall (2009) point out, small nations may allow for better cooperation hence why the narrative of smallness may be a key factor in leveraging additional funds. But bringing it full circle, small nations can perhaps remain vulnerable through this same mechanism.

The expression 'to punch above our weight' appears in Qatar as well as in Cuba (Grix and Lee 2013). While it is likely a form of 'newswire short-hand', its ubiquity raises important questions, not least of which is whether the constructed nature of scale is likely to ever be de-emphasised in the face of increased resources. In this light, it is worth asking whether policy reforms aimed at building resilience render New Zealand sport any less vulnerable.

One of the difficulties for small states arises from the pressures to establish organisational structures comparable to larger states (Raadschelders 1992). Although Finland may be more comparable in terms of population, size and resources, it is the systems of larger states that New Zealand sport policy officials choose to emulate. As discussed, this is partly due to geography (proximity to Australia) and history (colonial ties), but it is also due to the repeated interactions between the sports themselves. New Zealand therefore compares itself to the United Kingdom because the two nations share similar targeted sports: cycling, rowing and sailing. In this way, aspects of vulnerability and resilience become mutually constitutive; the comparison both affirms (in the case of medal-winning performances) that New Zealand punches above its weight *and* that it has comparatively fewer resources. The steady increase in high-performance sport funding thus presents a paradox. Whereas political claims over the past decades have suggested that New Zealand's sport system has been comparatively underfunded, this is certainly no longer the case – neither on a dollar per capita basis nor as a percentage of national GDP. Indeed, New Zealand's rapid investment increases make it increasingly difficult to maintain the claim that it is weak or vulnerable. Comparisons with the United Kingdom are thus essential for the purposes of legitimising the system because countries of comparable size and population spend far less.

But there are other potential consequences of having to continue 'punching above one's weight'. One consequence is that the storyline need not necessarily apply to state-sponsored Olympic sport but rather can be appropriated by any number of sporting interests. This is indeed the case in relation to Team New Zealand and the *America's Cup*, a professional sailing syndicate heavily supported by millions of government dollars that has little connection with the 'sport system' as most would understand it. Likewise, mega events like the World Cup 2011 and the Cricket World Cup 2015 are sources of pride, and demonstrate economic resilience internationally. While supplemented from other sources of the government budget (e.g. Ministry of Economic Development), these events and the infrastructure they demand may nevertheless disrupt, delay and even obscure the need for sport facility investment for community-based sport. Thus, just as the increase in budgets to elite sport is based in part on the deliberate positioning of New Zealand as 'small', the significant investment in sport mega events owes much to the imperative of maintaining a presence on the 'world stage' and to the image of a 'stadium of 4 million' people.

Conclusion

Houlihan (1997, p. 114) suggests that sport policies might be a response to 'cultural insecurity', an observation that may be particularly relevant to small nations. If we accept two premises – that sport contributes to the formation of national identity and that this in turn has the capacity to create unity and a proxy for 'homogeneity' conducive to economic growth (Campbell and Hall 2009), then small states in particular could stand to gain from investment in sport. As the saying goes however, the devil is in the detail, and therefore any assessment has to take into account the tensions around this form of resilience building. If the prevailing discourse remains around 'punching above one's weight', it renders appropriate the need for specialisation and the concentration of resources into a narrower range of activities, such as elite sport. However, the means through which consolidation, rationing and targeting can be accomplished must necessarily take place in an environment marked by close networks and fewer degrees of separation. Consequently, central sport agencies in small states like New Zealand may have to paradoxically invoke strategies to break the very communal bonds that provide them with the 'fertile' conditions for growth and competitive advantage.

This paper suggests that legitimations around smallness and vulnerability have shaped New Zealand's sport policy trajectory. The case illustrates how size can be used to induce a steady commitment to reforms and an increasing imbalance within sport policy objectives. Whether size encourages 'over commitment' is difficult to say for sure but the remedy of putting more eggs into fewer and fewer baskets is in itself a risk for smaller nations. At the same time, the increased investment to elite sport renders the claim of being small and underfunded untenable without continued comparison with the largest nations. In this way, state comparisons of 'like with like' will probably remain politically untenable.

Undeniably, a country's size is only one consideration in the analysis of policy systems. Scale makes a difference but the analytical difficulty lies in identifying exactly how and why it matters and with what effect. From the research taking smallness as a point of departure, both realist and constructivist approaches point to the importance of context in explaining phenomena. To this end, studies on small states can potentially pay more attention to the importance of close-knit networks and the modes of accommodation therein. If we extend the concepts of vulnerability from economic studies, there may also be a cause to consider the sport-specific sources of 'shocks' in small nations' sport systems. Indeed, how vulnerable are small nations to sport policy disasters like doping scandals or match-fixing? A small state's governance responses to risk (or the public reactions to a scandal) may help elucidate aspects of its insularity and resilience, as well as how it sees itself, its national sport policies and priorities.

Disclosure statement

No potential conflict of interest was reported by the author.

Note

1. Notably, as this article was being finalised, New Zealand won a non-permanent seat to the United Nations Security Council. Prime Minister John Key was quoted as saying the win was 'a victory for the small states that make up over half the United Nations membership' and that New Zealand would be 'determined to represent the perspective of small states at the Security Council' (Young and Trevett 2014).

References

Armstrong, H.W. and Read, R., 1998. Trade and growth in small states: the impact of global trade liberalisation. *The world economy*, 21, 563–585. doi:10.1111/1467-9701.00148

Bairner, A., 2001. *Sport, nationalism, and globalization: European and North American perspectives*. Albany: State University of New York Press.

Benedict, B., 1967. Sociological aspects of smallness. *In*: B. Benedict, ed. *Problems of smaller territories*. London: University of London/Athlone Press, 45–55.

Bolger, J., 1993. *Path to 2010: securing a future for New Zealanders to share*. Wellington: NZ National Party.

Bridgman, T. and Barry, D., 2002. Regulation is evil: an application of narrative policy analysis to regulatory debate in New Zealand. *Policy sciences*, 35, 141–161. doi:10.1023/A:1016139804995

Briguglio, L., Persaud, B., and Stern, R., 2006. *Toward an outward-oriented development strategy for small states: issues, opportunities, and resilience building*. Washington, DC: World Bank.

Browning, C.S., 2006. Small, smart and salient? rethinking identity in the small states literature. *Cambridge review of international affairs*, 19, 669–684. doi:10.1080/09557570601003536

Buchanan, P.G., 2010. Lilliputian in fluid times: New Zealand foreign policy after the cold war. *Political science quarterly*, 125, 255–279. doi:10.1002/j.1538-165X.2010.tb00675.x

Bullen, C., 2013. *High performance Sport New Zealand's philosophy: athlete-focused, coach-led, performance-driven* [online]. Available from: http://www.svenskidrott.se/ImageVaultFiles/id_40403/cf_394/Olympia_2.PDF [Accessed 7 January 2013].

Campbell, J.L. and Hall, J.A., 2009. National identity and the political economy of small states. *Review of international political economy*, 16, 547–572. doi:10.1080/09692290802620378

Chalip, L., 1996. Critical policy analysis: the illustrative case of New Zealand sport policy development. *Journal of sport management*, 10, 310–324.

Collins, C. and Downey, J., 2000. Politics, government and sport. *In*: C. Collins, ed. *Sport in New Zealand society*. Palmerston North: Dunmore Press Ltd., 201–221.

Cosgrove, A. and Bruce, T., 2005. "The Way New Zealanders would like to see themselves": reading white masculinity via media coverage of the death of Sir Peter Blake. *Sociology of sport journal*, 22, 336.

De Bosscher, V., Bingham, J., and Shibli, S., 2008. *The global sporting arms race: an international comparative study on sports policy factors leading to international sporting success*. Brussels: Meyer & Meyer Verlag.

Farrugia, C., 1993. The special working environment of senior administrators in small states. *World development*, 21, 221–226. doi:10.1016/0305-750X(93)90017-4

Forster, J., 2006. Global sports organisations and their governance. *Corporate governance*, 6, 72–83. doi:10.1108/14720700610649481

Gerrard, B., 2002. The muscle drain, coubertobin-type taxes and the international transfer system in association football. *European sport management quarterly*, 2, 47–56. doi:10.1080/16184740208721911

Grix, J. and Lee, D., 2013. Soft power, sports mega-events and emerging states: the lure of the politics of attraction. *Global society*, 27, 521–536. doi:10.1080/13600826.2013.827632

Gstöhl, S., 2002. Scandinavia and Switzerland: small, successful and stubborn towards the EU. *Journal of European public policy*, 9, 529–549. doi:10.1080/13501760210152420

Hall, S., 1986. The problem of ideology-Marxism without guarantees. *Journal of communication inquiry*, 10, 28–44. doi:10.1177/019685998601000203

High Performance Sport New Zealand, 2013. *Basketball high performance funding* [online]. HPSNZ. Available from: http://www.hpsnz.org.nz/news-events/basketball-high-performance-funding [Accessed 12 August 2014].

Houlihan, B., 1997. Sport, national identity and public policy. *Nations and nationalism*, 3 (1), 113–137.

Houlihan, B. and Green, M., 2008. *Comparative elite sport development: systems, structures and public policy*. 1st ed. Amsterdam: Elsevier/Butterworth-Heinemann.

Jackson, S.J., 2004. Reading New Zealand within the new global order: sport and the visualisation of national identity. *International sport studies*, 26, 13–29.

Jackson, S.J. and Andrews, D.L., 1999. Between and beyond the global and the local: American popular sporting culture in New Zealand. *International review for the sociology of sport*, 34, 31–42. doi:10.1177/101269099034001003

Jackson, S.J. and Scherer, J., 2013. Rugby World Cup 2011: sport mega-events and the contested terrain of space, bodies and commodities. *Sport in society*, 16, 883–898. doi:10.1080/17430437.2013.791156

John, A. and Jackson, S., 2011. Call me loyal: globalization, corporate nationalism and the America's cup. *International review for the sociology of sport*, 46, 399–417. doi:10.1177/1012690210384658

Katzenstein, P.J., 1985. *Small states in world markets: industrial policy in Europe*. Ithaca, NY: Cornell University Press.

Katzenstein, P.J., 2003. Small states and small states revisited. *New political economy*, 8, 9–30. doi:10.1080/1356346032000078705

Keat, R. and Sam, M., 2013. Regional implementation of New Zealand sport policy: new instrument, new challenges. *International journal of sport policy and politics*, 5, 39–54. doi:10.1080/19406940.2012.656684

Knight, G., Macneill, M., and Donnelly, P., 2005. The disappointment games: narratives of Olympic failure in Canada and New Zealand. *International review for the sociology of sport*, 40, 25–51. doi:10.1177/1012690205052163

Lowenthal, D., 1987. Social features. *In*: C. Clarke and T. Payne, eds. *Politics, security and development in small states*. London: Allen and Unwin, 26–49.

Ministerial Taskforce, 2001. *Getting set for an active nation: Report of the sport, fitness and leisure ministerial taskforce*. Wellington.

Miskimmin, P., 2012. The future of sport in small nations. *International symposium on the future of sport in small nations*. Dunedin: University of Otago School of Physical Education.

Neumann, I.B. and Gstöhl, S., 2004. *Lilliputians in Gulliver's world? Small states in international relations*. Institute of International Affairs. Reykjavik: University of Iceland.

Norman, R., 2004. Recovering from a tidal wave: new directions for performance management in New Zealand's public sector. *Public finance and management*, 4, 429–447.

NZAS and SPARC, 2005. *Re-igniting the SPARC: Looking back at Athens – forward to Beijing*. Wellington: Sport and Recreation New Zealand.

Pierson, P., 2000. Increasing returns, path dependence, and the study of politics. *The American political science review*, 94, 251–267.

Piggin, J., 2010. Is resistance futile? The effects of criticising New Zealand sport policy. *International journal of sport policy and politics*, 2, 85–98. doi:10.1080/19406941003634057

Piggin, J., Jackson, S.J., and Lewis, M., 2009a. Knowledge, power and politics: contesting 'Evidence-based' national sport policy. *International review for the sociology of sport*, 44, 87–101. doi:10.1177/1012690209102825

Piggin, J., Jackson, S.J., and Lewis, M., 2009b. Telling the truth in public policy: an analysis of New Zealand sport policy discourse. *Sociology of sport journal*, 26, 462–482.

Pope, C.C., 2014. The jagged edge and the changing shape of health and physical education in Aotearoa New Zealand. *Physical education and sport pedagogy*, 19 (5), 500–511.

Raadschelders, J.B., 1992. Definitions of smallness: a comparative study. *In*: R. Baker, ed. *Public administration in small and island states*. West Hartford, CT: Kumarian Press, 26–33.

Richards, J., 1982. Politics in small independent communities: conflict or consensus? *Journal of Commonwealth & Comparative Politics*, 20 (2), 155–171.

Richards, T.L., 1999. *Dancing on our bones: New Zealand, South Africa, rugby and racism*. Wellington: Bridget Williams Books.

Sam, M.P., 2003. What's the big idea? Reading the rhetoric of a national sport policy process. *Sociology of sport journal*, 20, 189–213.

Sam, M.P., 2012. Targeted investments in elite sport funding: wiser, more innovative and strategic? *Managing leisure*, 17, 207–220. doi:10.1080/13606719.2012.674395

Sam, M.P. and Jackson, S.J., 2004. Sport policy development in New Zealand: paradoxes of an integrative paradigm. *International review for the sociology of sport*, 39, 205–222. doi:10.1177/1012690204043463

Scherer, J. and Jackson, S.J., 2010. *Globalization, sport and corporate nationalism: the new cultural economy of the New Zealand All Blacks*. Bern: Peter Lang.

Scherer, J. and Sam, M., 2012. Public broadcasting, sport, and cultural citizenship: SKY's the limit in New Zealand? *Media, culture & society*, 34, 101–111. doi:10.1177/0163443711429234

Schienstock, G., 2007. From path dependency to path creation: Finland on its way to the knowl-edge-based economy. *Current sociology*, 55, 92–109. doi:10.1177/0011392107070136

Skilling, P., 2010. The construction and use of national identity in contemporary New Zealand political discourse. *Australian journal of political science*, 45, 175–189. doi:10.1080/10361140903296594

SPARC, 2002. *Our vision and direction: Strategies for success from 2006*. Wellington: Sport and Recreation New Zealand.

SPARC, 2005. *Brief to the incoming minister*. Wellington: Sport and Recreation New Zealand.

SPARC, 2006a. *Melbourne 2006: a review of New Zealand's performance at the 2006 Melbourne commonwealth games*. Wellington: Sport and Recreation New Zealand.

SPARC, 2006b. *Statement of intent 2006–2009*. Wellington: Sport and Recreation New Zealand.

SPARC, 2007. *Annual report for the year ended 30 June 2007*. Wellington: Sport and Recreation New Zealand.

SPARC & NZAS, 2006, 2010. *High performance strategy 2006–2012*. Wellington: Sport and Recreation New Zealand.

Sport NZ, 2007. *Coaches converge on capital* [online]. Scoop. Available from: http://www.scoop.co.nz/stories/CU0703/S00163.htm [Accessed 1 March 2014].

Sports Development Inquiry Committee, 1985. *Sport on the move: Report to the Minister of Recreation and Sport*. Wellington.

Sutton, P., 2011. The concept of small states in the international political economy. *The round table*, 100, 141–153. doi:10.1080/00358533.2011.565625

Thorhallsson, B., 2006. The size of states in the European Union: theoretical and conceptual perspectives. *Journal of European integration*, 28, 7–31. doi:10.1080/07036330500480490

Thorhallsson, B. and Kattel, R., 2013. Neo-liberal small states and economic crisis: lessons for democratic corporatism. *Journal of Baltic studies*, 44, 83–103. doi:10.1080/01629778.2012.719306

Thorhallsson, B. and Wivel, A., 2006. Small states in the European Union: what do we know and what would we like to know? *Cambridge review of international affairs*, 19, 651–668. doi:10.1080/09557570601003502

Tõnurist, P., 2010. What is a "small state" in a globalizing economy. *Halduskultuur – administrative culture*, 11, 8–29.

Wallis, J., 1997. Conspiracy and the policy process: a case study of the New Zealand experiment. *Journal of public policy*, 17, 1–29.

Whineray, W., 1995. *The winning way*. Wellington: High Performance Sport Review Committee.

Wivel, A. and Steinmetz, R., 2013. *Small states in Europe: challenges and opportunities*. Farnham: Ashgate Publishing, Ltd.

Young, A. and Trevett, C., 2014. *NZ wins seat on Security Council: 'Victory for the small states'* [online]. Auckland: New Zealand Herald. Available from: http://www.nzherald.co.nz/nz/news/article.cfm?c_id=1&objectid=11343853 [Accessed 18 October 2014].

Finland as a small sports nation: socio-historical perspectives on the development of national sport policy

Pasi Koski[a] and Jari Lämsä[b]

[a]Department of Teacher Education, University of Turku, Rauma Unit, Finland; [b]KIHU – Research Institute for Olympic Sports, Jyväskylä, Finland

Elite sports are an important part of most nations' culture and identity and international success in sport is highly valued. However, the increasingly important cultural, economic and political significance of sport has effectively created the equivalent of a global sporting arms race. This means challenges especially for the small nations who may have both limited populations and resources.

The aim of this essay is to analyse and understand the role of elite sports in one small nation – Finland. By almost any measure Finland has been a successful sporting nation. The nation's Olympic success was exceptionally high until the middle of the last century but success has been more difficult to achieve in recent times. This article examines the changes in Finnish sporting success and policy development in relation to the three phases of international sport: amateurism, totalisation and professionalism. During the golden and largely amateur era of Finnish sport, the main motivations for success were founded in national identity, hard work and 'sisu'. However, following this amateur era and facing increasing competition, there was a need for new structures, policies and resources. It was clear that a small country like Finland had to redefine international sport success and hence the emergence of totalisation followed by professionalism. However, these phases are challenging for nations with small markets and for sport systems that operate democratically and are dependent on voluntary civil activity. How can and should Finland adapt its structures, strategies and policies to compete in the new global arena?

Introduction

Elite sports are an important part of most nations' culture and identity and international success in sport is highly valued. On a national level, we like to compare how successful our athletes are compared with those from other countries (Green and Houlihan 2008, De Bosscher et al. 2009). This is particularly true in small nations where there may be fewer people participating in a narrower range of sports and where success is more difficult to achieve. However, sporting success in small nations has the potential to have a greater impact given that it may resonate with a greater percentage of the population. A range of factors including the geographical location and the seasonal requirements of various sports may determine the potential and possibilities of a small country in elite sports. These possibilities may also depend on the political and cultural status of elite sports in the country concerned. This could include how elite sports are valued by state government and the general public, the perceived career paths for young athletes, and the overall status of the sport sector compared to others. In addition, the structure and the efficiency of elite sport policies and training system of the country play a crucial role in the actual process of competition between countries (Green and Oakley 2001, De Bosscher, De Knop, Van Bottenbugh and Shibli 2006). Ultimately, one of the bottom lines is what kind of financial and other investments people and nations are prepared to make in elite sports.

For young nations, sports may play an important part in promoting independence and strengthening national identity. As the early twentieth century of Finnish history shows, success in the international sporting arena and the emergence of national sport heroes strengthened national pride, especially during the process of independence and after its birth as an independent nation (e.g. Heinilä 1987).

In terms of population, Finland is a small country (5.4 million inhabitants),[1] and therefore it offers an excellent site for the analysis of elite sport and its social status. Owing to its geographic location and history, Finland has long been considered as a kind of 'little brother' to its neighbouring countries, especially Sweden. Originally a part of the Swedish kingdom for about 700 years, and subsequently a Grand Duchy of Russia from 1809, Finland gained full independence in 1917. Influences from both of these cultures can still be recognised in Finnish society. The target-driven and perseverance-oriented nature of the Finnish nation have transformed it from a poor, agriculture-dependent country, from a European perspective, peripheral country, into an affluent Nordic social welfare nation with a high standard of living supported by strong education and technology sectors.

The rapid development and social changes within Finland are reflected in the role and status of elite sport in the country. Notably, the development of international elite sport in Finland and in other small sporting nations has been accompanied by a range of challenges. Often these challenges, when discussed in relation to a nation's size, are characterised using the metaphor of 'David against Goliaths'.

This article describes the long-term development of elite sport in one small country, Finland, which historically, is one of the most successful small sporting nations. The aim is to analyse and understand the role of elite sports development within the context of Finland, by examining the status and value of elite sports and by identifying the nature of sports policy that results from that development. The analysis applies Houlihan and Green's (2008) classification of megatrends in elite sports, Bale's (1991) model of the study of elite sport and Heinilä's (1984) idea of the process of totalisation. The first section of this article outlines the historical background, key moments and current context of elite sport in Finland. In turn, the article examines Finnish Olympic success and its development as well as the cultural status of elite sport. This is followed by analysis of the explanations offered for the changes within and the reactions to national sports policy. Finally, the conclusion reflects on the relevant observations from the perspective of the literature on small nations.

Periodisation of modern elite sport from a Finnish perspective

The modern, global and institutionalised sport system means that elite sport is practised around the world with an agreed set of rules, structures and ideologies, all of which makes international competition possible. John Bale (1991, p. 6) claims that nations are part of that global sporting system, in which the elements (e.g. nations, international sport organisations, nations, national sport organisations, cities, athletes) are linked in a way such that they are all dependent on one another.

Despite the growing amount of research indicating the homogenisation of sport around the world (Green and Oakley 2001), cultural differences among nations with respect to the

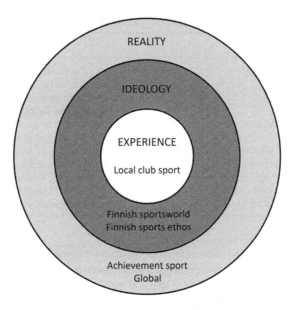

Figure 1. A three-tier model for the study of elite sport (Bale 1991, p. 11–13).

meaning and experiences of sport exist. For example, the experiences of Finns in elite sport reflect aspects of Finnish national character and culture, which are different from, for example, those of Sweden or Germany. The idea of national ideology affecting sport experience is presented in Bale's (1991, p. 9) three-tier model, where the national level functions as an ideological filter, which creates different kinds of cultural experiences (Figure 1).

This article considers the long-term development of elite sport in Finland. For our purposes, we have divided the development of international elite sport into three different periods: amateurism, totalisation and professionalism.

Amateur ideology has been one of the most contradictory principles in modern sports and can be seen as a reaction to the commercialisation and professionalisation of the British society in the nineteenth century (Allison 2001). Wikberg (2005, p. 34–36) illustrates the complexity of the concept by analysing four different aspects: (1) the moral aspect (ethics/morals); (2) the social aspect (class/occupation); (3) the economic aspect (income/compensation for expenses); and (4) the peripheral aspect (ethnicity/ traditionalism). In practice, the economic aspect, i.e. ban on pecuniary rewards, super-seded the other aspects. In the early twentieth century, amateurism replaced profession-alism especially after the Olympic movement adopted strict rules prohibiting professionalism. Finland, like the other Nordic countries, quickly adopted the Olympic sports ideology using it as the basis for its own sports architecture. This, however, meant that cash prizes had to be prohibited in all sports (Heikkinen 1977). After that point amateurism was viewed as the only legitimate form of sports participation. The approval of amateur rules meant that the power of sports organisations also grew. In principle, competitions were open to all, but the prerequisite for participation was membership in the local sports club. Consequently, at the national level the first period, amateurism, can be linked to nationalism and the development of sporting culture as a civic movement.

After World War II, international competitive sports gained significant attention. The split of the world into two competing ideological camps also played a role in initiating a

Table 1. Sport resources as related to resources of society at large (Heinilä 2004, p. 104).

Resources of elite sport	Resources of society
Number of talents in elite sports	Size of population – number of talents – level of nutrition – standard of living etc.
Achievement orientation in sport	Achievement as a common frame value
Sport funding	Level of national production
Effectiveness of sport authorities	Political order of society
The quality of sport sciences	The quality of science in general
The quality of medical services in sport	The quality of medical services in general
The quality of training and coaching	The quality of higher education in society
The ecological setting of sport	The geographical frame of the country etc.

new, more intensive level of international competitive sports. The transition from *amateurism* to a new system of competition was marked by the 1952 Helsinki Olympic Games, when the Soviet Union joined the Olympic movement and placed second on the medal table after the United States.

Heinilä (1984) referred to this new system and phase of development as totalisation, in order to characterise the increasing competition between contrasting national systems. In this sense, 'sport organizations are responsible for the promotion of elite sport to mobilise all relevant resources available in society for the production of high performance in international sport' (Heinilä 2004, p. 101). While the Olympic movement declared in its ideology that sport is supposed to be competition between equal individuals, within the system of totalisation, the focus was on the struggle between sports systems. At its extreme, this meant that the whole of society was harnessed to promote the nation's success in competitive sports. According to Heinilä (2004), there are several connections between the operational prerequisites of elite sports and the available social resources (Table 1).

In Finland, totalisation occurred during a period in which the welfare state expanded significantly and the resources of the public sector could also be utilised in sports. When the shift from amateurism towards semi-professionalism occurred at the beginning of the 1970s, Finland used both Western and Eastern connections to adopt new tools for elite sport development.

The slow erosion of amateurism eventually led to open professionalism at the Olympic Games. The transition was marked by a fully professional US basketball team, nicknamed the 'dream team', at the 1992 Barcelona Olympic Games. Since then, the world's best athletes, including professionals, have been able to participate in the Olympic Games.

Houlihan and Green (2008) summarise the key development features of elite sport with respect to three megatrends: (1) globalisation, (2) commercialisation and (3) governmentalisation. The most visible effect of globalisation is the strong growth in the number of countries that participate in international competitions. For instance, the number of countries that have participated in the Summer Olympics has doubled since the 1980s. Along with globalisation, national sport policies have become increasingly dependent on international policies and rules. Consequently, international sport organisations have developed into strong, economically powerful, units which are able to exercise influence on national-level actors by redistributing resources and controlling various events rights.

There are three different aspects to the commercialisation of sports: (1) brandisation of sports events, sports clubs and athletes; (2) expansion of financial profits from sports to outside actors, such as media; and (3) growth of sports-related business sectors, such as sports equipment. Arguably, greater and more open financial rewards than ever before have changed athletes' attitudes towards their sports careers. Sport is now considered a career choice, even in sports where actual professional competitions do not yet exist. Commercialisation has also meant that the management models of the business world have become an essential part of the operational cultures of sports organisations (Houlihan and Green 2008).

The third megatrend is governments' increasing interest in elite sports. In the past, sport was only seen as the beneficiary and user of public funding, but as the market value of large global sports events has increased, sport has become a part of the profit-making, cultural industry. During the past few decades, several countries with widely different social structures, including Australia, China, Denmark, Canada, Japan, New Zealand and Brazil, have significantly increased both their focus on, and financial investments in, elite sports. Indeed, they have all joined what has been referred to as the 'global sporting arms race' (De Bosscher et al. 2008).

For a small country, the development of modern elite sports has increased the requirement levels so much, especially in major summer sports, that not even an exceptional talent pool and total commitment of athletes is enough. To be successful nations need the support of an elite sports system with top level professional expertise (Heinilä 2010). Consequently, in the era of globalisation, nations have to draw upon their own national traditions and unique strengths that lead to success but also benchmark and learn about new strategies and systems that other countries have developed in their systems (Böhlke and Robinson 2009).

Finally, as shown in Table 2, Finland's Olympic success, based on the number of medals won at Summer Olympic Games, shows a clear trend over time. The difference between the golden age of Finnish elite sport (1907–1951) with an average of 23.8 medals in Olympic Games compared with the era of professionalism and an average of 3.7 medals, is striking. However, by comparison, success in the Winter Olympic Games has slightly increased. Potential reasons for the increase in Winter Olympics medals could be related to the smaller pool of nations committed to investing and the strong tradition and success that Finland has in winter sports like ice-hockey and Nordic skiings.

The background of Finnish elite sports

To be able to analyse the background of Finnish elite sports and to understand why sports and success in sports became so significant and highly valued in Finland, we need to review a few features that defined development, especially in the early twentieth century. These features include independence, national defence, demanding natural conditions, the protestant ethic, pursuit of equality in a poor and unequal country, development of a civil society, urbanisation, and sisu, the unique Finnish concept that relates to stamina.

Historically, the rise of the popularity of Olympic and competitive sports in Finland coincided with Finland's efforts towards independence, which became a reality in 1917. Earlier, local sports activities played an important role in ensuring that the nation was physically prepared to defend the country. For example, during a certain period of Russian rule, some sports and physical cultural practices had to be hidden or disguised behind the activities of various other associations. Indeed, formal sports organisations were banned as they were perceived as a military threat. For instance, the Finnish Gymnastic and Sport Association (SVUL) was established in 1900 but its activities were hidden until 1906, when sports organisations were eventually freed from the ban (Arponen 1981, p. 14–17). The nationalist cultured class of the country understood the significance of sports culture

Table 2. Periodisation of the Olympic sport and elite sport in Finland.

Period	1907–1951	1952–1991	1992–
REALITY: Olympic ideology as a global sport system	Amateurism – sport as individual hobby	Totalisation – competition between the systems, state amateurs	Professionalism – sport as a vocation and global phenomenon
Sign of the transition	1907: Amateur rules accepted by the Finnish gymnastic and Sport federation	1952: Helsinki Olympic Games. Cold war – the division of world into two opposite groups	1992: fully professional US basketball team 'dream team' wins Olympic gold. 1994: First official professional athlete in Finland
IDEOLOGY: domestic issues effecting elite sport policy	Nationalism Equality Sport as civic movement Elite sport valued as such Elite sport and media symbiosis	Welfare state Urbanisation Differentiation of sporting culture	Commercialisation Governmentalisation Health enhancing physical activity versus elite sport Commercialised media
Success of Finland at the Olympic Games (OG) and Winter Olympic games (WOG)	OG (8 games): 190 medals, average: 23.8 medals/OG WOG (5): 30 medals, average: 6.0 medals/WOG	OG(10): 89 medals, average 8.9 medals/OG WOG(11): 80 medals, average 7.3 medals/WOG	OG (6): 22 medals, average: 3.7 medals/OG WOG(6): 46 medals, average: 7.7 medals/WOG

for the nation and took deliberate actions to promote the cause. After being imported to Finland, sports ideology and popular physical cultural practices quickly spread across the country and reached all social classes. Many organisations, besides the sport clubs, such as workers' associations, voluntary fire brigades, temperance societies and youth associations, adopted sports as part of their activities (Halila and Sirmeikkö 1960).

In the first few decades of the twentieth century, sport offered the youth of an agriculture-based country new kinds of stimulating activities and also possibilities for social improvement. When urbanisation accelerated, sports and local sports clubs offered young people a form of community for a meaningful way to spend time and meet each other and thereby dissipate the feeling of rootlessness. As a result sport became a strategic sector in the development and maintenance of civil society. Finland's expanding and active club system, which was based on free civil activities, has played a central role in the development process of a democratic civic society by maintaining and educating the nation in its practices (Koski 1999).

Particularly before urbanisation, the harsh reality of Finland's challenging natural conditions and lifestyle (cold, darkness, etc.) has required perseverance, stamina and continuous hard work. The impact of such demands from one generation to the next have left their mark on Finns and Finnish culture. In Finnish society, respect for and appreciation of work has always been high. The natural conditions and, from time to time, also military threats, have tested the perseverance of Finns. Over time Finns have developed a special word and concept, *sisu*, which refers to this highly esteemed feature. *Sisu* also aligns well with the protestant concept of humbleness and diligence. The myth of Finnish *sisu* has also shaped Finns' attitude towards sports. *Sisu* loosely translates into English as an enduring strength of will, determination and perseverance in the face of adversity. Historically, Finnish power and energy often seems to rise from negation and negative experiences. This may be because Finland is a nation that often had to fight against powerful political enemies and found sport served as an important vehicle to find its place and status among nations.

Another factor contributing to Finland's early international sport success is that the nation was one of the purest evangelical Lutheran countries in the world in the sense that the protestant ethic was deeply rooted in the Finnish culture. Seppänen's (1981) analysis of the pre-1970s Olympic success of countries representing different religions clearly shows the superiority of the protestant countries. The protestant ethic emphasises the importance of hard work and diligence. Moreover, the protestant concept of salvation is based on the individual's own target-oriented religious struggle. Both of these concepts are in line with the ideology of competitive sports.

In elite sport, Finland was accepted into the Olympic movement as a 'sport' (versus political) nation as early as 1907, 10 years before the independence of the nation. Subsequently, amateur sports and Olympic success emerged as important tools for national identity building in Finland.

The Cold War era that followed World War II, also changed the nature of sports. International competitive activities were based on battles between national sports systems in a completely new way. At the beginning of this era, Finland's sports success collapsed. Later, although the nation's success never reached its previous levels, the Finnish sports system was able to utilise the resources of the growing welfare state and the country's relationships with both the East and the West so effectively that Finnish Olympic sports managed to achieve results that satisfied the nation during the 1970s and 1980s. In particular, the Summer Olympic boycotts in the 1980s fuelled Finnish people's illusion of continuous success and the functionality of the Finnish sport system.

The early 1990s revolutionised ideologies both in Finnish society and the Olympic movement. First, the collapse of the socialist system in Soviet Union in 1991 accelerated the process of Westernisation in many of its former alliance or neighbour countries, including Finland, which became the member of European Union in 1995. Second, Finland faced a deep depression in the early 1990s partly because of the collapse of the trade with the former Soviet Union and because of the poorly designed financial regulation. This crisis also crippled the largest central sports organisation in Finland, which led to major reform of the Finnish sport system. Third, in many Western countries, the development in elite sports were influenced by the professionalisation process and implemented through strong coordination, relying on expertise and centralised development of coaching, and strategic choice of sports, but Finland chose the opposite strategy of independent organisations and decentralisation. Consequently, the emphasis on public sport policies changed from sport to physical activity (Green and Collins 2008).

In twenty-first-century Finland, almost all the features noted above that have been essential to the development of sports have faded or changed their form. The protestant ethic is still a distinctive feature of Finland's culture but its influence has declined in the face of an increasingly pluralistic and secular society. Moreover, national independence and national defence are no longer the major issues they were 100 years ago. Finland's challenging natural conditions are still demanding, but thanks to new technologies and high standards of living, modern urbanised people do not encounter environmental challenges to the same degree. Not even the Finnish *sisu* is called for as often as in the old days. The appreciation of physical work and diligence is not as high among the population, which lives in an increasingly digital and less physical-labour-oriented era. And, similarly to many other nations, physical activity has also decreased significantly.

Finnish success in Summer Olympics: past and present

Before 1912, Finland had already participated in the Summer Olympics twice (1906 Athens; 1908 London) and achieved its first medals (a total of nine medals). The 1912 Olympic Games in Stockholm can, however, be considered a significant event for Finnish elite sports and for the development of Finland's national identity. At that time, Finland was still an autonomous Grand Duchy of Russia and participated in the games as part of the Russian team. In the opening ceremony, the Finns hung back from the main Russian team and marched behind with their own national 'sign'. In the actual games, Finland stormed the medal table. The comparatively small team won a total of 26 medals, which was a staggering share (8.2%) of the medals at that time. Finland was fourth in the medal table after Sweden, the United States and Great Britain (Sjöblom 2012, p. 17).

The most prominent individual athlete in the Stockholm Olympics was long-distance runner Hannes Kolehmainen, who won three gold and one silver medal. His achievements inspired the Finnish history writers to state that 'Finland was run on the world map' (Kaila 1926, p. 5). However, the reality is that media coverage of sports was not very comprehensive at that time, and Kolehmainen did not significantly increase the world's awareness of Finland around the world. The message was, however, more important for Finns (Viita 2003). A poor, isolated nation realised that they could succeed in international competitions. It could actually be argued that Finland was run into Finnish people's minds. After Kolehmainen, several long-distance runners (e.g. Iso-Hollo, Höckert, Lehtinen, Nurmi, Ritola, Salminen, Stenroos) popularly referred to as the 'Flying Finns' added weight to the statement. Finland's national identity was increasingly built through sports, and considering the time, this was an important factor.

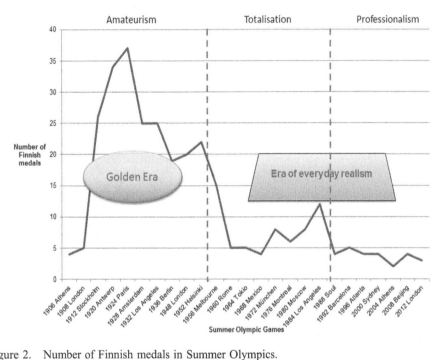

Figure 2.   Number of Finnish medals in Summer Olympics.

Long-distance runners soon became the torchbearers for Finland's national identity. There is one particular name that should be mentioned in this context: one of the most successful athletes in the Olympics history, Paavo Nurmi, who won a total of 12 Olympic medals, nine of them gold, between 1920 and 1928.

In proportion to the population, Finland's 458 Olympic medals suggest the nation ranks very high with respect to international comparisons (Medals per capita 2013). In the Summer Olympics list, Finland is ranked first in terms of medals per capita and, in the list which covers both Summer and Winter Olympics, ranks second, just behind Norway. Most Finnish success has been achieved in track and field events, having won a total of 115 medals, of which 57 were in long-distance running. Finnish performance has also been good in wrestling (83 medals) and cross-country skiing (73 medals). These three sports account for 53% of the total number of Finland's Olympic medals.

Figure 2 shows how Finland's medal score in the Summer Olympics has developed since 1906. The diagram can be summarised with respect to two periods. From the early twentieth century to Finland's own Olympic Games in Helsinki in 1952, the medal tally was impressive and this period could be described as the golden era of Finnish Olympic sports. The period that followed could be called the era of everyday realism. This refers to the fact that participants of the other countries started not only to participate in the games more actively but also to take the business more seriously. Myths that were created during the golden era about the extraordinary athletic capabilities of the Finns, were seen in a new light. What kind of factors explains such a clear change from one period to the other?

One obvious explanation for Finland's declining success in the Olympic Games is greater international competition. By this, we do not only refer to the totalisation and increased seriousness of competition but also to the simple fact that the number of countries and thereby the number of athletes competing in the Olympic Games has

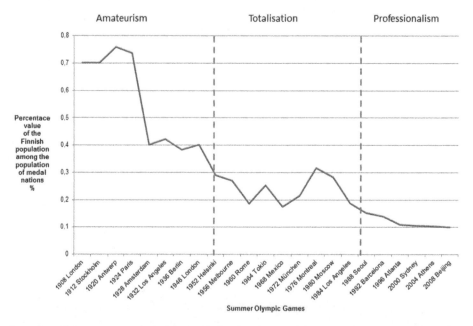

Figure 3.   The percentage of Finnish population in relation to the population of the medal nations in Summer Olympics.

increased significantly during the past 100 years. Based on the population coefficients of the countries that won medals in the 2008 Beijing Olympics, for example, it was seven times more difficult to win an Olympic medal in the first decade of the twenty-first century than it had been at the beginning of the twentieth century (Figure 3).

Figure 4 illustrates, using an index, the relative success of Finland in the Summer Olympics. The index is computed using a formula where the number of Finnish medals is

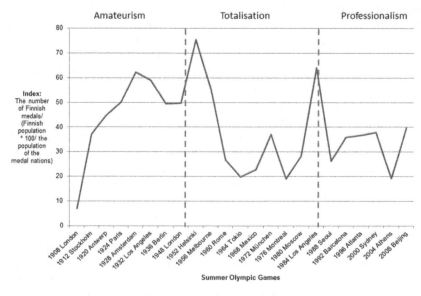

Figure 4.   Index: Finnish medals in Summer Olympics based on the proportional comparison of the Finnish population with the population of the medal winning nations.

112

proportioned to the amount of Finnish population as a part of the population size of all the medal nations.[2] This observation suggests that the fall in the success rate during the years is not as dramatic as in a comparison based on the mere number of medals. The difference between the two eras is, however, clear. This is true, especially if the high spike of Los Angeles 1984 is not counted. Finnish chances to win medals in those games were better because of the Soviet-led boycott. Seven Finnish medals out of total 12 were secured in sports where the absent countries usually had several medal candidates (wrestling, weightlifting, hammer throw, boxing).

It is completely understandable that in terms of sheer mathematics a small country has greater difficulties in maintaining continuous success in international elite sport. Notably, Finland's relative position in the global sports arena is not only weakened because of the growing number of competitors but also because of changing demographics. Put simply, given its population structure, Finland is one of the most rapidly aging nations in Europe (Giannakouris 2008). As the number of young people has declined, the number of potential candidates for a career in sports has also decreased or is decreasing. Adding to the challenge is the fact that Finland has not made strategic choices to invest in a few targeted sports, like other countries, including New Zealand, have done (Keat and Sam 2013, p. 48). Finland has continued to 'let all flowers bloom', which means that the number of sports has increased and the number of athletes per sport has decreased.

As the proportional number of potential medal candidates per Olympic Games is low, an emerging problem for successful small sport nations is that the pressure on an individual athlete to win medals may be unreasonably high. The situation may be worse for young athletes who are forced into high-level competition before they are ready. This often results in failure and public criticism, often destroying a promising sports career.

Changes in the appreciation and cultural status of sports in Finland

In Finland, sport has played an important role in building national identity and strengthening patriotism. However, since World War II, the significance of patriotism has weakened and values associated with individualism have gained ground. According to Suhonen's (2007) surveys, priorities such as good personal relationships and health have increased their importance in people's list of the most important values since the 1980s, whereas issues such as Finnish independence have become less important. The national project has also lost its significance in the European unification process. From the perspective of patriotism, the role of sports has also weakened in Finland. In a survey carried out in the early 1990s, the changing status and role of elite sports in society could be seen clearly (EVA 2003). On the one hand, the earlier stronger role of elite sports as the building material of Finnish identity was recognised, but at the same time the significance of elite sports was likely to weaken in the future.

According to Jokisipilä (2010), the weakening connection between success in sports and Finnish identity can also be seen as a signal of Finland's national identity having reached maturity reflecting a new set of social values and priorities. This phenomenon is in contrast to what has happened in the last 20 years, especially in many Anglo-Saxon countries, where the elite sport is still seen as a major source of national identity and governments prioritise elite sport in their policies (Green 2004, Green and Collins 2008, Grix and Carmichael 2012).

One explanation for the change in Finland's success rate in the Olympic Games is a general change in the sports culture of Finland. After the idealistic era of amateurism, the proportional significance of elite and competitive sports in the field of physical activities weakened considerably by the 1980s. The Finnish government had come to view sport and physical activities from a much broader perspective (Koski 1999). In particular, physical activity became a core concept in the Finnish sports policy and education, and at the same time the whole sector was increasingly characterised by greater diversification (Heinilä 1987, Heikkala and Koski 1999).

As previously noted, Finland's success in the Olympic Games had been largely achieved through individual sports, such as long-distance running, wrestling and cross-country skiing, but over time young people within an increasingly urbanised Finland were attracted to team sports. One of the trends, which Zacheus (2008) noted when analysing physical activity across generations of Finns, was that the popularity of and interest in team sports increased. This was true not only in terms of individual participation but also with respect to spectator sports. The change in the status of track and field and skiing can be seen clearly if we compare the levels of interest among people born in different decades (Koski 1998, Zacheus 2008). The older the age group, the more likely they hold an interest in those traditional individual sports. Correspondingly, the younger the age group, the higher the level of interest in ice-hockey and motor sports. From the perspective of Finnish Olympic success, this shift means fewer potential medals because many of the most talented young people select team sports where the number of available medals is smaller than in individual sports.

Even if the success rates in the latest Summer Olympics may show otherwise, Finland remains a relatively strong sports nation. This claim is supported by the fact that Finns managed to win around 200 world or European championship medals every year during the period 2005–2011. The number of adult world championship medals has been around 100 and the average number of champions is 30 per year (2000–2011). A closer analysis of the sports in which Finland has been successful shows that Finns have done well in nature- or motor-related sports. Finns have gained success in various forms of orienteering (in total 45 world championship (WC) medals in foot orienteering, 39 WC medals in ski orienteering and 38 WC medals in MTB orienteering, 2000–2011) and in car sports (41 WC medals between 2000 and 2011) or motorcycle sports (91 WC medals in 2000–2011) (Huippuurheilun faktapankki 2013). The physical environment in Finland offers an ideal training ground for these sports and Finland's cultural affinity with nature and technology also explains the success.

It is important to note, however, that many of the world championship sports that Finland now succeeds in, such as boot throwing or Finnish skittles, are not very popular internationally. Nevertheless, they are counted in the previous statistics because their national association is a member of the Finnish Sport Federation. In addition, Finns have developed other sports within a sort of carnival spirit and organised related world championship events. Some examples of these are swamp soccer, lake floorball, wife carrying, mosquito killing and mobile phone throwing. It is worth mentioning that these championships are not included in the above figures.

Prior to the 1980s, Finnish culture was characterised by a high degree of uniformity with respect to cultural values. During this era, Finland viewed itself as a homogenous society, reinforced by the national media, which featured successful athletes as national heroes suitable as idols for people and especially for youth. Hence, athletes were role models and sports played an educational role in Finland (Heinilä 2010). However, since the beginning of this millennium, the nature of sports heroes has changed considerably. An increasingly diversified culture and media have made successful athletes into celebrities comparable to other Finnish celebrities, rather role models based on their sporting achievements and character (e.g. ski jumpers Matti Nykänen and Harri Olli and boxer/

professional wrestler Toni Halme,). Instead of highly esteemed ideal citizens, athletes have increasingly become spokespeople for corporate sponsors and exploited for commercial gain. In the golden years of Finnish sports, sport served as a vehicle through which athletes could improve their social class and standing. The gentrification of the population and improved national educational achievement, however, has reduced the importance of this channel in part because Finland has become a highly education-oriented country (e.g. Rouhelo 2008). In such a society, unless a person is exceptionally talented, a career in sports is not a very sensible choice if it has to be achieved at the expense of education. In the past, one could easily find work after one's sports career, as there was plenty of unskilled work available. Moreover, there was no big social stigma connected with lack of education in a country where the work of most people did not require long formal education. Today, the competence requirements in the world of work are higher, and a career in sport often seems a risky investment owing to, amongst other things, its brevity. Within Finland's contemporary education-oriented society, young people have to compete for both study places and jobs. The continuous competition in everyday life may make a career and even a hobby within sports competition look less attractive than in the past (Salasuo and Koski 2010). In addition, because of the small marketplace of professional sport in Finland, the profession of coach is also a risky choice and hence their numbers are rather low.

One aspect that has significantly affected the cultural status of sports is that the public image of sport has weakened. Sport used to be regarded as an excellent environment for young people to grow both as athletes and as ideal citizens. However, the myth of sports as a panacea for society has slowly faded (Itkonen 1996). Over the past few years, there has been a steady stream of examples of the negative side of sports that has led to increased scrutiny of the public image of Finnish sports. For example, considering the issue of doping, the cases that have attracted the most publicity are those of Martti Vainio in the 1984 Olympics and the 2001 doping scandal in the world championships in skiing in Lahti, Finland, where several Finnish skiers were caught red-handed (e.g. Leino 1984, Vettenniemi 2010). The doping cases in skiing have caused several long legal processes and human tragedies, one of the saddest being the death of Mika Myllylä, three-time Olympic medallist and four-time world champion (SR/Olympic sports 2013). There have also been match fixing cases in football and Finnish baseball connected with betting (e.g. Paloaro 2001, Szerovay and Vehmas 2012). Some sports personalities have also been enticing targets for the media but their bad behaviour and ensuing publicity have undermined the public image of athletes as ideal citizens and role models. Maybe the best example of this is Matti Nykänen, the ski jumper who has won a total of 19 championship medals. During the past 20 years, he has been in the public eye for his prison sentences, alcohol abuse, relationship problems and violent behaviour (Heiskanen 2013). In a small country, where sports have been one of the most transparent parts of national identity, these kinds of events have tarnished both Finland's reputation and the social value of sports. As Tervo (2003) argues: 'There is no longer a clear consensus on the meaning of sports as the interpreter of the Finns' feelings of nationality.'

According to international research observations, Finnish pride for the country's achievements in sports is no longer on the same level as in Ireland, New Zealand or Sweden (Ministry of Education and Culture 2010, p. 27). The value and appreciation of sports have declined in Finland, and at the same time, the previous success rate has become a kind of burden. Quite often, the relative added difficulty to achieve success in sports today is not taken into account when public expectations and official government and sport organisation are set often based on the triumphs of the past decades. Owing to the demands caused by the development of professional sports, elite sport in Finland has also – consciously or unconsciously – distanced itself from the grassroots level and the educational role to which it was once dedicated (Koski 2009). This is unlikely to increase the appreciation of elite sport among the people who work at the grassroots level. This is particularly important within the Finnish sport system, which is heavily dependent upon voluntarism.

Sport policy reactions

In the 1920s, after Finland's declaration of independence, the first structures of public sport administration were created. Sport was included within the scope of the Ministry of Education (Vasara 2004, p. 10–53). Overall, the gap between the State and civil activities in sports has not been very wide: they have both wanted to reinforce the nation and national identity (Hentilä 1992, p. 133). Juppi (1996) characterises Finnish governmental sport policy in the first decades as supervising and patronising. However, following this period, the state loosened its grip. Juppi suggests that the role of the government transformed from 'the stern father' to 'the kind godfather'. This was partly due to the introduction of a government betting company in 1940, the profits from which were given to the State to distribute to a range of social programs including sport and physical activities.

One essential historical issue that guided Finnish sport policy until the 1990s is related to the fact that the nation was divided into two camps after the Civil War in 1918. The influence of this separation was seen in sports as well. The organisation of sports into one national movement, for instance, did not succeed; rather sport was divided into *language*- and *class*-based camps (Heinilä 1987, 1989). Several competing sports movements (bourgeois, working-class and Swedish-speaking people's sport movements), however, brought some consistency to Finnish sports attracting large masses of people. On the other hand, sport also became highly politicised and a part of political struggle. In Finland, the purpose of the amateur sport was not only to train better athletes but also it was given a national educational task of making young people into honest and respectable citizens (Koski 2007). Each sport movement had their own particular emphases in this work. This instrumental value assigned to sports led to a close relationship between society and sports in line with the corporate model.

The significance of physical activity became an important issue during the structural change in the Finnish economy in the 1960s. As people moved from rural to urban areas and their work became mechanical industrial or office work, they needed physically active leisure-time physical activity to counterbalance the lack of physical labour. The hegemony of competitive sport started to weaken in the 1970s and consequently physical culture in Finland found a new model (Vasara 1992, p. 369). In 1967 the concept of *Liikunta* was defined for official state administration, research and policy and refers to movement, motion and physical activity. *Liikuntakulttuuri* (sport culture) was seen to constitute four equal parts: sport for all, physical education, competitive sport and top-level sport (Koski 1999). According to this idea the government adopted a broader perspective with respect to physical activities and at the same time the belief in planning in public administration strengthened. Sport for all, international sporting activities and, in part, the sport sciences were increasingly under greater state control including monitoring and evaluation. In Finnish terms 'the stern father' raised his head up using the magic word of planning (Juppi 1996, Koski 1999). The Sports Act, enacted in 1979, consolidated the distribution of tasks that had long been applied: the task of the public sector was to create the necessary preconditions for sporting activities, and sports clubs are responsible for organising the actual activities (Liikuntalaki 1979). Economically government sports policy was based on the profit of the state betting company and, in particular, the profitable 'Lottery' that was introduced in 1970.

During the 1980s, along with the boom in consumerism, the government sports policy was liberalised and pluralised. From the perspective of Finnish national sport organisations, the 1970s was, according to Koski and Heikkala (1998), still a decade of amateurism with the subsequent 1980s referred to is named as the decade of institutionalisation. During this era financial resources as well as the number of personnel and various forms of activities of sports federations grew strongly and the initial phases of managerialism, such as marketing and other models from the business world, were implemented. Ultimately state and organisational actions were more systematised. Moreover, the public expectations for sport organisations increased and diversified, which meant that the associations could not concentrate solely on elite sport (Koski and Heikkala 1998, Heikkala and Koski 1999).

The concrete manifestation of the previously noted processes was the introduction of the so-called *results-based system* by the government in the early 1990s. According to the criteria for public support, the share of funding for elite sport was defined as one quarter. For sport for all was defined one quarter whereas the rest 50% was defined for youth sport. The new system underlined the process of differentiation in the national sports organisations (Koski and Heikkala 1998). The deep economic recession of the early 1990s meant that not only the public resources but also those of elite sport were threatened. At the same time, the old hierarchical structures of Finnish sport were renewed by a new network of service organisations. The new core organisation, the Finnish Sport Federation, was not to occupy a position at the top of the hierarchy but rather to be located at the centre of a network. In addition the main domains of sports culture were redefined and new organisations to support them created.

The key domains were youth sports (youth and children), adult sports, elite sport and adapted physical activities. A key development of the new organisation was that it changed the previous power relationships (Koski 2012). All the organisations in the new system were independent and there was enormous need for cooperation. Retrospectively it is easy to argue that the new structure and new strategies were not ideal for elite sport, especially because the Finnish Olympic Committee did not accept its new roles and responsibilities as a domain organisation.

The reforms implemented in Finland were unique when compared to international trends. Moreover, the principles of results-based management and the idea of domain organisations were also applied to civic activities (Koski and Heikkala 1998, Heikkala 1998). In many other countries, the change processes in sports emphasised coordination between the various actors, a concentration of power, and the creation of a uniform elite sports culture (Green and Oakley 2001). In Finland, changes moved in the opposite direction. Elite sports lost their status at the top of the sports hierarchy and they were unable to maintain the traditional ties between the various actors. Instead, the new independent actors, led by national sport federations, designed and developed elite sport on the basis of their own interests. Instead of membership-based relationships, the various actors created customer relationships characterised by short-sightedness and competition. The eventual shift to programme and project activities disintegrated the field further.

A central feature of the 1990s reform was a gradual transfer of power from the sports organisations to the government (Heikkala 1998). Houlihan (2009) describes this process, governmentalisation, as one of major trends in elite sport. In Finland, this process took a different form than in, e.g. United Kingdom, where the state created arm's length organisation of elite sport (UK sport).

In the past, the representatives of the Finnish national sport federations had a significant voice in the distribution of the government's sport subsidies, and on the local level, the representatives of sports clubs had participated in municipal decision-making. In the operational model adopted in 1995, the government took over the sports subsidy policy. Before the change, the resources had been allocated from the government to the national sport federations and from there to the sport-specific and regional organisations and to the local sports clubs. After the change, the government distributed the subsidies directly to about 130 national and regional sports organisations. This introduced a totally new kind of direct government-level lobbying (State sport council 1993, Ministry of Education 1996).

The Finnish elite sports organisations and actors did not fully understand the significance of the changes in the 1990s. Immediately after the change, the Finnish Olympic Committee, the government and all the central actors launched a comprehensive strategic review of elite sport. In this strategy and in the subsequent three other national elite sports strategies, the following challenges were recognised in the development of Finnish elite sports: lack of cooperation, coordination and shared practices, as well as unclear division of responsibilities (Huippu-urheilun tehostamisryhmä 1994, Huippu-urheilu 2000-luvulle 1998, Huippu-urheilu 2000-luvulla 2002, Ministry of Education 2004). According to the fifth strategy working group, which completed its work in 2010, the problem in the previous strategies had been the lack of a comprehensive vision as well as overlapping and uncoordinated development work (Ministry of Education and Culture 2010, p. 34).

Based on the proposals of the strategy working group, the Finnish Olympic Committee launched a two-and-a-half-year project to change the structure of elite sport. Five highly merited sport experts were selected to implement the project. The Ministry of Education and Culture funded the project with almost three million euros. The change process, called the 'athlete's path', was given the role of a reference framework on which all the measures to develop Finnish elite sports should be based. The result of the change process was that the role of the Finnish Olympic Committee was strengthened significantly as a development centre. In the future, the Olympic Committee will bear responsibility for success in elite sport together and, together with national sport federations, it will develop the knowledge capital of Finnish sports. Knowledge capital will be developed by means of the network led by KIHU Research institute for Olympic Sports, and it will support the early part of an athlete's path through 19 regional sports academies (Finnish Olympic Committee 2012). However, while Finland is building a more coordinated elite sport model, it is doing so much later than many of its main competitors.

Conclusions

This article described the long-term development of elite sport in one small country, Finland. The country was one of the early adopters of Olympic sport at the beginning of the twentieth century. The genesis and development of the Olympic Games was timely for a nation that taking its first steps towards independence and seeking to develop and express nationalism. Finnish athletes were amongst the first to take international sport seriously. The new field of sport offered an ideal platform for the development of cultural values and the formation of national identity. Early on, the ideals of amateurism offered an opportunity for a small country to be successful because its strong ideological influence challenged the domination of totalitarian sport systems and countries with large population.

Similar to other Nordic countries, sport was organised in Finland as a civic movement where the voluntary work was and still is the backbone of the system. Voluntary sports clubs play an important role among the local associations which had and have a role in building and confirming democratic civil society. When elite sport turned to the phase of totalisation, the limits of the voluntary system began to appear. However, the Finnish sport system, together with the state, adopted new resources and models of the more efficient elite sport systems from the East and West enabling it to achieve some success. The challenge has been much bigger during the period of open professionalism since 1990s. During the period of professionalism, several sport clubs have opted out of the target-oriented elite sport (Koski 2009). This has happened mostly because of limited resources. In a country with a small population the demographic and financial resources as well as the coaching expertise are insufficient for competing in a wide range of sports. In addition, being linked to the process of globalisation, professional sport often requires athletes to be mobile, forcing them to move away from their home country. At the same time, there appears to be a decline in the national appreciation of elite sport compared to Finland's golden sporting era.

Furthermore, other countries adopted strategies for the development of elite sport much earlier than Finland. In Finland, probably because of the deeply rooted ideal of equality and emphasis on pluralism, the focus on targeted sports has not even been a consideration. Thus, it is no surprise that this policy is reflected in success ratings as measured by Olympic medals. For example, although it is well-known as a traditional winter sports country, Finland only won five medals in Sochi 2014 whereas the Netherlands, for instance, won 24 medals just in speed skating.

In sum, the status of elite sport in Finland has, historically, largely been dependent on particular cultural affinities and their changes. For example, within the domain of physical activities, the relationship between the two main philosophies of 'mens sana corpore in sano' and 'citius, altius, fortius' or, stated another way, between the perspective of sport for all and elite sport, has been an enduring dilemma in Finnish sport policy. The result is that those who advocate for mass participation argue that investment trickles 'up' leading to success at the elite level whereas those who lobby to prioritise investment in elite sport argue that success at the international level will trickle down and that without a targeted funding policy elite sport will suffer. In many other countries, elite sport has at least a rhetorical role as the engine of the sport system, resulting in some policies directed at targeted sport investment.

Finland offers, and will continue to serve as, an interesting test laboratory for studying elite sports and national sports culture now and in the future. Finland's system is clearly different from the sports movement-based model of the other Nordic countries, but is also distinct from sport policy in Anglo-Saxon countries.

Although we consider Finland a special case, we must acknowledge that there are likely to be similarities in terms of the challenges and strategies adopted by other small nations although the nature of the challenges and responses will vary for a wide range of reasons including: history, geographic location and population demographics. No doubt sport can be a tool for nationalism and for binding the nation, especially during the first stages of independence (e.g. the former parts of Yugoslavia). For example, elite sport can play an important role and serve as a model for wider society, particularly during the early stages when the slower developing structures of society such as the economy are not ready for such a role.

While it is difficult to prove empirically, there remains a sense that in small nations, the influence of elite sports is relatively stronger than in big countries. In part this can be linked to the fact that success or failure in small countries often resonates with a larger proportion of the population. Small countries are more sensitive to fluctuations and to the consequences of certain individual cases as well. In the other words, issues such as economic fluctuations, changes in demographics, single cases of doping or other negative by-products, for instance, would probably have a greater impact on the status and well-being of elite sport in a small country than in the big ones. On the other hand, in a small country, one or two championships or Olympic medals could be enough for some years.

We assert that the totalisation and professionalisation of elite sports have weakened the possibilities of small nations to keep up with international competition. And as a result the global sporting arms race is much more suited to Goliath nations. The implications of investment in elite sport, and its potential social outcomes, have been discussed within many small nations (e.g. Dóczi 2011, Elling et al. 2012). A key emerging question is: are there any limits? If the Olympics continue to grow, will this result in some nations opting out and/or seeking alternative or additional regional competitions? Success is a relative question and continual success in international sport events is dependent upon media and sponsors. In future it may be that a greater number of more specialised events that ensure greater equality of competition will appeal to the key stakeholders.

Disclosure statement

No potential conflict of interest was reported by the authors.

Notes

1. In this article, Finland is defined as a small country on the basis of its population. Geographically (338,400 km^2), Finland is the seventh largest country in Europe, but the number of inhabitants (5.4 million) makes Finland the most scarcely populated country in Europe (16 inhabitants/km^2).
2. The number of Finnish medals in Summer Olympics/(n = Finnish population/n = the population size of all the medal nations).

References

Allison, L., 2001. *Amateurism in sport. an analysis and a defense.* London: Frank Cass.
Arponen, A.O., 1981. *Suomen urheilu SVUL 1900–1980* [Finnish sport SVUL 1900–1980]. Hanko: Hangon Kirjapaino.
Bale, J., 1991. *The brawn drain: foreign student-athletes in American universities.* Urbana: University of Illinois Press.
Böhlke, N. and Robinson, L., 2009. Benchmarking of élite sport systems. *Management decision*, 47, 67–84. doi:10.1108/00251740910929704
De Bosscher, V., et al., 2008. *The global sporting arms race. An international comparative study on sports policy factors leading to international sporting success.* Oxford: Meyer & Meyer Sport.
De Bosscher, V., et al., 2009. Explaining international sporting success: an international comparison of elite sport systems and policies in six countries. *Sport management review*, 12, 113–136. doi:10.1016/j.smr.2009.01.001
De Bosscher, V., et al., 2006. A conceptual framework for analysing sports policy factors leading to international sporting success. *European sport management quarterly*, 6, 185–215. doi:10.1080/16184740600955087
Dóczi, T., 2011. Gold fever (?): sport and national identity – the Hungarian case. *International review for the sociology of sport*, 47, 165–182. doi:10.1177/1012690210393828

Elling, A., Van Hilvoorde, I., and Van Den Dool, R., 2012. Creating or awakening national pride through sporting success: a longitudinal study on macro effects in the Netherlands. *International review for the sociology of sport*, 49, 129–151. doi:10.1177/1012690212455961

EVA, 2003. Mitä mieltä suomalainen? EVAn asenne tutkimuksien kertomaa vuosilta 1984–2003 [What's your opinion Finn? Summary of the EVA public opinion surveys 1984–2003]. EVA. Available from: http://www.eva.fi/wp-content/uploads/2010/06/Mita_mielta_suomalainen.pdf [Accessed 12 Dec 2013].

Finnish Olympic Committee, 2012. *Huippu-urheilun muutosryhmän loppuraportti 2012* [The final report of the elite sport reform group] [online]. Helsinki: Suomen Olympiakomitea. Available from: http://eklu-fi-bin.directo.fi/@Bin/1a0ed56c8293eb3585392e92a00b48f6/1396610154/application/pdf/308272/HuMu_loppuraportti.pdf [Accessed 12 Dec 2013].

Giannakouris, K., 2008. *Population and social conditions*. Eurostat, European Commission. Available from: http://epp.eurostat.ec.europa.eu/cache/ITY_OFFPUB/KS-SF-08-072/EN/KS-SF-08-072-EN.PDF [Accessed 10 Jan 2011].

Green, M., 2004. Changing policy priorities for sport in England: the emergence of elite sport development as a key policy concern. *Leisure studies*, 23, 365–385. doi:10.1080/0261436042000231646

Green, M. and Collins, S., 2008. Policy, politics and path dependency: sport development in Australia and Finland. *Sport management review*, 11, 225–251. doi:10.1016/S1441-3523(08)70111-6

Green, M. and Houlihan, B., eds., 2008. *Comparative elite sport development: systems, structures and public policy*. Oxford: Butterworth-Heinemann.

Green, M. and Oakley, B., 2001. Elite sport development systems and playing to win: uniformity and diversity in international approaches. *Leisure studies*, 20, 247–267. doi:10.1080/02614360110103598

Grix, J. and Carmichael, F., 2012. Why do governments invest in elite sport? A polemic. *International journal of sport policy and politics*, 4, 73–90. doi:10.1080/19406940.2011.627358

Halila, A. and Sirmeikkö, P., 1960. *Suomen Voimistelu- ja Urheiluliitto SVUL 1900–1960* [Finnish gymnastics and sport federation SVUL 1900–1960]. Vammala: Suomen Voimistelu- ja Urheiluliitto.

Heikkala, J., 1998. *Ajolähtö turvattomiin kotipesiin* [Finnish sports federations and associations in transition]. Acta Universitatis Tamperensis 641. Tampere: Tampereen yliopisto.

Heikkala, J. and Koski, P., 1999. *Reaching out for new frontiers*. Jyväskylä: University of Jyväskylä.

Heikkinen, A., 1977. *Ammattilaisesta amatööriksi; Suomen hiihtourheilun ensivaihe* [From professional to amateur; the First steps of skiing as sport in Finland]. Oulu: Pohjoinen.

Heinilä, K., 1984. Totalization process in international sport. *In*: M. Ilmarinen, ed. *Sport and international understanding. Proceedings of the congress held in Helsinki, July 7–10, 1982*. Berlin: Springer-Verlag, 20–30.

Heinilä, K., 1987. Social research on sports in Finland. *International review for the sociology of sport*, 22, 3–24. doi:10.1177/101269028702200102

Heinilä, K., 1989. The sports club as a social organization in Finland. *International review for the sociology of sport*, 24, 225–248. doi:10.1177/101269028902400304

Heinilä, K., 2004. *Centennial international sport in critical focus*. Jyväskylä: Minerva.

Heinilä, K., 2010. *Liikunta- ja urheilukulttuurimme. Eilen – tänään – huomenna* [Finnish sports culture. Yesterday – today – tomorrow]. Helsinki: Kalevi Heinilä.

Heiskanen, B., ed., 2013. *Mitä Matti tarkoittaa?* [What does matti mean?] Turku: Savukeidas.

Hentilä, S., 1992. Urheilu järjestäytyy ja politisoituu [Organisation and politization of Sport]. *In*: T. Pyykkönen, ed. *Suomi uskoi urheiluun: Suomen urheilun ja liikunnan historia* Liikuntatieteellisen Seuran julkaisu nro 131. Helsinki: VAPK -kustannus, 133–153.

Houlihan, B., 2009. Mechanisms of international influence on domestic elite sport policy. *International journal of sport policy and politics*, 1, 51–69. doi:10.1080/19406940902739090

Houlihan, B. and Green, M., eds., 2008. *Comparative elite sport development: systems, structures and public policy*. Oxford: Butterworth-Heinemann.

Huippu-urheilun teostamisryhmä, 1994. Huippu-urheilu 2000. *Strategia huippu-urheilun kehittämiseksi* [Elite sport 2000. Elite sport development strategy]. Helsinki; Huippu-urheilun tehostamisryhmä: Opetusministeriö, Suomen Olympiakomitea and Suomen Liikunta ja Urheilu.

Huippu-urheilu 2000-luvulla, 2002. *Strategia suomalaisen huippu-urheilun kehittämiseksi 2002–2006* [Elite sport in the first decade of the 21st century]. Helsinki: Suomen Olympiayhdistys.

Huippu-urheilu 2000-luvulle, 1998. *Strategia huippu-urheilun kehittämiseksi* [Elite sport to the 21st century]. Helsinki: Suomen Olympiakomitea, Opetusministeriö and Suomen Liikunta ja Urheilu.

Huippu-urheilun faktapankki, 2013. Jyväskylä: KIHU. Available from: www.kihu.jyu.fi/fakta pankki/faktaalueet/tulostus.php?id=228&otsikko=Menestys [Accessed 10 November 2013].

Itkonen, H., 1996. *Kenttien kutsu. Tutkimus liikuntakulttuurin muutoksesta*[The call of fields. The study about the change of sport culture]. Tampere: Gaudeamus.

Jokisipilä, M., 2010. Huippu-urheilu hakoteillä [Elite sport way off beam]. *Kanava*, 7, 36–39.

Juppi, J., 1996. Ankara isä vai kiltti kummisetä [Stern father or kind godfather]. *Liikunta & Tiede*, 33, 8–10.

Kaila, T.T., 1926. *Hannes Kolehmainen. Suomalaisen suurjuoksijan elämä ja saavutukset* [Hannes Kolehmainen: the life and achievements of the great Finnish runner]. Porvoo: WSOY.

Keat, R.A. and Sam, M.P., 2013. Regional implementation of New Zealand sport policy: new instrument, new challenges. *International journal of sport policy and politics*, 5, 39–54. doi:10.1080/19406940.2012.656684

Koski, P., 1998. Hiipuuko hiihto, uupuuko yleisurheilu? Penkkiurheilu ei ole perinnelaji [Is cross country skiing and track and field fading out? Spectator sport breaks with tradition]. *Liikunta & Tiede*, 35, 4–7.

Koski, P., 1999. Characteristics and contemporary trends of sports clubs in Finnish context. *In*: K. Heinemann, ed. *Sport clubs in various European countries* Series Club of Cologne. Vol. 1. The Club of Cologne. Stuttgart: Hofmann Verlag, 293–316.

Koski, P., 2007. Liikunnan ja urheilun seuratoiminta nuorisotyönä [Sports club activities as youth work]. *In*: T. Hoikkala and A. Sell, eds. *Nuorisotyötä on tehtävä. Menetelmien perustat, rajat ja mahdollisuudet*. Helsinki: Nuorisotutkimusverkosto, 299–319.

Koski, P., 2009. *Liikunta- ja urheiluseurat muutoksessa* [Sports clubs in change]. Helsinki: SLU.

Koski, P., 2012. Finnish sports club as a mirror of society. *International journal of sport policy and politics*, 4, 257–275. doi:10.1080/19406940.2012.656852

Koski, P. and Heikkala, J., 1998. *Suomalaisten urheiluorganisaatioiden muutos. Lajiliitot professionaalitumisen prosessissa* [National sports organisations and the process of professionalisation]. Department of Social Sciences of Sport, research report no. 63. Jyväskylä: University of Jyväskylä.

Leino, E., 1984. *Martti Vainion tuskien taival: raportti juoksijasta, syyttömistä ja syyllisistä* [Martti Vainio's journey of agony: report on runner, innocents and guilties]. Helsinki: WSOY.

Liikuntalaki, 1979. Sport act [online]. Available from: http://www.finlex.fi/fi/laki/alkup/1979/19790984?search[type]=pika&search[pika]=liikuntalaki%201979 [Accessed 10 Nov 2013].

Medals per capita, 2013 [online]. Available from: www.medalspercapita.com/#medals-per-capita:all-time [Accessed 17 Nov 2013].

Ministry of Education, 2004. Huippu-urheilutyöryhmän muistio [Report of elite sport working group]. Opetusministeriön työryhmämuistioita ja selvityksiä 2004:22.

Ministry of Education, 1996. *Liikuntajärjestöjen avustusjärjestelmä – työryhmä II: nmuistio* [The state support system of sport associations – report of II working group]. Opetusministeriön työryhmien muistioita 44: 1996.

Ministry of Education and Culture, 2010. "Sanoista teoiksi," Huippu-urheilutyöryhmän ajatuksia suomalaisen huippu-urheilun kehittämiseksi ["From words to action," the ideas of elite sport working group towards the development of Finnish elite sport]. Opetusministeriön työryhmämuistioita ja selvityksiä, 2010:13. Helsinki: Opetusministeriö.

Paloaro, M., 2001. *Sopupelien varjot* [The shadows of match fixing]. Tampere: Pilot-kustannus.

Rouhelo, A., 2008. *Akateemiset urapolut. Humanistisen, yhteiskuntatieteellisen ja kasvatustieteellisen alan generalistien urapolkujen alkuvaiheet 1980- ja 1990-luvuilla* [Academic career paths. The early career phases of generalists in the fields of humanities, social science and education in the 1980s and 1990s]. Turun yliopiston julkaisuja, sarja C, osa 277. Turku: University of Turku.

Salasuo, M. and Koski, P., 2010. Miten kilpaurheilu istuu nykynuorten sielunmaisemaan – näkökulmia liikuntasuhdetta vahvistaviin ja heikentäviin tekijöihin [Has elite sport a place in life of the youth of today – perspectives to the supporting and weakening factors of physical activity relationship]. *Liikunta & Tiede*, 47, 4–9.

Seppänen, P., 1981. Olympic success. A crossnational perspective. *In*: G.R.F. Luschen and G.H. Sage, eds. *Handbook of social science of sport*. Champaign, IL: Stipes Publishing, 93–116.

Sjöblom, K., 2012. Autonominen Suomi olympiadiplomatian pyörteissä [Autonomous Finland in the riffles of Olympic diplomacy]. *In*: R. Forsman and V. Tikander, eds. *Tehtävä Tukholmassa. Suomi olympiakisoissa 1912*. Keuruu: Otava, 13–17.

SR/Olympic sports, 2013 [online]. Available from: http://www.sports-reference.com/olympics/ath letes/my/mika-myllyla-1.html [Accessed 3 Apr 2014].

State sport council, 1993. Ehdotus liikuntajärjestöjen valtionavustusten jakoperiaatteiksi uudessa yhteistoimintaorganisaatiossa [Proposal for government subsidies allocation formula of sport associations in a new cooperative organisation]. Valtion liikuntaneuvosto 1991–1995. Järjestömäärärahajaosto. Helsinki.

Suhonen, P., 2007. Suomalaisten eriytyvät ja muuttuvat arvot [Differentiating and changing values of the Finns]. *In*: S. Borg *et al.*, eds. *Uskonto, arvot ja instituutiot. Suomalaiset World Values -tutkimuksissa 1981–2005*. Yhteiskuntatieteellisen tietoarkiston julkaisuja 4. Tampere: FSD Tampereen yliopisto, 26–46.

Szerovay, M. and Vehmas, H., 2012. Sopupelaaminen on jalkapallon globaali ongelma [Match fixing is a global problem in football]. *Liikunta & Tiede*, 49, 18–22, .

Tervo, M., 2003. *Geographies in the making. Reflections on sports, the media, and national identity in Finland*. Volume 32:1. Publications of the Geographical Society of Northern Finland and the Department of Geography. Oulu: University of Oulu.

Vasara, E., 1992. Toiminnan ja ohjauksen kilpajuoksu [Race of operation and direction]. *In*: T. Pyykkönen, ed. *Suomi uskoi urheiluun: suomen urheilun ja liikunnan historia*. Liikuntatieteellisen seuran julkaisu nro 131. Helsinki: VAPK -kustannus, 369–391.

Vasara, E., 2004. *Valtion liikuntahallinnon historia* [The history of state sport administration]. Liikuntatieteellisen Seuran julkaisu nro 157. Helsinki: Liikuntatieteellinen Seura.

Vettenniemi, E., ed., 2010. *Hiihto & häpeä. Lahti 2001 mediaskandaalina* [Crosscountry skiing & shame. Lahti 2001 as a media scandal]. Jyväskylä: Jyväskylän yliopisto.

Viita, O., 2003. *Hymyilevä Hannes. Työläisurheilija Hannes Kolehmaisen sankaruus porvarillisessa Suomessa*. [Smiling Hannes, The heroism of worker-athlete Hannes Kolehmainen in a bourgeois Finland]. Keuruu: Otava.

Wikberg, K., 2005. *Amatör eller professionist. Studier rörande amatörfrågan i svensk tävlingsidrott 1903–1967* [Amateur or professional. Studies about the issue of amateurism in competitive sport in Sweden between 1903–1967]. Stockholm: Sisu idrottsböcker.

Zacheus, T., 2008. *Luonnonmukaisesta arkiliikunnasta liikunnan eriytymiseen. Suomalaiset liikun-tasukupolvet ja liikuntakulttuurin muutos* [From natural everyday exercise to a personalized exercise experience. Finnish physical generations and the changes in physical culture]. Turun yliopiston julkaisuja, sarja C, osa 268 [Publications of the University of Turku, Series C, Volume 268]. Turku: University of Turku.

Sport, policy and politics in Lebanon

Nadim Nassif[a] and Mahfoud Amara[b]

[a]Department of Psychology, Education and Physical Education, Notre Dame University, Zouk Mosbeh, Lebanon; [b]School of Sport, Exercise and Health Sciences, Loughborough University, Loughborough, UK

Lebanon offers an interesting context for the study of sport policy as there is a lack of literature on sport policies in developing countries, and particularly, in small- and multi-confessional societies. Hence, the aim of this study was to illustrate how the dynamic of power between the state and the political parties/confessional communities is reflected in the national sport system. In particular the paper seeks to provide some insight into the mechanism in place to implement the concept of 'balance of power' or so-called mosaic society within the national sport system, looking specifically at structure and resource allocation.

Introduction

The successive foreign powers that occupied the country and the multitude of different religious communities that have coexisted inside Lebanon (Salibi 1993) have not only contributed to the emergence of a modern nation that enjoys very rich cultural and religious diversities, but also founded a republic governed by a fragile balance of power. It was under the umbrella of this inherent legacy of internal tensions, and the almost 'natural' dependency of the Lebanese Government on foreign powers, that the independence of Lebanon was declared in 1943 (Salibi 1965, 1993).

To establish a republic where the main characteristic would be a fair division of powers between the various communities, it was therefore officially decided henceforth that the President of the Republic would be a Christian Maronite, the Prime Minister, a Muslim Sunnite and the Assembly President, a Muslim Shiite. The other smaller communities (Druzes, Christian Orthodox, Christian Catholics, Armenians, etc.) would also have a quota in the government (Bustros 1973). At that time Lebanese politicians thought that this compromise was essential to secure political stability. This explains why Lebanon is a unique country, and it is next to impossible to find, in the whole world, a small place of 10,452 square kilometres, and a population of less than 10 million, embracing 18 different religious communities. However, despite these measures aimed at establishing a balance of power, tension remained between different communities and it had often led to major conflicts, which in turn resulted in an ongoing unsteady political and economic situation.

The tension and competition between different religious communities are also apparent in the sporting domain. Indeed, although there is no official distribution of powers according to religious affiliations inside the national sport system, compromises are, however, informally in place to promote an internal 'peaceful climate' within various sport institutions. These informal arrangements and tacit agreement between different protagonists, allow every community to have influence in the national sport system, although very often this led to situations of mismanagement and division, which in turn have strongly affected the implementation of sport policies in the country.

In terms of structure, we start by providing an account of the political system. In the second part we identify the key features of the national sport system. The final part is devoted to the analysis of political interference in sport particularly in relation to structure and resource allocation.

The Lebanese political system

The multi-confessional political system is the principal trait of Lebanese society. There are 18 different communities in Lebanon that can be clustered under three main groups:

(1) Muslims which constitute 59.7% of the population (Shi'a, Sunni, Druze, Ismaeli, Alaoui);
(2) Christians which represent 39% of the population (Maronites, Orthodox, Melkites, Catholics, Armenian orthodox, Syrian Catholics, Armenian Catholics, Syrian Orthodox, Roman Catholics, Chaldeans, Assyrians, Copts and Protestants); and
(3) other small minorities representing 1.3% of the population.

With this large palette of religious groups on such a small geographical surface, and taking into account the legacy of the civil war from 1975 till 1989, establishing a government that is able to establish and maintain 'harmony' between different communities has become a major issue. In fact, the authors of the constitution, although aware of how difficult it is, have always had the spirit and the will to establish a non-confessional state. Therefore, it was agreed that a secular state (*laïque* according French tradition) separating between religion and political affairs should be gradually established as stated in the 1926 constitution, the 1943 national pact and the *Taef* agreement signed on 22 October 1989 by different protagonists of the civil war and ratified later on by the Lebanese Parliament.

However, the constitution failed to resolve certain ambiguities that have made the principle of 'just equilibrium' between communities hard to accomplish. Indeed, even though the preamble (9th, 10th and 19th paragraphs) clearly indicates that religious beliefs and diversities should not, under any circumstances, interfere with the path that the government is taking; articles 22, 24 and 95 indicate also that equal participation of religious groups in the heart of the state is mandatory to eradicate *confessionalism*. These measures have many times proven to be contradictory, making it hard thus to consolidate consensus and national unity.

After the dismantlement of different militias by the Syrian army in 1990, most armed factions reclaimed themselves as political parties thus turning the Lebanese political system to a mixture of consociationalism and confessionalism (Reiche 2011). This designation was first used to explain how different religious groups in the Netherlands were able, at the beginning of the twentieth century, to overcome their rooted political differences in order to ally themselves and rule together. Consociationalism has, later on, spread and included other political systems like those of Belgium, Canada, Colombia, Lebanon and India.

On the other hand confessionalism is a system of rule where the authority is distributed among different communities, whether ethnic or religious, according to their size. It is used today to describe mainly the unique case of the Lebanese political system.

The 18 religious communities recognized by the constitution have two main functions:

(1) Responsibility over all legal matters related to personal status (like marriage, divorce, children custody and heritage).
(2) Access to political positions attributed to them on a proportional basis, as discussed earlier.

The *Taef* accord came as a reiteration of the 1943 National Pact and introduced changes to (questionably) the benefit of the increasing Muslim population. Muslims and Christians have the same number of seats in the Parliament whereas the National Pact attributed a 6/5 ratio to the Christians. Moreover, the powers of the President were narrowed while giving more powers to the Prime Minister in co-signing the decrees.

Similarly, the Doha accord signed on 23 May 2008 had put an end to the political vacuum which lasted for a year and a half, confirming thus the principle of the *Taef* agreement but also led to the formation of a government of national unity formed by ministerial positions distributed as follows: 16 from the majority, 11 from the opposition and 3 named by the President. The Doha agreement also stipulated that the various parties forming the government should guarantee not to resign or obstruct any actions undertaken by the government.

One can argue however that both the Doha and the *Taef* agreements reinforced the communities' roles as 'states within the state'. The influence of religious communities is to be found today in various sectors in Lebanese society. We can cite, for instance, the media sector, where each community has its own TV and Radio channels:

(1) 'Future TV', supporting the ideology of the Future party, was founded and financed by the former Prime Minister Rafik El-Hariri.
(2) 'Al Manar' channel supported by Hezbollah.
(3) 'NBN TV' supported by Amal party.
(4) 'OTV' takes the side of the Free Patriotic Movement.

Based on the above discussion the questions to be asked are as follows: how does sport mirror the political and communitarian oppositions within Lebanese society? Does sport prolong this ultra-confessional tendency? Can the latter be found in sport institutions and does it affect the sport policy process? To answer these questions two aspects are considered in the subsequent section:

(1) Roles and objectives of various actors in the national sport system
   (a) What roles do they have?
   (b) What relations do they maintain?
(2) The funding of the Lebanese sport system
   (a) Where does the money come from?
   (b) How is it allocated?

To answer these questions, in addition to document analysis, including Parliamentary debates, laws, government reports and newspaper articles, interviews were undertaken by the first author of this paper with personalities from the government, the Parliament and the national sport movement.

National sport system in Lebanon

Having introduced the political system in Lebanon in the first part of this paper, this section focuses on the national sport system, including the policy measures around the organization of sport and roles of various actors. During the first part of the post-war period, that lasted almost a decade (1991–1999), the Lebanese government took no official measure in favour of sport. The advisor to the Ministry of Youth and Sports in the late 1990s, the former Lebanese champion in boxing and member of the Lebanese basketball team, Joseph Sacre, proposed a plan to reform the Lebanese sport system. The structure suggested by Sacre (1990) includes the following departments: the General Directorate of Youth and Sports (under the authority of the Ministry of Education); Lebanese National Olympic Committee, National Sport Federations; University Sport; School Sport; and Sport Associations.

Worth noting, this proposed structure was never established.[1] Actually, no law related to the function of the Lebanese sport system was passed between 1991 and 1999. The period was marked, instead, by the establishment of a series of independent, separate and non-coordinated measures.

In 1993, the higher education sector granted universities the first permits to begin establishing physical education and sport programmes.[2] Later on in 1997, according to decree 10227, physical education and sports was registered as an official school subject in the Lebanese school curriculum.[3] The first drafted law aiming at defining national sport organization was submitted under the decree 247 signed in 2000,[4] which transformed the General Directorate of Youth and Sports into the Ministry of Youth and Sports (MYS). A Sport and Scouting unit was created inside the Ministry of Education in order to develop school sports. The monitoring of the National Olympic Committee (NOC), National Federations and Sports Associations has henceforth become the privilege of the newly established Ministry, whose budget was voted upon and whose actions were supervised by the Youth and Sports Committee in the Lebanese Parliament. The latter was formed at the same time as the Ministry of Youth and Sports, in 2000.

In December 2001, the decree 6997 was ratified by the Lebanese government,[5] which defines the rules of every sport institutions whether the NOC, Sports Federations and Sports Associations, including the relation of these structures with the Ministry of Youth and Sports. With this decree the political institutions no longer have direct authority over the LOC (Lebanese Olympic Committee), which is directly accountable to the International Olympic Committee (IOC). Although, to preserve the national sovereignty, the MYS has the authority to recognize and dissolve national federations, whereas the LOC, despite its autonomy, has the authority to recognize sports that are part of regional Games such as the Pan Arab Games, the Mediterranean Games and the Islamic Solidarity Games, which are not necessarily organized under direct patronage of the IOC.

In 2004, the Youth and Sports Committee in the Parliament voted law 629 that elaborated the regulations governing the internal functioning of the MYS.[6] In 2005, a collaboration programme between the French Embassy and the MYS was signed and two French sports experts, Henri-Pierre Gazzeri and Jean-François Isnard, were nominated in 2005 to study the possibility of creating a coaching diploma (inspired by the French coaching diploma) in Lebanon. On 27 March 2007, the last law to date concerning the

Lebanese sport system was signed. The decree 213 came to replace the decree 6997 signed in 2001.[7] The main difference between the two is in relation to university sport.

University sport

The decree 213 placed the Lebanese Federation of University Sport (LFUS) under the authority of the Ministry of Education. The President of the LFUS, Nasri Lahoud, opposed the decision, on the basis that Article 14046, signed in 1946, stipulated that the LFUS was an independent federation recognized by the Lebanese government. According to George Nader,[8] former basketball player, sports teams' director in Notre Dame University and General Secretary of the LFUS, the Ministry of Education wanted to set the foundations of a 'new' federation for university sports and thus to dismantle the LFUS. Furthermore, in Nader's terms, the Ministry of Education wanted to manipulate university sport without proposing any budget, and hence the decision was definitely based on political motives. It should be mentioned that the LFUS President is the sibling of the President of the Republic, Emile Lahoud (who was still the President in 2007, when the decree 213 was signed), the political rival of the Future party, which controls the Ministry of Education. Thus, the dispute over university sport constituted one of the arenas of conflict between, on the one hand, the Future party, founded by former Prime Minister Rafik El-Hariri who was assassinated on 14 February 2005, and President Emile Lahoud accused of being the 'henchman' of the Syrian regime, the prime suspect in the assassination of Hariri, on the other hand.

School sport

The other problem concerning the decree 213 is in relation to school sport. The MYS as well as the Youth and Sports Committee in the Parliament believe that school sport must be under the MYS, given that it could constitute a pool of talents for national sports federations.[9] Unlike university sport, school sport used to be under the Sports and Scouting Unit (SSU) of the Ministry of Education and Higher Education since the decree 247 was signed in the year 2000. However, with the signature of the decree 213, the MYS and the Youth and Sports Committee in the Parliament hoped to change this by 'annexing' school sports to the MYS. In order to develop school sports, the Ministry of Education signed, on 26 January 2011, the decree 147/3/2011 aiming at 'transforming' the Sports and Scouting Unit of the Ministry of Education into a 'future' Lebanese Federation of School Sports, which is formed and financed by the school sports associations. Hence, schools willing to be part of this federation ought to form sports associations and pay annual enrolment fees. Using this money, the federation would be able to organize inter-schools league competitions. On the contrary, Adnan Hammoud, director of the SSU assumes, according to section 4 of Article 629 of the MYS, that all activities pertaining to school sports must be the privilege of the Ministry of Education. Therefore, this federation must also belong to the Ministry of Education. Politics comes again into play. In Hammoud's point of view, the problem is definitely political: 'the MYS is controlled by the Amal party, while the Ministry of Education belongs to the Future party, and both parties are rivals'.[10]

The first conflict between the two structures took place in July 2010, when the Pan Arab School Games were held in Beirut. The MYS declared that it had to be in charge of the competition. According to Adnan Hammoud, the decree 147/3/2011 is 'the drop that flooded the vase'. He also declares that:

certain people want to *put their hands* on the Lebanese Federation of School Sports because they know that it will become the largest in Lebanon, in terms of the number of affiliated sports associations, and they can, thus, *stuff their pockets* with the great amounts of money that will flow from the participation fees in the federation (emphasis added).

Sport and confessionalism

The over-representation of religious communities in Lebanese sports at the expense of developing a transparent and functional structure is, according to Jihad Salame,[11] candidate for the position of Minister of Youth and Sports for the 2013 legislative elections, strongly present in the national sport movement. All governmental institutions in the country follow, in reality, the same rule. Hence, many people are 'parachuted' into certain positions within certain federations because they represent or are supported by a political party. In consequence, 90% of people working at sports federations are not 'the right people at the right places', according to Salame, but rather the result of 'arrangements under the table' performed by various politicians. Several athletes openly declared recently in the media that the sport sector is the victim of 'bad management' and 'corruption'.[12]

This phenomenon of confessionalism in Lebanese sport was clearly highlighted in the studies of Blanc (2004), Boukhater (2004) and Reiche (2011) as well as Nseir's thesis (2012). Football and Basketball, the most popular sports, are cases in point. As illustrated in Tables 1 and 2 below, football and basketball clubs are strongly affiliated to political and religious parties divided into two main coalitions: the 14th of March and the 8th of March movements. The former whose principal leader is Saad El-Hariri, Sunni, son of the assassinated former Prime Minister Rafik El-Hariri, is a coalition between Future Movement, Sunni party, and the

Table 1. Sport, confessional belonging and political affiliation: example of first division football clubs for the season 2009–2010.

Club's name	Confessional belonging	Political affiliation
'Al-Ahli' Sidon	Sunni Muslim Club	Future Party (March 14)
'Al Ahed' Beirut	Chiite Muslim Club	'Hezbollah' (March 8)
'Al Ansar' Beirut	Sunni Muslim Club	Future Party (March 14)
'Al Islah Bourg Shemaly' Tyr	Chiite Muslim Club	'Amal' Party (March 8)
'Sagesse' Beirut	Christian Maronite Club	Lebanese Forces (March 14)
'Al Mabarra' Beirut	Chiite Muslim Club	(March 8)
'Shabab Al Ghazieh'	Chiite Muslim Club	'Amal' Party (March 8)
'Nejmeh' Beirut	Club previously belonging to the Chiite Muslim community, now belonging to the Sunni Muslim community	Future Party (March 14)
'Racing' Beirut	Christian Orthodox Club	Future Party (March 14)
'Safa Sporting Club' Beirut	Druze Club	Progressive Socialist Party (March 14 at first, later moved to March 8 in January 2011)
'Shabab Al Sahel' Beirut	Chiite Muslim Club	(March 8)
'Tadamon' Tyr	Chiite Muslim Club	(March 8)

Source: Reiche (2011, p. 264).

Table 2.   Sport, confessional belonging and political affiliation: example of first division basketball clubs for the 2009–2010 season.

Club name	Communal belonging	Political affiliation
'Anibal' Zahle	Christian Maronite Club	Free Patriotic Movement (March 8)
'Antranik' Antelias	Christian Armenian Club	'Ramgavar' (March 14)
'Blue Stars' Beirut	Christian Maronite Club	Free Patriotic Movement (March 8)
'Champville' Deek-El-Mehde de	Christian Maronite Club	Free Patriotic Movement (March 8)
'Sagesse' Beirut	Christian Maronite Club	Lebanese Forces (March 14)
'Hoops' Beirut	Chiite Muslim Club	(March 8)
'Kahraba' Zouk	Christian Maronite Club	Lebanese Forces (March 14)
'Al-Moutahed' Tripoli	Sunni Muslim Club	Safadi Foundation (March 14)
'Al-Riyadeh' Beirut	Sunni Muslim Club	Future Party (March 14)
'Sporting Club' Tebnine	Chiite Muslim Club	'Amal' Party (March 8)

Source: Reiche (2011, p. 264).

Lebanese Forces and the Phalanges, which are Christian Maronites parties. They claim to be 'anti-Syrian', 'anti-Iranian', 'pro-Saudi' and 'pro-Western', whereas the latter is mainly composed of 'Hezbollah', 'Amal', Shi'a parties and the Free Patriotic Movement, Christian Maronite. They are accused of being 'pro-Syrian' and 'pro-Iranian' (Reiche 2011).

In 2003, an interview with a coach of squash also revealed that some decision-making positions within certain federations are granted in order to preserve the 'equilibrium' among various communities (Nassif 2010). The coach suggested 'all federations are formed in conformity with this equilibrium. Some belong to Maronite Community while others belong to Sunni community or to Shi'a, etc...'. To illustrate this, Table 3 represents a list of Presidents and general secretaries of 32 Lebanese federations in 2003.

In 2003, among the 32 federations, only four combine Muslims and Christians. That is around 12.5% of the total number of federations. Similar phenomenon can be noticed for 2008 and 2009, as illustrated in Table 4.

Among the 32 federations listed, seven combine Muslims and Christians, a ratio of 21%. Although the percentage of federations combining Muslims and Christians increased after 2003 (from 12.5% to 21%), around 80% of federations are still managed by Presidents and general secretaries from the same community. Nseir (2012) looked at the religious belonging of all the members of Lebanese federations in 2009. Among the 34 federations included in the census, 16 (47%) have a ratio exceeding 80/20% in favour of one of the communities, while 24 (70%) have a ratio exceeding 70/30% in favour of one community. Only one federation had a 50/50 ratio. Thus, it is evident that *confessionalism* is strongly spread in various sports institutions in the country. The fact that a sport is dominated by one religious community reduces significantly the number of people interested in it. Generally, athletes, referees and trainers are more prone to choose a sport which is managed by people of their own community. For instance in football, the second most practiced sport in Lebanon, among the 133 associations affiliated with the federation, 85% are composed by Muslim members (Nseir 2012). Furthermore, according to a research concerning table tennis, among the 22 associations affiliated with the federation during the 2009–2010 season, over 71% were Christian (Nseir 2012).

In January 2013, it was announced in the media that the election for the Lebanese Olympic Committee will be taking into account the confessional belonging of each member. The lobbying of the political parties created a situation where the President of the Committee had to be Christian, the General Secretary Muslim Sunni and the treasurer Muslim Shi'a.[13] It will be interesting to know what would be the reaction of the IOC

Table 3. List of the federations along with the confessional belonging of their Presidents and general secretaries for the year 2003.

National federation	Confessional belonging of the President	Confessional belonging of the general secretary
Athletics	Christian	Christian
Volleyball	Christian	Christian
Tae Kwon do	Christian	Christian
Rowing	Christian	Muslim
Skiing	Christian	Christian
Water Skiing	Christian	Christian
Gymnastics	Christian	Christian
Cycling	Christian	Christian
Weight Lifting	Muslim	Muslim
Shooting	Christian	Christian
Badminton	Muslim	Muslim
Swimming	Christian	Muslim
Squash	Muslim	Muslim
Fencing	Muslim	Christian
Equestrian	Christian	Christian
Kick-boxing	Muslim	Muslim
Archery	Christian	Muslim
Karate	Christian	Christian
Basketball	Christian	Christian
Tennis	Christian	Christian
Handball	Muslim	Muslim
Table Tennis	Christian	Christian
Football	Muslim	Muslim
Wrestling	Muslim	Muslim
Boxing	Muslim	Muslim
Wushu	Christian	Christian
Sailing	Christian	Christian
Chess	Muslim	Muslim
Canoë-Kayak	Muslim	Muslim
Muay Thai	Muslim	Christian
Dance sport	Christian	Christian
Paralympics	Muslim	Muslim

Source: The Lebanese Olympic Committee (table and information were provided by the assistant of the former president of the Lebanese Olympic Committee (approved by the president of the Lebanese Olympic Committee)).

towards this new plan with regard to questions of Olympic values, equality and the preservation of the NOCs from political intervention.

In the subsequent section we address the other important element, which informs the power relations and politico-religious dynamics within the national sport system, which is funding and resource allocation.

The funding system of Lebanese sport

It is accepted that every budgeting cycle should normally include the following four main phases (Lee *et al.* 2008): preparation and submission; approval; implementation; and auditing and evaluation. Before the Ministry of Youth and Sports was established (following the decree 247) these phases were respected and applied in Lebanese national sport

Table 4. List of the federations along with the confessional belonging of their Presidents and general secretaries for the years 2008 and 2009.

National Federation	Confessional belonging of the President	Confessional belonging of the general secretary
Taekwondo	Christian	Christian
Wushu	Christian	Christian
Canoë Kayak	Muslim	Muslim
Muay-Thai	Muslim	Muslim
Dance sport	Christian	Christian
Karate	Christian	Christian
Handball	Muslim	Christian
Volleyball	Christian	Christian
Basketball	Christian	Christian
Table Tennis	Christian	Christian
Kick-Boxing	Muslim	Muslim
Squash	Muslim	Christian
Gymnastics	Muslim	Christian
Shooting	Christian	Muslim
Football	Muslim	Muslim
Water Skiing	Christian	Christian
Badminton	Muslim	Christian
Archery	Christian	Muslim
Swimming	Christian	Christian
Weight Lifting	Muslim	Muslim
Boxing	Muslim	Muslim
Wrestling	Muslim	Muslim
Tennis	Christian	Christian
Skiing	Christian	Christian
Equestrian	Christian	Christian
Sailing	Christian	Christian
Cycling	Christian	Christian
Rowing	Muslim	Muslim
Fencing	Christian	Christian
Chess	Muslim	Christian
Athletics	Christian	Christian
Paralympics	Muslim	Muslim

Source: The Lebanese Olympic Committee.

system, but in non-continuous and unsystematic manners. By definition, continuous and systematic should mean a clarified budgeting that 'mechanically' repeats itself in a cyclical routine. In the United Kingdom, for instance, for every pound spent on the lottery, 33% are allocated to a fund called the 'National Lottery Commission'. These funds cover the expenses for heritage, community, education and sport. This is how British sport organizations, for instance UK Sport, is financed. In turn, UK Sport distributes funds to sports federations according to their size (number of licensees) and international performance. In Lebanon, this financing method was never adopted prior to the year 2000. Government grants were mainly allocated to the organization of different sports events such as for the construction Sport City in 1957 to host the 1957 Pan Arab Games and the Mediterranean Games in 1959. Funds were also allocated to host the Pan Arab Games in 1997 and the Asian Cup in 2000 (Nassif 2010).

The year 2000 was a turning point for the financing system of Lebanese sport, with the signature of the decree 247 and the establishment of the Ministry of Youth and Sport.

Consequently, a Parliamentary Committee of Youth and Sport, responsible, henceforth, for voting the budget allocated to the MYS, was created. The committee participates in the preparation and approval phases of the budget allocated to sport, in collaboration with the government. Once the approval is obtained, the government allocates the funds to the MYS in order to complete the implementation phase. Yet, one of the main gaps in the budgeting cycle has been the absence of auditing and evaluation, which led to malfeasances within various sports organizations. According to MYS officials, an annual report indicating which federations and sports associations deserve the financial aid, given their performance, is submitted to the MYS.[14] However, when it comes to the implementation phase, it is common for the Ministry to receive 'phone calls' from high profile politicians requesting a share of the funding to their 'friendly' associations and federations.[15]

During a Parliamentary session in 2010, the President of the Youth and Sports Parliamentary Committee, Deputy Simon Abi Ramia, demanded every sport association and federation to submit a financial report for 2010.[16] This constituted a historical event given that it was for the first time that an audit was seriously considered. According to Abi Ramia, the measure taken is essential to establish transparency within the Lebanese sport system, which is traditionally 'tainted' with corruption. In Abi Ramia's terms, the difficulties related to the implementation of this measure are the result of the 'politicisation' of different associations and federations 'belonging', in majority, to politico-religious communities. Although every religious community in the Parliament must have a quota according to its demographic weight, sport is in fact exempt from this law. However, 'on the field', sport remains informally structured according to political and religious allegiance. Sport Federations are under the 'protection' of political leaders and affiliated religious groups. The politicization of sport, a by-product of the confessional system, remains one of the main obstacles to good governance in sport in Lebanon.

In order to fight this 'anomaly' in the system, MYS along with the Youth and Sports Parliamentary Committee is currently studying a law that would 'force' the Minister to decide about the spending for only 20% of the budget. The other 80% would automatically be allocated to the Lebanese sport movement (Lebanese Olympic Committee, sport federations and associations) based on performance and number of participants and would therefore be protected from any political interference.[17] According to Hassan Chararah, advisor to MYS, this would prevent political parties from influencing the Minister's decision to support sports federations and associations that are connected with his/her political party and religious community. The outcome of the law project is yet to be seen. Similarly, in April 2011, Antoine Chartier (President of the LOC) requested the 32 federations, recognized by the LOC, to submit a financial report for the year 2010.[18] This request, like the one by Deputy Abi Ramia, did not receive any response because of the 'political back up' that national sport federations can receive from political parties.

A funding system of the Lebanese national sport movement officially exists, but it is still dictated by political interference that stand in the face of adequate spending based on criteria of performance and efficiency. This funding system also suffers from the absence of a rigorous method of auditing and evaluation, which favours political interventions and 'arrangements'.

Conclusion

As illustrated in the paper the political system in Lebanon which is based on *confessionalism* is mirrored in the national sport movement and is impacting directly on its integrity. The interference of politics to serve the interests of different religious communities is impacting on mass sport participation as highlighted in the struggle between Ministry of Youth and Sports and Ministry of Education over the control of sport in schools and universities. The over-representation and dominance of one religious community over one sport is limiting the recruitment of participants and talents from other communities, as exemplified in football and basketball. The distribution of funding that favours sports associations and federations which are 'under political protection' and the absence of rigorous auditing and evaluation are tarnishing the image of the sport movement, and hence discouraging private investors, who are already traditionally 'shy' when it comes to sport, to invest in community and elite sports. In addition, sport is not attracting a significant fan base due to inter-religious violence, as clearly stated by Jean-Pierre Katrib, head of public relations for the Loubananouna, a federalist lobby group seeking a federalist solution to Lebanon's sectarian tensions:

> Even our basketball teams are divided along the confessions. The Christian Blue Stars played the Sunni Riyadeh team the other day, and to rile each other up, Christian and Islamic religious slogans were being chanted on either side. (Abi-Habib 2007)

The inefficiency in the structure and the lack of public and private funding are constraining the development of sport in Lebanon and performance in international competitions. As clearly indicated by Stanton (2012, 2115) 'since 1947, Lebanon has fielded a team for every Olympic competition except 1956, yet has won only four Olympic medals: two silvers and two bronzes, for men's wrestling and weightlifting'. Since 1991, only eight athletes were able to qualify for the Olympic Games, with no one winning a medal. Slovenia, independent since 1992, with half population than Lebanon, won 22 medals. The only sport that achieved an international success is basketball. The national team qualified three times to the World Championship (2002, 2006 and 2010). This is mainly due to the contribution of players from Lebanese diaspora in Europe and North America, and a strong professional league with the presence of the former National Basketball Association players which has helped to boost basketball's popularity (Wood 2010). Confronted with both internal political tensions and a growing instability in the region, the effort of the government has been primarily oriented towards the rebuilding of sports infrastructures destroyed by the war and Israeli bombings and the repositioning of Lebanon in the world's map in staging regional sports competitions such as the Pan Arab Games in 1997, the Asian Cup in 2000 and the Francophone Games in 2009. Beirut, the capital, will host the next edition of the Pan Arab Games in 2015. This endeavour might however be compromised by the political and economic situations and particularly the armed conflict in neighbouring Syria, which is impacting directly on the country. With the amplification of sectarian violence in Syria, Lebanon has now to deal with an unprecedented influx of Syrian refugees and heightened sectarian tensions between Sunni and Shi'a armed groups.

Acknowledgement

This project could not have been accomplished without the support of the interviewees in Lebanon and Prof Michel Raspaud, 'Sport et Environment Social' Université Joseph Fourrier, Grenoble, France.

Notes

1. Interview with Adnane Hammoud, director of the Sport and Scout Unit of the Lebanese Ministry of Education, 18 March 2011.
2. Interview done on 26 March 2011 with an employee of the Lebanese Ministry of Education.
3. Interview with Nizar Gharib, President of the office of the training of the managerial staff in the Center of Education, development and research (this institution is under the guardianship of the Lebanese Ministry of Education, 7 April 2011.
4. Interview with Adnane Hammoud, director of the Sport and Scout Unit of the Lebanese Ministry of Education, 18 March 2011.
5. Interview with Andrée Nassour, administrator in the Lebanese Ministry of Youth and Sports, 18 December 2005.
6. Interview with Andrée Nassour, administrator in the Lebanese Ministry of Youth and Sports, 18 December 2005.
7. Interview with Hassan Chararah, advisor of the Lebanese Ministry of Youth and Sport, 18 March 2011.
8. Interview with George Nader, General Secretary of the Lebanese University Sport Federation, 24 March 2011.
9. Interview with Hassan Chararah, advisor of the Lebanese Ministry of Youth and Sport, 18 March 2011.
10. Interview with Adnane Hammoud, director of the Sport and Scout Unit of the Lebanese Ministry of Education, 18 March 2011.
11. Interview with Jihad Salame, candidate for the position of Youth and Sport Minister, 6 October 2011.
12. Interviews conducted with different Lebanese athletes from February to September 2003.
13. Interview with Jihad Salame, candidate for the position of Youth and Sport Minister, 19 November 2013.
14. Interview with Raymond Touma, Financing director of the Lebanese Ministry of Youth and Sports, 18 March 2011.
15. In terms of corruption, in the year 2009, Lebanon occupied the 133rd position among 180 in the list of the least corrupted countries by the International Transparency. In 2012, Lebanon occupied the 188th position (The Telegraph, 17 November 2009).
16. Interview with the deputy Simon Abi Ramia, President of the Lebanese Youth and Sports Parliament Committee, 19 February 2010.
17. Interview with Hassan Chararah, advisor of the Lebanese Ministry of Youth and Sport, 18 March 2011.
18. Interview with Jihad Salame, candidate for the position of Youth and Sport Minister, 6 October 2011.

References

Abi-Habib, M., 12 July 2007. Divided Lebanon debates federalism [online]. Available 7 March 2011 from Ajazeera English: http://english.aljazeera.net/news/ middleeast/2007/06/200852 5184747179802.html [Accessed 15 October 2010].
Blanc, P., 2004. Le sport au Liban: un révélateur de la société. In: Sports et politique en Méditerranée. Les Cahiers de Confluences, December, 159–161. Paris: L'Harmattan.
Boukhater, L., 2004. Basket au Liban. Outre terre, Revue Française de Géopolitique, 8, 129–130. doi:10.3917/oute.008.0129
Gazzeri, H.P. and Isnard, J.F., 2005. The protocol of the cooperation between the French Embassy and the Lebanese Ministry of Youth and Sports for the implementation of coaching programs. Beirut: Lebanese Ministry of Youth and Sports.
Lee, R.D. Jr, Johnson, R.W., and Joyce, P.G., 2008. Public budgeting systems. 8th ed. Sudbury, MA: Jones and Bartlett.
Nassif, N., 2010. Sport policy in Lebanon, 1975 to 2004. Saarbûcken: LAP LAMBERT Academic Publishing.
Nseir, G., 2012. Des communautés et des sports au Liban Enjeux des regroupements sportifs et des rencontres Intercomunautaires. Thesis (PhD). Strasbourg University

Reiche, D., 2011. War minus the shooting? The politics of sport in Lebanon as a unique case in comparative politics. *Third world quarterly*, 32 (2), 261–277. doi:10.1080/01436597. 2011.560468

Sacre, J., 1990. *Report submitted to the Lebanese Government*. Beirut: Lebenese Government.

Salibi, K., 1965. *The modern history of Lebanon*. Worcester: The Trinity Press.

Salibi, K., 1993. *A house of many mansions. The history of Lebanon reconsidered*. London: IB Tauris & Co Ltd.

Stanton, A.L., 2012. Pioneer of Olympism in the Middle East: Gabriel Gemayel and Lebanese sport. *The international journal of the history of sport*, 29 (15), 2115–2130. doi:10.1080/ 09523367.2011.631005

The Telegraph, 17 November 2009. Transparency International's 2009 corruption index: the full ranking of 180 countries [online]. Available from: http://www.telegraph.co.uk/news/newstopics/ mps-expenses/6589735/Transparency-Internationals-2009-corruption-index-the-full-ranking-of-180-countries.html [Accessed 13 December 2013]

Wood, J., 2010. Beirut, Lebanon, where former NBA basketball players fulfill hoop dreams, the Christian Science Monitor (6 April). Available from: http://www.csmonitor.com/World/Global-News/2010/0406/Beirut-Lebanon-where-former-NBA-basketball-players-fulfill-hoop-dreams [Accessed 18 December 2013].

Index

Note: **Boldface** page numbers refer to figures and tables, page numbers followed by "n" denote notes.